Springbok Rugby

UNCOVERED

Springbok Rugby

UNCOVERED

Mark Keohane

ZEBRA

Published by Zebra Press
an imprint of Struik Publishers
(a division of New Holland Publishing (South Africa) (Pty) Ltd)
PO Box 1144, Cape Town, 8000
New Holland Publishing is a member of Johnnic Communications Ltd

www.zebrapress.co.za

First published 2004

3 5 7 9 10 8 6 4 2

Publication © Zebra Press 2004
Text © Mark Keohane 2004
Cover photograph © Getty Images/Touchline Photo

PUBLISHING MANAGER: Marlene Fryer
MANAGING EDITOR: Robert Plummer
EDITOR: Ronel Richter-Herbert
COVER AND TEXT DESIGNER: Natascha Adendorff
TYPESETTER: Monique van den Berg
PRODUCTION CONTROLLER: Valerie Kommer

Set in 10 pt on 13.5 pt Plantin Light

Reproduction by Hirt & Carter (Cape) (Pty) Ltd
Printed and bound by Paarl Print, Oosterland Street, Paarl, South Africa

ISBN 1 86872 917 6

To my wife Karin ... the dream of a rugby World Cup
was mine and the sacrifice the last three years was all yours.
Thank you.

Contents

Acknowledgements

For the people who never doubted my integrity and judged me purely on my journalistic abilities, I'd like to thank David O'Sullivan of 702, Colleen Louw of Cape Talk, Archie Henderson of the *Cape Argus* and Rob Houwing of *SA Sports Illustrated*. I would also like to thank Gavin Rich for his unwavering support and defence of my situation.

Jason Probert must be thanked for his infectious enthusiasm for new media and for cheerleading my way into cyberspace. M-Web and News24 have provided wonderful support in this regard.

Shaun Johnson for his inspirational words at a time when I most needed them, and for urging me to write this book and so close a chapter in my life. I wouldn't have done this otherwise.

I'd like to thank Rian Oberholzer for his unfailing honesty in all my dealings with him, and particularly for sticking to the truth when the pressure was almost unbearable.

I must also thank Harry Viljoen for giving me the opportunity to work with the Springboks, and Rudolf Straeuli with whom I initially enjoyed a good working relationship.

My biggest thank you on this project must go to my editor Ronel Richter-Herbert. Thank goodness she's a rugby fan. Also, thank you to Robert Plummer, managing editor at Zebra Press.

My biggest acknowledgement of the past three years is extended to those players who put their bodies on the line in the name of South African rugby.

Introduction

It's a big moment for any Springbok when he is given his match jersey on the eve of a test. To add extra meaning to the occasion, Harry Viljoen would invite a respected former player to join the squad, spend half an hour with the players, regale them with an inspirational tale or two, and then hand out the test jersey to each of the match 22. It was not an original idea. Other international teams were doing it too, and many of those foreign players spoke highly of the ritual. With the Boks it did not take place before every test, as it sometimes depended on location and the availability of an invited player. Rudolf Straeuli, upon succeeding Viljoen, continued the practice.

In 2000 Gary Teichmann, modest and inspirational leader of the Boks during their unbeaten run of seventeen tests, was playing his rugby in Newport, Wales. He would be the first to address Viljoen's Boks on the eve of their test against Wales in Cardiff. It was a very revealing occasion, because a year earlier Teichmann had been axed both as No. 8 and Bok captain. One of the reasons given for his ousting was that the players had lost faith in him as a leader.

It certainly did not seem like it that evening. Teichmann, on entering the room, received a standing ovation. The applause lasted a good minute, which seems an awful long time when thirty-odd people are crammed into a small team room. Teichmann, humble as ever, spoke for less than two minutes. He did not preach or refer to his test-playing days. Many of the players seated in front of him had been his disciples for two international seasons. He felt it unnecessary to say too much. He told the players that they had nothing to fear from the Welsh. He said the Welsh weren't good enough to beat the Boks. Focus on yourself and not them, was his message.

A week later François Pienaar addressed the squad in Windsor on the night before the England test. The players clapped as Pienaar entered the room; with Teichmann they had cheered. There would be no standing ovation for Pienaar. The respect for Teichmann was obvious, and Viljoen felt strongly about honouring those players who had contributed so much in the green and gold jersey. I was fascinated by the response of the players to the two men who had led the Boks to their most significant victories post-1992. But I was most inspired by a man who had done wonders for South African rugby before and after 1992. Only Morné du Plessis could eclipse the Teichmann moment.

Players are aware of Du Plessis' reputation, and have high expectations every time he speaks. On this Friday night, he delivered. There was no self-indulgent reflection on his Bok career, either as a player or as manager of the 1995 World Cup winners. He told the boys a story. It was about meeting basketball legend Michael Jordan at an awards function. Du Plessis spoke of Jordan's presence, how he commanded the stage and how he owned the conversation, room and space in which he moved.

'He was larger than life, bigger than the occasion and bigger than his chosen sport of basketball ... he was also incredibly approachable,' said Du Plessis, who asked Jordan how he motivated himself to keep on performing and raising the standard.

Jordan's response went something like this. He said that during the warm up he would look into the crowd and seek out young faces. He would then pick one that had anticipation and joy written all over it. His goal for the night would be to keep the joy on that youngster's face. When the final hooter sounded he would look to that kid and judge his expression. If the kid was smiling, he had succeeded. If not, his effort on the night had not been good enough.

The players were enthralled by the story. Du Plessis said that there would be many youngsters at Newlands. He urged the players to pick one and to follow a similar ritual to Jordan's. 'Make sure he or she is smiling at the end of the game,' he said. 'And if for some reason they are not, go back next week and work harder because the South African youngster will come out again to back you. That is the privilege of playing for the Springboks. You will always have unconditional support from those youngsters.'

The following day a young Bok team beat Wales 19-8 at a wet Newlands. Youngsters, soaked and cold, left the ground with smiles on their faces.

I get annoyed when I hear people say we need to revive the pride and passion in the Bok jersey. It is nonsense. We need to get some intelligence into our game, but pride and passion have never gone away.

Some Bok players have not been good enough. Don't confuse that with a lack of passion. I was irritated when former Bok lock Kobus Wiese, to name but one former South African international, commented after the Boks' World Cup quarter-final exit that there was no passion in the display and that the players did not want to win as badly as the All Blacks. Wiese, of all people, should know better. He has played in that jersey many times. No Bok player goes out to lose deliberately, and each player I worked with feels incredible pride when he puts on the green and gold. Only once in three years did I witness Bok players giving up in a test, and that was against the All Blacks in Pretoria in 2003. It had as much to do with the match preparation as it did with the match itself.

During my time with the Boks there was both the glorious and the inglorious. Lacking passion was not why the Boks lost more times than was acceptable. Players, who never selected themselves, were not good enough, coaching was at times inadequate, preparation was erratic and confusing, game plans were exposed for lacking substance and on occasion the opposition was just too good. But each time a player was given a jersey, there was immense pride in the achievement.

You only had to witness the reactions of Joost van der Westhuizen and Mark Andrews, South Africa's most capped test Boks, to know what the jersey meant to them. Andrews used to smell the jersey, and his face would break into a half-moon smile. The first time he was given a Bok jersey with his name embroidered on the back, on the eve of the 2001 Tri-Nations test against the All Blacks in Cape Town, he stared at it for some time. Bob Skinstad, captaining the Boks for the first time at Newlands, asked Andrews what he thought of the innovation. 'I don't know,' said Andrews. 'It feels like we are breaking tradition.' Skinstad responded: 'I see it as making tradition.'

The Bok jersey has lost its aura internationally. This we can no longer dispute. But it has not lost its gloss for the South African rugby player. You can only appreciate this when you view it from within the same room. The Boks must consistently beat the best to win back the opposition's respect. The right selections have to be made, and a game structure that plays to our strengths and not the perceived weaknesses of the opposition would be a good starting point.

I spent three years with the Springboks as their communications manager. It shattered the innocence of my schoolboy dreams because there was no escaping the ugliness of professional sport, the fallibility of the player and the politics of South African rugby. It tore strips off my childhood image of the Bok mystique, because human failings crush any fantasy. Springbok players are not machines; they are as mortal as you and me. We turn them into heroes and shape them as perfect illustrations of our sporting aspirations. They are our alter egos, and because of this we simply won't accept failure.

We curse them for not being role models when they never asked to be. We lambaste them for not being good enough when they never selected themselves. We blame them for our depression on a post-test Monday, and we eulogise them for making some Mondays seem so magnificent.

My son Oliver is four years old. He loves the Springboks. He adores Corné Krige because he was the captain, and his logic is such that the captain had to be the biggest, strongest and best player. I want my boy to dream about that green and gold jersey. I want all South African boys to have a Bok dream. But I also want the game to be transparent and the agendas of those in charge of the Boks to be consistently exposed.

It is not the players' lack of passion that threatens the future of the Springboks.

Issues such as selection, discipline, coaching appointments, contracting, transformation, the media, referees and individual agendas all contribute to an explosive cocktail.

What you are about to read is not the three-year diary of someone who travelled with the Boks, but an insight into those issues that undermine Bok rugby and the individuals who put our game at risk. Test defeats will not spell the end of South African rugby. Those provincial presidents and administrators who run the show by division and not in the interests of national unity are killing the Springboks. They know who they are.

I

Cloak and dagger
Tri-Nations 2003

16-52: a crushing defeat, and the Springboks' worst ever against the All Blacks. This was the scoreline at the end of the 2003 Tri-Nations test in Pretoria, and no sooner had the final whistle blown than the jokes were out, about the date of Jan van Riebeeck's arrival at the Cape. The jokes hurt the Bok players, and the ridicule acted as motivation for the squad when they arrived in Dunedin for a rematch three weeks later.

The build-up to the Pretoria test had been a shambles. Rudolf Straeuli got it wrong that week. He played mind games with the players, did not communicate effectively, and exhausted the squad's energy on sideshows when the only focus should have been on beating the All Blacks.

Excuses were offered after the match, varying from a failure to convert early pressure into points to the outrageous suggestion that the team did not have confidence in the replacements selected for the test.

There was no substance to that excuse. Fullback Brent Russell, on for seventy-seven minutes against Australia the week before, was outstanding. Ashwin Willemse, returning after injury, was the pick of the Bok backs against the All Blacks. If there was a lack of confidence within the team, it was with the selection of André Snyman, picked on the basis of his international experience, whose defensive alignment had been questioned by specialist defence coaches Frank Ponissi and Ray Mordt. They were concerned about Snyman's ability to read the play and to understand the attacking lines of a side such as the All Blacks.

These reservations had been expressed prior to Snyman's selection for the first test of 2003 against Scotland in Durban. Straeuli did not listen then; he certainly was not going to listen now. He had huge faith in Snyman, and picked him despite the player's shocker in that test. The rest of the team was unchanged from the one that had beaten Australia in Cape Town.

Team selection was not the reason for the Bok bashing in Pretoria. But the difference in preparation between the Cape Town and Pretoria tests was vast, and very pertinent to their outcome. In Cape Town before the test against Australia, distressed players met privately as a group in reaction to Straeuli and his support staff's management style in the season's first three tests. Captain Corné Krige was appointed to convey their message to the coach. The players were apprehensive, and felt that they were being policed and treated like kids. They wanted more freedom, more time off and to operate in a more relaxed environment. They felt they were being spied on and that their every move was being monitored.

Straeuli had introduced a security presence in consultant Adriaan Heijns, who joined the Boks officially at the start of the 2003 season. Heijns, a former South African Police Services Task Force commander, ran his own security company. He came highly recommended, having headed up the stadium security at the 1995 World Cup.

The players were wary of Heijns because they knew he was as much an information provider to Straeuli as he was a security presence for the squad. Straeuli was big on discipline within the team context, but the players felt his attitude towards discipline was skewed. They believed he spent too much time worrying about inconsequential issues when his energy could have been channelled more positively.

Straeuli's greatest failing is his inability to listen. The players had stomached too much, and they spoke to Krige during the players' meeting in Cape Town. Straeuli had asked me to meet with Krige to document all the player concerns. The players wanted management to worry less about whether they wore the right colour T-shirt and were seated for breakfast at eight in the morning fully clothed in their Bok tracksuit, and focus more on the game plan and finalising the match 22.

They also wanted all the extra players who were involved in squad training and SA 'A' matches to be separated from the test match 22. They wanted to be alone in the week building up to the test match, and were fed up with the uncertainty of not knowing whether they were in the test squad or the South African 'A' squad.

The senior players appreciated why Straeuli had assembled almost fifty players so close to the Tri-Nations opener against the Wallabies. World Cup documentation had to be signed and accreditation photos had to be taken. They also accepted that he wanted all fifty to train together that week, as the 'A' side had a match against Namibia in Windhoek. What irked them was that by the following Monday evening the match 22 had still not been finalised.

The players wanted breathing space, and they wanted a decision from the coach. They also requested the luxury of a few alcoholic drinks at the Wednesday team dinner without feeling that this indulgence would harm their future selection. Straeuli and Krige met, and the captain calmly spelt out where the players felt matters could be improved. Straeuli conceded, confirmed the team on the Tuesday morning and sent the extra players home. You could sense the change in mood and atmosphere. Now twenty-two players knew they were the chosen ones who had to win it for South Africa on Saturday. No player had to look over his shoulder any more. There were no mind games during that week, and the players, superbly led by Krige, settled into test match mode.

Straeuli joked to management that the players wanted it this way, so now there could be no excuses come Saturday.

'Well,' I responded, 'there is nothing like watching the lunatics running the asylum.'

And how well they ran it in the latter part of the week. They enjoyed the final two practice sessions and took an active interest in the theory sessions, as every single one in the match 22 knew what his role was. There were no hangers-on they needed to worry about. Each player could zone in on the opposition instead of worrying about the shadow of the additional players Straeuli had drafted in to sustain the pressure and add to the uncertainty of test match selection.

The preparation that followed was near perfect. Every player I spoke to in the week was very confident that the test would be won. The media, understandably, were sceptical of the Bok prospects. Journalists were dismissive of their chances on the basis of three very poor performances against Scotland and Argentina.

This upset Straeuli. He disliked the intensity of the Cape media, finding them to be negative and out to 'get' him. I told him the press coverage was mild when compared to what Carel du Plessis, Nick Mallett and Harry Viljoen had endured. Straeuli did not care about comparisons. He wanted newspapers removed from the team room. He did not want the players reading the local papers. It was a taste of things to come as the pressure intensified in 2003, but that week the players were in control.

De Wet Barry had been picked out of nowhere to play at inside centre. He was never in the initial pre-season squads and did not feature prominently in the selections. Barry had been included in the general squad of fifty, but Ray Mordt and Frank Ponissi rated him the most solid of the midfielders after working with the SA 'A' backs for a day. Straeuli had drafted Barry into the 'A' squad for the two matches against Argentina and Namibia, but never started him in either of them.

Ponissi and Mordt also rated Robbie Fleck very highly, and they pushed for his inclusion. Straeuli was not interested, and instead wanted Trevor Halstead. Ponissi and Mordt felt Halstead was a liability on defence because he could not grasp the defensive patterns. According to them, Halstead had been shown up badly in the two Scotland tests. Barry offered solidity and had been in the international environment since 2000. He was also the regular provincial centre partner for first choice No. 13, Marius Joubert.

Rudy Joubert, the Bok assistant coach and backline specialist, favoured Wayne Julies, whom he had coached at Boland, but there were concerns about Julies' fitness. He had hardly played in a year, and Mordt and Ponissi argued that it would be a risk to play him.

Joubert felt Julies could easily slot in with his former provincial colleague Marius Joubert. Neither Rudy Joubert nor Straeuli gave Gcobani Bobo any consideration for a starting role. They were not impressed with his performance against Argentina, and criticised him for lacking pace and not making his tackles against the Argentinians. Match statistics showed him missing six tackles, three of which were in one movement that had led to an Argentine try.

But Straeuli felt he could not drop Bobo from the match 22 due to political sensitivities, and he had also told the media in the build-up to the season how highly he rated Bobo, persisting with his line that he saw only the player and not his colour. Yet he showed no inclination to start with him in the first test against Scotland, despite the forty-one votes Bobo received in the Super 12 weekly selections. Halstead could muster only seven, and also did not often start as a first-choice player with the Sharks.

If Straeuli had been true to the selection process he had established during the 2003 Super 12, Bobo should have started the early tests because he received the most votes at inside centre. But Straeuli finally settled on Barry, and told the media he had always been part of his plans. The last time Barry had played test rugby was in the Tri-Nations in August 2002. Straeuli did not pick him for the end-of-year tour in 2002, and ignored him for the first three tests of 2003. There had been very little communication with the player.

The media were quick to react negatively to the Barry selection, if only because he had not been a Straeuli selection factor for more than a year. I spoke to both Straeuli and Barry. We had to spin the story that Barry had always known he would start the Tri-Nations test against Australia, and that Straeuli, comfortable with Barry's ability, merely used the first three tests to examine the depth available to him at inside centre.

I asked Barry to stick to this theme during his press interviews in order to impress on the media that the coach had been in constant communication with him, and that he knew where he stood despite his lack of game time. Straeuli's credibility was taking a battering with every team selection because there was no consistency from one week to the next. Each week it was a case of spinning a tale to convince the media that it all made sense. Some weeks they would buy it; at other times they would quite rightly laugh at the madness of it all.

Barry faced the media, charming them with his politeness and clarity on team selection. He told the reporters that he had nothing to prove because he had been earmarked to play Australia, and that the coach knew his capabilities. Barry brought structure to the back division and positively influenced flyhalf Louis Koen's approach to defence.

Mordt, the defence coach, was pleased Barry had been selected. He trusted the player's ability, and immediately there was an increase in the aggressiveness of the backs at training on the Wednesday. The guys went to dinner that evening and drank wine with their meal. Some had a few beers. It was pleasant and professional. No one got drunk and everyone was back at the hotel by 11 p.m.

I invited Straeuli, Mordt and a few other management members for a drink in the Cullinan Hotel bar. The mood was positive, and the coaches were pleased with the manner in which the squad had trained. I complimented Straeuli for being amenable to the players' demands. Everyone seemed convinced we would win. I guess it has something to do with a Springbok player's belief that Australia cannot win in South Africa.

In my three years with the Springboks, they won all three home Tri-Nations matches against Australia. I can't explain it. There is no scientific explanation as to why they believe they can't lose at home to Australia, just as there is no real explanation why they feel they cannot win in Australia. Cape Town, being at sea level, offered the Australians some hope, but not enough to worry the Boks. They were confident of beating Australia.

Straeuli was still wary of the Cape Town media, and questioned the wisdom of staying in the city for another week to prepare for the All Blacks test, which was to be played in Pretoria. In 2001 and 2002 the squad had stayed in Durban and flown to Pretoria and Johannesburg respectively for test matches twenty-four hours prior to kick-off. On both occasions the Boks had beaten Australia. I reminded Straeuli of this, and also of how unobtrusive the media in Durban usually were when the squad trained there and the test was not played in Durban. In both years the build-up was laid back and peaceful. Few sports editors were prepared to send their writers to Durban when the test was taking place in Johannesburg or Pretoria. That night Straeuli made the decision to move the preparations to Durban. It made sense, given his reservations.

The coaches, logistics manager Mac Hendricks and I felt it was the right thing to do, but when I asked Straeuli on the Thursday before the Newlands game whether he had informed the squad of his decision, he said he would only do so after the match, as he did not want to take their focus off the test. An added complication was that many of the players had already flown their partners to Cape Town, and had made arrangements to spend the Sunday with them in the city. But that would be Saturday evening's dilemma.

On Friday the media caught me off guard at the final pre-test press conference. They wanted my response to an attempted hijacking involving Bob Skinstad, asking why the player had been out close to midnight. I had to think on my feet, saying we were pleased Skinstad was okay. I knew nothing about the incident, but reckoned if he had been injured it would already have been news. So I insisted that Bob's safety was our main concern, and that we were just glad he was not hurt. I then asked the journalist what information he was privy to. That is how I found out that Skinstad, a mate of his, Tim Mitchell, and Mitchell's wife had been held up when they dropped Skinstad off at his girlfriend's parents' place in the Cape Town suburb of Claremont.

The media wanted to know why Skinstad had gone out and was not with the squad. I explained that because he was not in the match 22, he was not staying with the squad at the team hotel in Cape Town. Skinstad was unavailable for the Australian test because of a viral infection he had contracted on the eve of the SA 'A' match against Namibia the previous week. I also said that it was not a crime for Skinstad to go out and have a meal with mates. He was not fit enough to play, as he had been ill in bed for a few days because of the infection, but he was well enough to have a meal and a glass of wine.

The media accepted the explanation, and reported on the incident without commenting on why Skinstad was not at home wrapped up in his winter woollies.

Straeuli approached me after the press conference and told me that we needed to put out a release about Skinstad, but that we had to keep it away from the squad. Straeuli had found out about the incident earlier in the day, and I asked him why he hadn't told me. He said he had been uncertain about the reported events, and had therefore not taken the matter further.

I left it at that and never even bothered to put out a release. The squad heard about the incident in the course of the Friday, and naturally it was a talking point that day.

Skinstad, had he been fit, was to have started at No. 8 against Australia. As it turned out, he never played under Straeuli again.

The players, allowed some freedom that week, were probably the most relaxed I had seen them for a test of that magnitude. There was no false bravado, no mouthing off to each other about the opposition or trying to talk each other up.

On the Saturday, Barry was destructive in his defensive play, and Australia's management would suggest afterwards that the Boks had had access to their game plan. It was not true, but there had been an attempt to videotape their final captain's run at Newlands. Straeuli had instructed Heijns to have the session taped secretly. Heijns, through a contact at Western Province, had obtained access to one of the private suites, and Bok video analyst Dale McDermott waited there for the Aussies to arrive.

McDermott taped only ten minutes of the warm up before getting an attack of conscience. He reported back that he had been spotted by some of the Australian squad and had left. Straeuli never told me that the session was going to be taped, but within management everyone talked, and McDermott mentioned privately that he had been uncomfortable with the plan. There was no video footage. The players would only hear about the spying allegation later in the Tri-Nations. They were oblivious to such management schemes.

The Boks won a match they never looked like losing. In an awful 2003 season it was to be their best performance, and it was inspired by Brent Russell, who replaced the injured Jaco van der Westhuyzen three minutes into the match. The squad had been under immense pressure after the indifferent performances against Scotland, whom they beat twice, and Argentina, whom they beat once.

Now they had beaten a team who still paraded as the world champions after their 1999 World Cup triumph in Cardiff.

It was an incredible feeling to be on the sideline with the players as they counted down the clock. There was non-stop banter from the bench to the XV on the field. They were urging the players on. Big hits were made, and the Aussies were kept in their own half for the final two minutes. Only four points separated the two teams, but our boys were never going to let them into our half.

It was my 100th test involving South Africa (seventy covering the Boks as a press man, and thirty with the team as communications manager) and a significant one for me. My first official test match as a rugby writer was the 26-3 defeat to Australia at Newlands in 1992, and more than a decade later we had beaten Australia 26-22 at the same venue. As a Cape Town boy, and having watched rugby at Newlands from the railway stand as an eight-year-old, it could not get better.

Management are given a test jersey every third test. Mac Hendricks, the logistics manager, arranged to have my initials put on one of the match jerseys for the day with a '100' under the Bok emblem. It is the jersey that still means the most to me.

The spirit in the change room after the victory was fantastic and the boys were upbeat. They had taken heaps in the past month and now they felt vindicated. They did it their way, and they won it their way. As is custom, SARFU president Silas Nkanunu entered the dressing room a few minutes after the final whistle. The players were huddled in a circle and Straeuli was speaking. He invited Nkanunu into the huddle and asked him if he wanted to address the players, who were the happiest they had been all season.

Nkanunu – and God alone knows what possessed him to say it – blurted out that the performance was not good enough. He said that the Boks had to raise the bar and he wanted to see improvement. Then, as an afterthought, he congratulated them on beating a team that at that stage were the world champions. There was stunned silence and the entire mood changed.

The players, sadly, had very little respect for Nkanunu. It was based on moments such as this one, and on occasions when he incorrectly identified players, for example referring to André Vos as André Venter. On one embarrassing occasion he asked for Bob Skinstad to speak in the absence of Corné Krige at the after-match function against France in Marseille in 2002. Krige was held up because of routine drug testing. Skinstad, Silas had to be told, was not on tour! He was at home recovering from injury.

The celebrations at the hotel after the Cape Town win against Australia in 2003 were marred when Straeuli told the squad we would be travelling to Durban the next day. It was up to the squad to sort out who would go on the early flight, and who could fly in later that afternoon. Many in the squad were annoyed.

Players want structure in their lives, and in a team set-up they want constant communication of what is going on.

The week in Durban prior to the test against New Zealand was to prove chaotic in terms of team unity and confidence boosting. There was no structure and very little effective communication. Straeuli obsessed about players being lulled into a comfort zone, which probably explains why in twenty-three tests he never selected the same XV in successive test matches.

It was his belief that you have to keep the player guessing, creating an uncertainty that never allows the player to slip into the dreaded comfort zone. With this in mind, Straeuli would not name the match 22 for the test against the All Blacks, and told the players he would only settle on the substitutes on the Thursday. He had planned a practice match between the Sharks and an SA selection XV for the Thursday, but told no one in the squad.

Straeuli invited several fringe players to the week's training, which immediately unsettled the existing squad. He named the starting XV early in the week, but would not give the players confirmation of the bench. In the week, all twenty-six national squad members were involved in the preparation, while another team of players was arriving at regular intervals to train with the national squad.

On the Tuesday, the Boks trained a contact session against a local club side. Straeuli mixed and matched the combinations. On the Wednesday there was more contact between the national squad and the fringe players. Again he juggled combinations.

The players first heard whispers of a practice match against the Sharks on the Wednesday. During training at the gym in the morning, Sharks players informed some of the Springboks that a match would be taking place on the Thursday. Straeuli kept it secret from the players until Wednesday afternoon. It was a way, he said, of ensuring that the players would not go out on the Wednesday night. He also wanted the media to know nothing about the match.

The seven reserves from the Australian test were put on match alert on Wednesday, and for the next twenty-four hours prepared to play a match on the Thursday. The starting test XV continued with their preparation and were given the Thursday off. Players were irritated with the mind games. For instance, the match squad of twenty-six were required to attend some meetings, while in others, only the match XV were needed. The mentality was outrageous. On one occasion Skinstad wanted to enter the team room during a squad meeting, and Straeuli told me to keep him out. I told Skinstad that the coach did not want him in the meeting. He gave a despairing look, shook his head in disbelief and walked away.

The clandestine nature of the Thursday match reached ridiculous proportions. None of the players knew where the game would take place. Heijns' crack security team escorted the team bus on a route that would first take the Bok Invitation squad to Absa Stadium, where the Sharks squad would be picked up. Both teams, in the same bus, then took a lengthy drive, under security surveillance, to Durban University Sports Grounds.

An official practice match, refereed by Tappe Henning, was played. The odd varsity student watched the game, but no one else was allowed in. Security did not have to worry because no one knew of the match. Straeuli had picked a team that included Conrad Jantjes, Fabian Juries, Anton Pitout, Dries Scholtz, Wayne Julies, Gcobani Bobo, André Pretorius, Enrico Januarie, Craig Davidson, Bob Skinstad, Joe van Niekerk, Luke Watson, Pedrie Wannenburg, Selborne Boome, Geo Cronjé, John Smit, CJ van der Linde and Dale Santon.

The national scratch XV led two tries to one for most of the hour-long exercise before the Sharks struck back to win three tries to two. In the last quarter there was a lot of mixing and matching between the two sides. The match was physical, and injured players Skinstad, Van Niekerk, Smit and Pretorius were given the chance to prove their fitness. Test reserves Davidson, Bobo and Santon were not used in the match, but participated in the exercise as reserves.

I suggested to Rudolf that we inform the media about the match so as to avoid any negative publicity. The details were bound to get out. The spin we put on it was that a match had taken place, and that its primary goal had been to gauge the fitness levels of World Cup contenders Skinstad, Smit, Pretorius and Van Niekerk – players who Straeuli had named earlier in the year as World Cup certainties if they were fit. Straeuli had therefore created a match to test their fitness. This is what we told the media on the Thursday evening in a hastily arranged session with South African journalists staying at the team hotel. The line we gave to the media was that Van Niekerk had been sensational in the match, and Pretorius had showed his class. Skinstad had struggled with fitness, as had Smit.

Straeuli wasn't prepared to risk Van Niekerk or Pretorius in the match against New Zealand, despite them easily passing the 'fitness test'. The coach was thrilled that he had pulled off the staging of a match while managing to keep it a secret. He now knew that he could take Van Niekerk and Pretorius to Australasia. That evening, Straeuli confirmed that the bench against the All Blacks would be unchanged from the Australian test. The players who had been involved in the exercise were mentally drained. They now had only a day to prepare for the test against the All Blacks.

The Boks were to fly to Johannesburg on the Friday afternoon. That morning the players were informed, through Mac Hendricks, that they would not be staying at the Palazzo Hotel in Fourways according to the original schedule. The players were not told where they would be staying on the Friday night. It caused further uncertainty, which disrupted the flow of the preparation. Players wanted to know how they could get their match tickets to friends, family and partners. Some players were waiting for their boots to be delivered to the Palazzo, and others had arranged to meet people on the Friday evening prior to the test.

Superstition and routine play a big part in most rugby players' preparation. Many, as a ritual, go to a movie. But by 8 p.m. on Friday evening they did not even know where they would be staying. After the captain's run at Loftus, the players and management were driven to a location forty kilometres outside Pretoria. They did not know the name of the place, and once they'd arrived, no one was allowed to invite anyone to the venue.

On arrival the players ate dinner and went to bed. All they had with them was an overnight bag. Their luggage had been sent to the Palazzo, where the squad would stay on Saturday night. Straeuli wanted the squad to focus on the test match without the presence of the usual 'hangers-on' at the team hotel, who irritated him. For each of the players who tried to be positive about the Friday night location, there was another who was extremely put out. Sure, they had a bed to sleep in, but everything that was familiar to them had been removed and their rhythm had been disrupted. Straeuli's plan to take them out of their comfort zone had certainly worked.

Rapport journalist Louis de Villiers phoned me at 9 p.m. that evening to meet up for a beer. I said that I was forty-odd kilometres outside of Pretoria at a resort. He laughed. 'My God,' he said, 'if your coach doesn't believe his players can hack the pressure of being in central Pretoria on the Friday night of a test, how are they going to deal with the pressure of the All Blacks?' De Villiers told me he feared the worst for the test match. I don't think he knew how bad things were and just how awful it was going to be the next day.

In my three years with the Boks, it was the most bizarre build-up to a test match – and it happened to be against the All Blacks. On the Saturday of the test, prior to departure for the ground, Straeuli told the players that he had changed hotels to keep them on their toes, to focus them and to take them out of their comfort zones, as that was what the All Blacks would be doing to them in the next few hours. He said he did not need interruptions from every hanger-on at the hotel.

He then asked the squad if they really believed they could beat the All Blacks, and emphasised that this was something only they could determine. Straeuli felt they did not believe it was possible, and challenged them to prove him wrong. As a motivational talk, it definitely was alternative.

During the drive to the stadium, a sense of uneasiness pervaded the atmosphere. No one talked in the bus. The players were not tense, but they were distant. The week had been emotionally draining, and more unnecessary strains awaited them at Loftus. Players were not sure if their match tickets had been picked up, others were anxious that their boots would not be delivered to the ground, and some worried about other issues that may appear minor now, but on match day have a huge influence on the psyche of a player.

Brent Russell couldn't find his gum guard and didn't know if his parents had received the tickets to the game. He also couldn't get hold of them, and emotionally he was all over the place. Lawrence Sephaka was another player who was trying to find out whether his gear, which he would need for the test match, had arrived at the Palazzo. Several players also complained of not getting enough sleep because of the uncomfortable mattresses – Sephaka even asked for two Red Bulls to wake him up.

A few players were talking on their cellphones barely an hour before kick-off in an attempt to clarify arrangements. Pedrie Wannenburg was on his cellphone to his girlfriend forty minutes before kick-off. He defended it as a pre-match ritual, but Corné Krige was furious, saying it was unacceptable. The cellphone issue would be addressed later in the Tri-Nations.

In the meantime, the All Blacks had selected their match 22 on the Sunday evening after arriving in Durban, and had trained all week in isolation with minimal distraction. The Boks were mentally stuffed around all week by their own coach, as well as indirectly by their management team.

Prior to kick-off I stood next to the field, briefly chatting to All Black legend Sean Fitzpatrick. He asked me who was going to win. Before I could answer, he said: 'Think with your head, not your heart.' He was very confident that the All Blacks would win. 'It is our pack against your backs,' I said. 'If we dominate your pack ...'

I never finished the sentence because he smiled and said it was not going to happen.

My lasting memory of that test is the Bok pack disintegrating. The All Blacks smashed us 52-16, and the final fifteen minutes were the feeblest I had experienced during my time with the Boks. In the 53-3 defeat at Twickenham, the players had gutsed it out until the end. In Pretoria, the heartland of Calvinist rugby defiance, players gave up in a Bok jersey. It was the first time I ever saw that happen. It would also be the last.

Krige was shattered. He had given everything, but his last act was to be buried on his backside as his opposite number, All Black loose forward Richie McCaw, ran over him in the final minute of the game. He felt insulted, and appalled that his teammates had jerked tackles, turned their backs on play and thrown in the towel. Corné held nothing back afterwards. He expressed his disgust in the team huddle. Straeuli said he would speak about the game when emotions had calmed down. I had been part of a few empty moments in Bok change rooms, but this was the lowest. All that compared in terms of hollowness was being in the change room at Murrayfield in Scotland in 2002 after we had lost 21-6. Then, there had been the excuse of a Bok team that would have ranked somewhere between a B or C team. Here, Straeuli had picked what he felt was the best team, except for the injured Marius Joubert and Joe van Niekerk. There were no excuses. There couldn't be.

That evening some of us were guests at Nelson Mandela's 85th birthday celebrations. For a few hours we could forget about rugby and marvel at the Madiba magic. But at 8 a.m. on the Sunday morning, there was no escape. Team manager Gideon Sam called a management meeting, which was standard procedure. Initially, all issues relevant to the week in Durban were tiptoed around. When it came to general matters, Gideon asked me if I had anything to report back from the players. It was the norm to chat to Corné prior to the meetings and put any issues on the table. I was frank and said the players felt that the week had been a debacle. Their biggest criticism was for the lack of communication regarding the practice match, the change of hotel venue and the general mind games.

Rudolf took the criticism very personally, but it was a confrontation that was long overdue. When I say confrontation, there was no heated exchange. Rather, the communication problem was addressed. Team doctor Uli Schmidt was equally outspoken. He was very disillusioned about what had happened in Durban, as well as with the approach to the test match. For the first time, many in the management team spoke up about issues that were troubling them.

Management felt that they were powerless to influence the performance of the players, yet every week had to take responsibility for what happened on the field. They wanted to be judged according to their portfolios. The general feeling was that the chaotic approach to the Pretoria test had given the players an excuse, allowing them to blame a management structure which, in that week, did not seem to know its head from its tail.

Straeuli took the criticism badly. His response was to ask if the complaints were a vote of no confidence in him as a coach, and, if so, he would have to step down. No one responded. There was silence. Gideon called the meeting to a close, as the squad had to attend a birthday celebration for Silas at the team hotel. Many players did not want to be at the brunch. They had no choice; they had to attend.

At the brunch I spoke to the managing director of SA Rugby, Rian Oberholzer. I gave him some insights into the meeting, and he wanted to know what the consequences had been. There had been none. But hopefully a bit of introspection would take place before the squad assembled for the away leg of the Tri-Nations, and perhaps the assistant coaches would be more forceful in pushing for those selections they felt could improve the team.

Rudy Joubert made it clear to Rian he would not have picked half the backline that played against the All Blacks in Pretoria. Rian's response was to tell him to stop being a 'yes-man' then, and start backing what he believed in. Rian wanted to see a change in approach from the backs. He had reluctantly supported Straeuli's sudden decision to get rid of backs coach Tim Lane a week before the start of the international season. Now he wanted to see the benefits of the decision. This would never happen, because in the remaining Tri-Nations matches, as well as in the World Cup matches against England and the All Blacks, the Bok backs would not score a try.

Selection was problematic. Two matches out from the World Cup, Straeuli was still unsure what his best starting XV was. He certainly had not settled on a game plan, but he hid behind the mask of the World Cup. When Oberholzer questioned him, he asked to be judged on the World Cup. When the media wanted answers, he said people would only remember the World Cup and that he was not prepared to show his hand in the Tri-Nations. He tried to buy time with promises of something spectacular at the World Cup. It never materialised, because all the planning that had been done the year before and everything that had been put in place in 2003 had changed. And it would continue to change ... by the week.

And yet everything had looked so promising in the Spring of 2000, when I walked into the offices of SA Rugby for the first time ...

2

Turning buffalo into businessmen

Harry Viljoen's vision for Springbok rugby

When Harry Viljoen succeeded Nick Mallett as Springbok coach in September 2000, his one big advantage was his wealth. Rugby players are impressed with wealth. When Harry sold his blueprint to the players of how the game should be run in South Africa, they looked at his fortune and concluded that his proposal had to be lined with gold. In many respects, it was. It was a good blueprint, based on a lot of research and many discussions with highly successful and influential business- and sportspeople.

Rod Macqueen, the 1999 World Cup-winning Wallabies coach, was a good friend of Viljoen's. They had exchanged many thoughts on how to improve the game. In Macqueen's opinion, the Boks lacked rugby intelligence. He often told Harry that the Boks possessed neither finesse nor intellect on the field. They were all brute strength. The Boks played for one-off wins and relied on bullying the opposition into submission. They lacked consistency in getting winning results because they did not have the capacity to think.

Viljoen told the Bok players of an occasion when he and Macqueen were on a game park drive soon after Viljoen's appointment as Bok coach. They saw some buffalo. 'Look Harry ... there's your players ... big, strong and fucking dumb,' Macqueen had said.

Macqueen aside, Harry also spent time in the States during his business travels, studying various professional sports codes and conducting his own research – another benefit of being wealthy. Harry went where he wanted to go. If SARFU resisted, he paid for the trip himself. In the weeks before his appointment, he cut short a holiday trip to the south of France to spend time with Tim Lane at Montferrand and John Connolly at Stade Français.

Viljoen, having been out of the game for three years, undertook a crash course in rugby trends. He spent a fortnight in France and England. He lusted for knowledge, knowing that he had to bring something new to the South African game. Harry was adamant that the 'extra' he was looking for could not be found in South Africa. He asked me, as his newly appointed personal advisor, to study the successes of various international teams, and I borrowed whatever was applicable and incorporated the information into a formula I believed could be beneficial to the Boks.

Kevin Roberts, chief executive of Saatchi & Saatchi, had co-written the book *Peak Performance*, which focused on business lessons learnt from leading international sports teams and organisations. Roberts had formed a strong association with the All Blacks during his time with Steinlager in the mid-1990s, and was a member of the New Zealand Rugby Football Union executive. I knew his opinion would be invaluable, as he also had a strong affiliation (again because of sponsorship) with Australian rugby league side Manly.

Bayern Munich, the Chicago Bulls, the San Francisco 49ers and Williams F1: they were all sports models that could contribute to Viljoen's 2001 Springboks. I also found much of value in the achievements of Netball Australia and Australian Women's Hockey, and I was very keen to tap into the mind of Aussie Rules coaching guru Kevin Sheedy. He had transformed the way the game was played at Essendon. I arranged a meeting between Viljoen and Sheedy in April 2001.

Former All Black coach John Hart was another brilliant business mind in the world of sport. Hart agreed to see us during the Australasian trip. Harry also did not want to discard the achievements of Nick Mallett and Alan Solomons. Despite occasional personality clashes with Solomons during their time at Western Province and the Stormers, Harry had a very high regard for Solomons' rugby expertise. He rated Solomons' work ethic, intelligence and commitment to South African rugby very highly.

By taking bits and pieces from a number of different sports codes and merging them with Harry's ideas and some of my own, we created a basic formula to improve South African rugby. Rian Oberholzer was enthusiastic. Harry, it seemed, was bringing something new to the South African game. The challenge would lie in whether he could stay true to his gut instincts and overcome the obvious obstacles the conservative element within the South African game posed.

For the blueprint to work in South African rugby, absolute focus and full-time commitment would be required. One also had to be alert twenty-four hours a day, as those carrying the knives don't sleep. Harry's initial enthusiasm did not take long to wane. Rugby politics and the media would prove too much for him, but at the outset he was all glitz and glamour. The players loved it. Harry spoke 'business' to them. Unfortunately, not many of them understood the lingo, but his approach was so radically different to what they had known before that they quickly bought into the idea of a Springbok 'company', run independently from SARFU.

But running a Springbok 'company' was not practical in 2001, because SARFU chief executive Rian Oberholzer was putting the finishing touches to the formation of SARFU's professional arm, SA Rugby (Pty) Ltd, of which he would become the first managing director. The word 'company' was soon buried and replaced with 'business unit'. The Springboks would be a business unit, run by Harry, but still answerable to Rian and the SARFU executive. However, SARFU's national executive was hesitant. The emphasis on a 'business unit' scared them. They thought it an attempt to make the Boks an elitist and separate group within SA Rugby.

Their resistance was soon broken down when Oberholzer explained the principle behind the idea, which was to promote professionalism within the Bok team, give players greater responsibility and reward them well for any successes. The SARFU executive – and later the professional arm's board of directors – would still control the Boks. Viljoen was not privatising Bok rugby, nor was he taking it away from the people. He was trying to move it away from incompetent committee-driven men who had been involved in amateur rugby, and who interpreted professional rugby as finally being remunerated in the form of sipping cocktails while attending rugby matches.

Viljoen's appointment to succeed Mallett had been finalised the week before the SARFU executive confirmed it. The appointment was effected through typical business methods. Rian Oberholzer did not contact Viljoen. Instead, a leading businessman with links to SA Rugby was involved to sound out whether he was interested in the job.

Once Oberholzer knew that Viljoen wanted the job, he started convincing executive members of the merits of the appointment. He did a selling job on each one individually, but ran into a few hurdles. Keith Parkinson was in favour of a coaching combination of Viljoen and André Markgraaff, as that would appease the conservative northern provinces. In 2000, Parkinson, junior vice-president of SARFU, was a huge fan of Markgraaff's. Arthob Petersen, an executive member of SARFU and another friend of Markgraaff's, also wanted him involved. The executive knew that they could not reinstate André Markgraaff as head coach, as the country was not yet ready to accept the disgraced former Springbok coach following his resignation in 1997 after a racist incident. Viljoen would be the image presented to the world, and Markgraaff would be the guy who actually did the coaching.

Viljoen was initially opposed to having Markgraaff involved, but then had a change of heart, and told Oberholzer he would include him. However, at the time, Markgraaff ruled himself out as assistant coach, because, he said, of my involvement. In my ten-year career as a rugby journalist I had been critical of him, and had broken the story about him calling black rugby administrators 'kaffirs', which had led to his resignation three years earlier. Harry had asked me to join his management team if he was appointed, to advise him on transformation, among other things. Markgraaff told *Rapport* that he could not work with me, although he later told me that he had been misquoted. Oberholzer cautioned

Viljoen against involving Markgraaff, as he was concerned that Markgraaff would dominate Viljoen. Markgraaff would reintroduce the ox wagon, when Viljoen was talking about spacecrafts.

Oberholzer also had one reservation about Viljoen, which was that he would do a runner when the going got tough. And he was wary of Markgraaff waiting in the queue to take over. Viljoen assured Oberholzer that this was one rugby challenge he would see through to the end.

For me, the week leading up to Viljoen's appointment was filled with personal drama. I had resigned all my media interests, informing my editors that I would be joining Harry. If he were appointed to the Bok job, then I would work with him. If he were not, then I would work for his company, Edge Investments. I knew he had pretty much secured the Bok job, so my decision to work with him was based on the rugby option.

The papers ran the story of my appointment, which upset both Oberholzer and Viljoen, as it put them in a difficult position. It meant another bridge had to be crossed for Viljoen to be confirmed as coach. The executive members were opposed to my appointment because of my past criticism of SARFU, which is putting it mildly. Some of them hated me. SARFU vice-president Ronnie Masson and Parkinson led the protests, and Arthob Petersen was at the forefront of the black opposition. Parkinson would never accept my role with the Boks. Masson was more accommodating. We met, and he spent half an hour telling me exactly what he thought of me, and making his dislike clear. I offered no defence, as I could not change what I had written. I thought it was irrelevant debating whether I had been right or wrong.

He accepted this, and said that while we would not be friends, he would always support me for the sake of the coach and the Boks. In the next three years, Masson was always true to his word. He backed me on a professional level, even if we hardly spoke socially.

The black administrators were put out because I had called them gravy-trainers in a column a few months before linking up with Harry. I blamed them for 'selling out' their players, as well as everything they had fought for during the days of segregation and apartheid. The moment the white administrator gave them a business class air ticket, match tickets and invitations to every event, they forgot what the fight for equality was all about. They forgot about their players. This view was only reinforced during my time at SA Rugby.

Oberholzer called Viljoen on the Thursday, the day before the coach was to be announced, and told him to get rid of me, as my involvement was a complication. Viljoen then called me, and said that the executive would not give him the job if I were involved; it was his choice to make. Viljoen had just come from a private meeting with Parkinson at the Holiday Inn on Cape Town's foreshore. He told me Parkinson had said that if I were linked to the Boks, it would be difficult for them to appoint him. Parkinson was not willing to lend him his support, and no guarantees could be given that he would get the job.

I was shattered, and did not know what to say. I asked Harry to ring me back once I'd had time to think about it. We spoke again a few minutes later, and I told him that the call was his to make. I was not going to pull out. He had approached me and sold me on an idea, and I had accepted. He had to decide whether or not he was prepared to back me, or do as the executive wanted. The executive meeting was due to start at 10 a.m. on Friday. Parkinson wanted an answer from Viljoen by eight in the morning. If I was out, he would guarantee Viljoen complete support at the meeting; if I was still involved, Viljoen would be on his own.

Harry and I again talked on the phone, but I refused to relent. I was not going to make the decision for him; he had to do it. Harry wanted me to understand the political nature of the decision, and put me on hold while he phoned Rian on a separate line. On speakerphone, while I listened, Oberholzer told Viljoen to fire me, get appointed, and then rehire me. I have a high regard for Oberholzer as a rugby administrator, but I also know the politician in him. Once the conversation ended, Viljoen asked me what I thought of Rian's suggestion. I did not find it acceptable. Either Harry backed me, or he called off our arrangement. He said he would phone me in the morning, and, when he did, he told me he had made up his mind: he would stick with me, and if he did not get the job, then so be it. He had made a commitment to me, and he was a man of his word.

I was relieved and flattered at the same time. Viljoen arranged to come to my house at 11 a.m. to prepare for the press conference. If he had the job, then we'd be on our way. If he didn't, we'd go for lunch. Oberholzer called Harry after midday to tell him he had the job. There would be a 2 p.m. press conference, and Rian advised Harry that it would be wise to leave me at home. But Harry insisted that I be there, which was the kind of treatment that inspired loyalty. I felt committed to giving Harry every ounce of energy I had in the future.

When Viljoen got the job, in September 2000, he had a fortnight to prepare himself for the Bok tour of Argentina, Ireland, Wales and England. All he wanted was to survive the tour with minimal damage. The changes he proposed could only be effected in 2001. At this stage, André Markgraaff had accepted Viljoen's invitation to join the squad as assistant coach.

A squad of forty would tour, and Viljoen allowed himself to be guided by the incumbent selectors, François Davids and Wynand Claassen, and assistant coach Jake White. At the outset of the tour, Viljoen said that his influence would not be evident, although when you look back on the Viljoen era, it was the only time the Boks showed anything resembling change. The Boks won three of the four tests, and beat the Barbarians in a thriller at the Millennium Stadium.

Before the tour, Harry Viljoen spoke to the senior players at length about their time with Nick Mallett, wanting to know both the good and the bad about his tenure as coach. The feedback was mixed. Beyond a doubt, Mallett had impressed the players as a coach. They highly approved of his knowledge of and passion for the game. But they criticised his people skills. The players felt that he was too single-minded in his approach. He did not listen to their opinions, and no environment existed within which to challenge ideas.

Mallett's people management style, according to the players, was in complete contrast to Viljoen's, who spoke of empowerment and equal contribution for equal reward. Although it may have worked in Viljoen's business world, he was to find out very quickly that dealing with rugby players was very different.

Viljoen met briefly with Mallett before taking the tour. Mallett spoke and Viljoen listened, but did not take much away from the meeting. Viljoen also arranged sessions with the best coaches in South Africa. He wanted to know their feelings on the Boks. In October 2000, Viljoen still believed Ian McIntosh, the former Sharks and Springbok coach, could contribute to the Boks, and he asked McIntosh to accompany the team to Argentina as a consultant.

From a rugby perspective, McIntosh excelled in his knowledge of the game. But he was set in his ways, and this concerned Viljoen. He felt that McIntosh was not prepared to venture into the unknown. McIntosh had unparalleled experience and a mind that understood test rugby. Viljoen, yet to be involved in a test, would learn how hard and unforgiving the arena of test rugby was. Viljoen also flew Australian technical expert Barry Honan to Argentina, whom he paid himself.

Viljoen is a master salesman, and he was desperate to make a dramatic impression on the players. He wanted something to trigger their minds, to show them that the only way to improve was to chase the unknown. I was asked to arrange for the delivery of forty rugby balls from Gilbert, SA Rugby's official ball supplier. Each player would have his own ball.

On meeting the squad for the first time, Viljoen said that the one thing he had been critical of as a rugby supporter was South African players' apparent lack of skills. According to him, no one was prepared to coach the players and work on their skills. Practice, he told the players, was the only way to improve skills. 'Repetition' became his buzzword during the first week. When he gave each of the players a ball, he told them not to lose it. 'This is why you play this game ... to have the ball in your hand,' he said. 'Learn to love it. Learn to enjoy the feel of having it in your hand. Perhaps then you won't give it away in the tackle, throw it away when there is nothing on and kick it away aimlessly.'

At first the players struggled with carrying the ball everywhere. Just remembering to pack it in their bag was an effort. These were small teething pains, and Viljoen felt he had ignited something, especially when he told the players that the Boks would become the first team in test rugby's history to complete eighty minutes without kicking a ball.

The players did not believe him at first, until they started training for the test in Buenos Aires. Everything was about ball retention and phase play. Every drill was designed to improve body positioning in the tackle, ball placement, offloading in the tackle and retaining possession. The first week in Argentina, the players trained twice a day. No time was set aside to improve their fitness. Instead, Viljoen focused on improving their skills level in most of the practice sessions.

In his discussions with Rod Macqueen, Viljoen had spent a lot of the time absorbing information. Defensive patterns had improved in the game, and Viljoen was adamant that the only way to break down the best defences was through patience, outstanding ball retention skills and game breakers who could think on their feet. He called it 'breaking the wall', an Australian description for beating the defence.

Viljoen wanted the players to run into space instead of into the face of the opposition, and avoid making unnecessary contact. McIntosh agreed that the idea could work, but not at the expense of forsaking the basic elements of the game. The forwards still had to do their primary job of winning the ball before they could think of playing with it. McIntosh is a prophet of momentum, which is all he spoke to the players about for a week. Each theory session was designed for them to understand the world of momentum. They had to know why they were taking the ball back into the traffic, why a split second in recycling made such a difference to the effectiveness of the next phase and what constituted a mismatch in numbers.

McIntosh's theory was that to dominate a game and dictate terms, a team had to be on the front foot. You only achieve that through momentum, and you can only achieve momentum by having more numbers in attack than the opposition. For this to happen, you suck the opposition in to the point of breakdown, force numbers to the breakdown by attacking the pillars next to the breakdown, and through this you try to create mismatches, where your backs are running at their forwards. Then you strike.

McIntosh did not believe in taking the ball wide when there was no momentum. A physical team with the ability to offload in the tackle and skilled in contact situations could successfully implement the theory of momentum. In that week players worked on the basics of rugby. There was nothing extravagant about the intended style of play against Argentina, but something exceptional was going to happen: the Boks would not kick the ball. McIntosh and Markgraaff had one reservation about this approach: the fitness of the team. They did not think the Boks were conditioned to play a ball-in-hand test for eighty minutes. Both appealed for balance in this approach, and tactical awareness of the situation. Viljoen said it was possible to go eighty minutes without kicking.

McIntosh went home a day before the test because of other commitments, and while Viljoen respected his rugby knowledge, he felt McIntosh was too old school for his environment. In hindsight, Viljoen's attitude was a mistake, because McIntosh, in a technical and advisory capacity, would have benefited the squad.

Honan introduced analyses some of the Boks had never seen. He broke down the scrumhalves' passes to a hundredth of a second, and with the help of video clips showed the scrumhalves the negative impact on play in any delay. They couldn't argue with the evidence. Honan supported his opinion with fact.

Honan was very good. Alan Solomons had used him with the Stormers, so the Cape-based players had experience of working with him. Viljoen valued Honan's input, but thought he overstepped his professional boundaries. Within a few days Viljoen felt that Honan wanted to be the coach. He was not invited back.

And so we travelled to the River Plate Stadium to play the Pumas in the second test in front of 57 000 fans. It was like going to a soccer match. Our players had never experienced such hostility on arriving at a ground. People swore at the players as they got off the bus, youngsters made taunting gestures and the noise level was deafening. The Boks were in an unfamiliar zone. Not only did they have to beat the Pumas, they had to do so without kicking. It was Percy Montgomery's first test at flyhalf, and he touched the first ball after fifteen seconds. The Pumas kicked off, the Boks won the ball, it was shifted back to Montgomery and he sent it down the line. The Boks were caught in possession, held onto the ball and were penalised: 3-0 to the Pumas.

Markgraaff was beside himself.

'Harry,' he said, 'we have to kick the ball.'

Viljoen said it was still early days. He wanted to see how much belief there was in the side, and he would only know if they rose to a seemingly impossible challenge.

For the next thirty-eight minutes the Boks played some of the most incredible rugby, exhibiting skills previously thought to be the ownership of the Australians. One try included eleven phases, and in the build-up to another one, twenty-one passes were made, half of them in the tackle, over a distance of 60 metres. The Pumas were finished by halftime. It took them fourteen minutes to emerge for the second half. Our players were equally exhausted, and here Viljoen made a critical error in judgement.

Markgraaff wanted the Boks to change the game plan in the second half, kick to the corners, slow the game down and finish off the Pumas. It made perfect sense. But Viljoen said that there was still forty minutes of ball-in-hand rugby to be played. And the players themselves, stunned at their own ability to play half a test without kicking the ball, did not want to kick it now. They wanted to win the eighty-minute challenge. They wanted to create history. Markgraaff worried that it might be the wrong kind of history. The Boks had never lost to the Pumas. He was scared that it would all go wrong and the Boks would lose. The debate on the stands continued between Markgraaff and Viljoen.

'Harry, can I tell them to kick it? Harry, we are getting ourselves into shit. We need to kick it.' Markgraaff was right. Australian referee Scott Young penalised the Boks regularly in the first fifteen minutes of the second half, and the Pumas were potting the goals. Within twenty minutes they had closed the gap. The crowd burnt flags, papers and whatever else they could put a match to. There was no coach's box to sit in, and the coaches, support staff and the players not involved in the game were all seated among the crowd. The locals swore and spat at us, and tossed cooldrink bottles in our direction. It was a different experience from being at Newlands.

Markgraaff was frantic going into the final ten minutes. Viljoen tried to remain calm, but he was troubled. The Pumas were on the attack. One point separated the teams. It was our line-out throw. Montgomery was standing in the in-goal area, and left wing Pieter Rossouw was so deep he was beyond the deadball line. Viljoen had to concede the dream.

'Tell them to kick the ball. Tell them to kick the fucking ball.'

Before he could even utter the second line, Markgraaff was on the two-way radio screaming to Jake White: 'Kick ... kick the ball! Harry says tell them to kick!'

White, standing next to the line-out, motioned for a player to go down, which gave him time to go on the field and pass Montgomery the message.

'The coach says kick it as far you fucking can.'

Montgomery asked him if he was sure.

'Just kick the fucking thing,' White ordered.

Montgomery hammered it downfield. The Boks had kicked the ball out of hand for the first time after seventy-three minutes of the test. Braam van Straaten would add a long-range penalty with a few minutes to spare, and the Boks won by four points. They had escaped, but Viljoen felt that seventy-three minutes was seventy-three more than the players had thought possible. For him, it was a victory of the power of the mind.

The rest of the tour was set up for a revolutionary display, but this never materialised. Markgraaff's pessimism and failure to buy into Viljoen's way of playing the game had an effect on Viljoen. McIntosh had returned home, and when we arrived in the United Kingdom, it rained almost every day. According to Markgraaff, there was no time to focus on skills, and conditions were not conducive to phase play. He told Viljoen that we had to play conservatively, just try to win, and bring about all the changes in 2001. Viljoen agreed. He would never rekindle the kind of enthusiasm among the players that we experienced in Argentina, although the final forty minutes against a star-studded Barbarians team was on par with what we saw in the first forty minutes against the Pumas.

Back in South Africa, Harry flew the senior players to Cape Town. Harry did things differently to what had gone before. On the tour he had treated the players with respect and related to them as colleagues. Now he entertained them at his business offices at the Victoria & Alfred Waterfront. André Vos, captain of the Boks, Mark Andrews, Joost van der Westhuizen, André Venter and Corné Krige were the senior players Harry invited to the first meeting. He wanted to know their feelings about South African rugby and, in particular, the set-up around Springboks.

Andrews was the most outspoken. He had carefully prepared for the meeting and made use of his laptop, speaking with conviction about the evils in South African rugby and the concerns he had as a player. He felt the players were treated like pawns, were too easily discarded, weren't consulted often enough and were shown very little respect. Few players were more passionate about the Bok jersey than Andrews, but playing under five Bok coaches in six years had turned him into a cynic. Andrews was very negative, and doubtful that things could change within South African rugby.

Krige, Van der Westhuizen and Vos were dissatisfied with the fact that players were always the last to know about anything relevant to Bok rugby, and they all questioned the contracting system, the reality of transformation's ideology and the money allocated to the Springboks. They wanted a share in the gate money, but did not have the answer when asked what the consequences would be when they lost. The players wanted to be treated like businessmen, but they were told in no uncertain terms that it could not be a case of 'we are a business' when the salaries had to be paid, but 'it is only a sport' when responsibility had to be taken for poor results.

It was a healthy discussion, and the players spoke freely about the potential of the Boks and the formation of a business unit. Understandably, they focused on money and the allocation of funds to the Springboks. Also, all of them wanted to feel special for having made the Bok team, and felt the green blazer had been cheapened because everybody was wearing it, be it the team's computer analyst, the under-19 captain or the SARFU executive.

They wanted something distinctive to set them apart as the national team. We suggested small changes to the blazers, which would have a major impact on the players' attitude. The word 'Springbok' was added to their blazer pocket and test jersey. You had to have played a test to be able to wear the blazer with the wording and badge. The words 'South African Rugby', and not 'Springbok', would identify management.

In 2000, everyone played in the same jersey. We had to fight to have the jerseys of the SA 'A', SA under-23, Sevens, SA under-21 and SA under-19 teams changed. By 2002, all the jerseys and blazers of the junior teams had been altered. Rian Oberholzer was amenable to all the changes and understood the rationale behind them. He convinced the executive to agree to all of it. Without his support, it would never have happened. The word 'Springbok' would also be added to the test player's tie; non-test players and management would have a Bok emblem on their tie, but no wording. Seniority was rewarded by acknowledging test caps. A player in the squad would be ranked from 1 to 26 on seniority, and that would be how they were numbered once in camp. It may seem trivial to the outsider, but to these very influential Boks, it meant everything.

In the next two seasons, Joost and Mark Andrews enjoyed a wonderful battle to see who would receive kitbag No. 1. They also wanted acknowledgement of where they fitted into the Springbok hierarchy. The number they were given was something to be proud of, because it was theirs for life. We suggested that this be the number that goes on their training jersey. They loved the idea, and it was implemented when the squad got together six months later.

The players felt that the wearing of the green blazer had lost its meaning. They were always dressed in the green blazer, whether they travelled to matches or attended functions. They wanted to look more businesslike and less like school-boys. Harry's ideas were catching on. We proposed that they wear suits, and only wear the green blazer to a test match. This would honour the occasion and restore pride in the green blazer. The players agreed. Again, in principle, it was a valid argument. Practically, it was more complicated. Executive members who opposed the idea suggested that Harry was trying to do away entirely with the green blazer and other Springbok traditions.

But, in fact, the players at the initial meeting had asked for a system that would strengthen the traditions, marry them to the corporate world and together create a distinctive new Bok identity. They argued that they were given no buy-in to their own destiny or appearance. They were told what to wear, how to play and when to be at training. Their input was minimal, and coaches and administrators refused to discuss important issues with them.

Andrews felt that, after nearly a decade of playing test rugby, surely he ought to know a thing or two? Viljoen agreed. It was always his contention that the players had to have a greater say in the running of the side. He informed the players that he wanted regular communication with them, and that he would call a squad meeting, or seminar, in January 2001 to sell the business unit concept to all the contracted players, whom he had inherited from Mallett until the end of 2001. Viljoen had no choice but to honour the contracts and work with all the players. The meeting with the senior players was very professional, and they had clearly never experienced such an approach from a rugby coach.

The 2001 season was shaping as the most exciting ever in South African rugby's professional era. For the first time, indications were that the Boks would be a professional outfit. My job was to research other sporting codes, put together a one-day seminar, and arrange trips to Australia, New Zealand and, if necessary, the United States. Viljoen wanted to meet with influential leaders in the sports world. It was an incredibly exciting time.

Rian Oberholzer backed every idea. He craved change, and embraced Viljoen's reforms without reservation. Financially he gave Viljoen everything he wanted. Oberholzer fought with his executive, and then the board, to acquire the personnel he believed Viljoen needed to make the Boks world champions in 2003.

Even André Markgraaff was caught up in the early-year frenzy of borrowing ideas and formulating new ones, trying to settle on something that would be unique to the Boks of 2001. The unlikely pairing of Viljoen and Markgraaff had shown some promise during the tour, and in January and February 2001 there were signs that they had forged a working relationship that I, among others, had thought impossible.

January 2001 was to prove very significant for Viljoen and his players. The seminar was held at the Cape Sun Inter-Continental Hotel, and Viljoen flew in the players, the most relevant sponsors and media partners SuperSport. A topic that had to be discussed was contracting, as the players were always unhappy about the process. Viljoen's predecessor, Nick Mallett, had settled on a yearly retainer, divided into an A, B and C category. On top of this, the player received a match fee of R20 000 and a win bonus of between R5 000 and R10 000, depending on the opposition.

A-category players earned R700 000, B-category players R600 000, and C- category players R500 000. The national side plays an average of twelve tests a year. An A-category player in 2000 could earn a million rand if he played in all the tests and the Boks were successful in only 50 per cent of them. Viljoen, ideally, wanted the system changed. He wanted players to be rewarded for their efforts, and thought it wrong to group players. Statistics showed that in 2000 some players had earned R600 000, having played in only two or three tests. Others, who had played in every test, earned less.

Viljoen's goal was to do away with the retainer, as he felt this rewarded mediocrity and did not inspire excellence. He wanted to pay the player a match fee in excess of R100 000, with a decent win bonus. Viljoen was a believer in incentive. Our rugby had operated on retainers, and winning statistics of 50 per cent proved the folly of the system.

Oberholzer had become disillusioned with the contracting issue. It had been a problem with every coach, and SARFU and the players never found common ground. Players felt that SARFU should take all the financial risk, while SARFU believed the risk should be shared. The South African Rugby Players' Association (SARPA) made a lot of noise, but could not offer a solution that satisfied both parties.

Viljoen put on a wonderful sales display at the seminar. He spoke of a business unit and of independence. He spoke about money. He insisted that the business unit would be run in offices separate from SARFU's, that the Boks would have their own budget and that money saved would be reinvested in the squad. The players would be the beneficiaries, not SARFU. Viljoen wanted the players to promote excellence within the squad, and to force out hangers-on or players who were not good enough. He wanted players to stop protecting their mates, and he illustrated the benefits by using financial equations. He put it to the players that a mediocre teammate was costing them money, and a contracting system that lumped everyone together in one category was detrimental to the players who wanted to excel.

The players were shown video and Powerpoint presentations to illustrate Viljoen's ideas for the business unit. Rian had already agreed that the business unit should be situated away from the SARFU offices, and for six months the unit was run from Cape Town's central business district. Players would be given business cards and laptops, and were expected to communicate along professional lines. They would be tutored on punctuality, precision and life skills, as well as other essential tools in the business world. Viljoen promoted the philosophy that a better all-round person guaranteed a more efficient rugby player.

He encouraged players to express themselves and to grow; Viljoen wanted personalities in his team, and he yearned for a squad of professionals. In theory, it was revolutionary for South African rugby. But, in the next year, Viljoen the idealist and theorist would be crushed. Internal politics and the media contributed to his defeat, but he committed rugby suicide long before the media put the knife in.

In January 2001, though, the Boks were a brand about to be revolutionised, and Viljoen masterminded the signing of all squad contracts in one evening. He waited until 8 p.m. The players had been fed on a diet of excitement and expectation, entertained by sponsors' promises, and finally sat down to a feast. The evening session began after dinner, and by then the players were emotionally drained. Viljoen delivered the coup de grâce. The players were to see him one by one, in alphabetical order, and he would present each player with his season's contract.

He told the players that it was a 'take-it-or-leave-it' situation. Those who did not think for themselves, or who preferred agents to do their thinking for them, asked if they could get back to him with an answer. Viljoen said no.

Grant Esterhuizen was the first to ask to consult with his agent. Viljoen said that was fine, but he wanted an answer before the end of the evening. He told the players that he neither spoke to agents, nor dealt with them. Viljoen's philosophy included treating the players like directors, and he expected them to have decision-making abilities. Viljoen did not speak to his business directors through agents; he expected the same courtesy from his Bok players. Player and coach had to trust one another; if the player could not speak openly to the coach, then he should not be in the squad.

Viljoen offered players set fees. Whereas Mallett had had two categories – R700 000 or R600 000 – Viljoen offered some players R700 000, and others as little as R200 000. These figures would be reviewed three times a year, with the player capable of either increasing or reducing his retainer in the course of the season. Performance would be key. Viljoen also wanted to improve the match fee and win incentive.

The players were very taken aback by Harry's approach. They were given a glimpse of the ruthless businessman in him – the guy who had come to make a deal, and was only going to leave once it had been closed. Viljoen needed the players' signatures. In the five years since the 1995 World Cup Springboks had signed their contracts, no Bok squad had collectively signed contracts – one of the more bizarre situations at SA Rugby. Contracts were prepared and presented, but invariably never signed, because of disputes between SARFU and the player's agent.

Players queued in alphabetical order. Some were upset, and Esterhuizen was among those who called his agent. Viljoen did not care, and Esterhuizen eventually signed that evening.

Japie Mulder's contract retainer was cut from R600 000 to R400 000, and he was pissed off, as he alleged Viljoen had promised him during the 2000 end-of-year tour that there would be no reduction. Mulder was further angered when Joost told him and other players that his contract remained untouched, and that he would still be on a R700 000 retainer. Mulder confronted Viljoen about it.

They discussed the issue like adults, but it was the first sign for Viljoen that he was not operating in a business environment. This was Springbok rugby. Money was both a motivator and an evil. Later that evening, Viljoen spoke to me about his disappointment in Mark Andrews. He thought he had given Andrews a lifeline by backing him after Mallett had been about to put an end to his international career.

By rights, Andrews should not have been offered a contract. Viljoen started him on R600 000, to be reviewed in six months. Viljoen also guaranteed Andrews that he would look after him if he performed well on the field. Viljoen's room was next to Andrews', and he later overheard Andrews in conversation with his wife. The player was disgruntled that he was on a lower retainer than Van der Westhuizen.

Viljoen felt that Andrews should have shown more appreciation. The previous coach was about to retire him, and all he could do now was complain. Viljoen was naive, and it bit him badly as the year unfolded. Rugby players are mercenaries, loyal only to whoever is coaching at the time. They will applaud their coach until he is ousted, then kick him when he is down and hail his successor as a breath of fresh air.

After Mallett, Viljoen was the wind of change the players desired. After Viljoen, Rudolf Straeuli was the stability the players sought. After Straeuli's rigid approach, Jake White now symbolises sanity ... and so it continues in Bok rugby. But Viljoen was overly sensitive to the media and players' attitudes, and took any kind of rejection or criticism very badly.

Players will use the media to further their cause as much as the media will use the player. Inevitably, disgruntled players complained to the media through their agents. The day after the seminar, the media reported that the players had been forced to sign a contract, and that the contracts were therefore meaningless. Agents harshly criticised Viljoen's methods, and anonymous players grumbled about the whole affair.

Viljoen knew who these players were, yet never held it against them. He selected them because he felt they were the best in their position. Harry dismissed the media reports as the knee-jerk reaction of one or two upset players. He had wanted thirty-odd signatures, and had closed the deal. A clear message had also been sent to agents and the media that there was a new attitude in Bok town.

Viljoen's private wealth gave him the confidence and freedom to do as he pleased, but his wealth and business acumen were also the reasons why the media never accepted him. They resented his attitude towards the press in general and his disregard for them as individuals. War had been declared, but at this stage of the game, Viljoen was pumped up enough to believe that he had the stomach for a battle he knew would get ugly. It would reach a climax in June 2001, against France …

3

An uneasy alliance

Harry Viljoen and André Markgraaff

On 23 June 2001, South Africa played France in Durban. It was a war. The players were physically sore and emotionally fragile after losing the week before. Now they won 20-15, but Harry showed very little euphoria. The series was drawn 1-1, but everyone was just relieved that it had not been lost. Harry believed there was nothing to celebrate. He was wrong, because the players felt the win was typical of test wins. France, despite the protests of the South African media, were a quality side, which they went on to prove in the next twelve months when they won the Six Nations, and beat England, Australia, New Zealand and South Africa in Paris.

The press, many of whom had been opposed to Harry from the time of his appointment, was relentless in the week building up to the Durban test. I told him to ignore the opinions of people he did not respect. This was the real world of professional sport: if they like you they will excuse your every failing; if they have a problem with you, the best win will not be good enough. Harry is a sensitive guy. In his social circle, it is one of his endearing qualities. In South African rugby, it is a character flaw, and a weakness quickly identified by the media. Harry's sensitivity always triggered a reaction, as he would seek out his critics for an explanation of their opinions. On the eve of the Durban test, he told a journalist that he had lain awake contemplating resignation. This, after one home test defeat!

The comment only gave Viljoen's detractors additional ammunition. The pressure on the team was already enormous because of the high expectations before the game. Most of it was self-induced by management as a result of their pre-season claim that they would be taking the game to 'another level'. The Plettenberg Bay training camp, the Boks' international pre-season get-together, had created a hype that was never realised in any of the eleven test matches in 2001.

It had all started off so brilliantly in Johannesburg in the first test against France a week earlier. The Boks kicked off, won back the kick-off, the ball was immediately moved to the grandstand side of Ellis Park, and flyhalf Butch James threw a long pass that bounced favourably for Breyton Paulse on the right wing.

The French defensive line, stretched by the length of the pass and bounce of the ball, was unsure. Paulse danced his way through a series of tackles and scored. All of this took seventeen seconds. At this point, a sledgehammer should have been taken to the Ellis Park lighting system to put an end to the game. Instead, the French pack used a sledgehammer to dismantle Harry's world, and won 32-23.

Tim Lane, the Wallabies' 1999 World Cup-winning backs coach and recently appointed backs coach to the Boks, had been in the country for forty-eight hours, and had attended only one Bok training session. Now he was in a Bok dressing room after a home test defeat. The Harry who had been sold to him as the saviour of South African rugby had been larger than life. The Harry he was now looking at was a vulnerable impostor. In an attempt to rally the team, Viljoen attempted a sales speech on how the defeat would test the character of the squad. It fell on deaf ears. He did not believe the words himself, because no one had thought the Boks would lose.

André Markgraaff admitted to feeling physically sick later that evening. The Afrikaans media were camped outside the change room. Harry went out, and they wanted him to have a go at the referee. He wouldn't, saying the referee had not beaten the Boks, which only added to the tension. Returning to the team bus that evening was another new experience. The bus, emblazoned with images of players, was under attack and had been for some time. Drunken supporters had urinated against it, people had pelted it with beer cans, and a group of thugs had tried to rock the bus onto its side with the driver behind the wheel. Stadium security was called to ease tensions and clear the way before the team made the short journey to the bus.

That evening's initiation of the new Boks was like a birthday celebration in a morgue. Viljoen, in particular, wanted the ritual ended as quickly as possible. He wanted to go to bed and forget the day had ever happened. Everyone had overestimated the strength of the Boks and the perceived inexperience of the French – except Lane, who as head coach of Montferrand had spent the past eight months coaching a third of the French side.

'There are a lot of blokes making their test debuts,' he had told the players. 'They will give their left ball to win at Ellis Park. They feel they have nothing to lose, and don't be fooled by the make-up of the team. They are the form players in France.' The Boks had believed their own hype, despite post-match protests that they had 'respected' the French challenge.

In his final pre-match talk, Viljoen had asked the players how many tries a good team averages per test match. They said four. He answered: 'Today we score eight.'

It sounded wonderful, but no one believed it was possible. Viljoen told the team to 'think bigger' than they had ever done before. When the Boks scored a try after seventeen seconds, it suggested the advent of a new age in Bok rugby. Then they lost control of the test, and never looked like winning it again. The players, bombarded with new information during the ten days' training camp at Plettenberg Bay, hit a blank. They forgot everything, went back to the bad habits with which they were familiar, and scrambled to stay in the game.

A few days before the test, Harry and captain André Vos had been the guest speakers at a corporate breakfast. John Robbie was the master of ceremonies, and in typical Robbie fashion he put on a great show, talking enthusiastically about the 'New-Age Boks', the scientific approach, the foreign influence and the frenzy surrounding the team.

Vossie lapped it up, saying it was brilliant to be involved. He told Robbie and the audience how much the Boks had learnt, and then made a fatal mistake. He said: 'I've learnt more in the last two weeks than I have in most of my career.'

It was all Robbie was waiting for. Earlier, Vos had spoken about the introduction of cycling to training, and how it was bonding the team and keeping them 'humble'. Robbie then cut Harry and Vossie up.

'Bicycles,' he said. 'That's wonderful. But what happens if the wheels come off against France?' There was no answer, and there would be no answer when the wheels indeed came off at Ellis Park.

Markgraaff, in particular, was critical of Vos' leadership and his contribution as a player. He urged Harry to drop him. Markgraaff reminded Viljoen that he had long held the view that Vos should never have been selected in the first place. On the end-of-year tour in 2000, Markgraaff had advised Viljoen to get rid of Vos. Viljoen had felt that it would be unfair to axe him without giving him a chance. He wanted as much continuity as possible on that tour, and in his opinion Vos had done more than enough to justify an extension in 2001.

Viljoen was not convinced that Vos was the answer at No. 8, which was why he only announced him as captain for the first two tests. But he was concerned that there was no one else to fill the gap. Bob Skinstad was the only player Viljoen believed capable of introducing the 'x factor' into the Bok team. But Skinstad's fitness was in doubt after he missed the 2000 season because of injury. Viljoen was not going to make the call on Vos until he was convinced that Skinstad was physically fit enough to play eighty minutes of test rugby.

Viljoen retained Vos for the Durban test, as dropping the captain after the Ellis Park defeat could have been interpreted as a panic reaction. Dropping him after a winning test would be more palatable, when Viljoen hoped to explain the decision to a slightly friendlier media. But Harry was getting fed up with the negativity surrounding Vos. Markgraaff was on his case, I was encouraging him to make the change sooner rather than later, and Jake White also felt that Vossie should go.

One night in Durban Harry snapped, and told Jake, Markgraaff and me that he did not want to talk about Vossie any more. But Markgraaff's patience had run out. The confrontation between Vos and Markgraaff was only days away. Harry wanted players to question things and to think for themselves. Markgraaff was from the old school where coaches coached and players played.

When Vos suggested to Markgraaff that the team miss a scrumming session on the Monday because the players had not recovered from the onslaught of the French, Markgraaff told him in no uncertain terms who the forwards coach was. 'You have been "coaching" the team for the past two weeks and we have seen the results,' Markgraaff said sarcastically. 'Now I am coaching them.'

Markgraaff was disillusioned. Players' opinions were considered equal to or even more important than that of the coaches. He was uncomfortable in that kind of team environment, and did not enjoy the Australian influence of Tim Lane and defensive coach Les Kiss. He felt they only reinforced Harry's ideal to move away from the power-based Bok game to a pattern that relied on phase play and skill. Viljoen knew he had to make a call on Vos. He had admitted in private that Vos was not his ideal No. 8. He was not tall enough, did not possess the ball skills to be effective in Viljoen's dream game plan, and was not dynamic enough.

The only problem was that Viljoen loved everything about Vos' character. He was loyal, the ideal team man, and passionate about the Boks and South African rugby. As a person, Vossie was very popular with the media, the South African public and within the squad. France had exposed the lack of height among the Bok loose forwards, with Vos, Corné Krige and Rassie Erasmus dwarfed by the French back row. France exploited this at both the line-out and kick-off.

Skinstad had shown up well in all the fitness tests. His attitude throughout the Plett camp was good, and he was willing to play his way back into the team. Prior to afternoon training, Viljoen informed Vos that he was no longer the captain. Skinstad had been offered the captaincy earlier in the afternoon, and only accepted after making a call to his mentor and former provincial coach, Alan Solomons.

The decision was relayed to the squad at afternoon training. Viljoen called the players into a huddle, and bluntly informed them that Skinstad was the new captain. Vos was out. Vos saved the situation by thanking the players for their support, and urging them to get behind Skinstad. He offered Skinstad his support in front of the squad.

The manner in which the team was informed was not ideal, and could have been more professional. Rassie and Corné were put out. Both had been strong candidates to captain the team, considering themselves certainties in the side. They were the two favoured by Markgraaff to take over from Vos. Now they were on the outer, and they showed little enthusiasm for training that afternoon. You could hardly blame them.

The players were stunned by the decision, and fifteen minutes after they returned to the hotel, my phone started ringing. Players had phoned their media connections. The story was out that Vos had been dropped as captain and that

Skinstad was in. The media wanted either confirmation or a denial. The only way to salvage the situation was to formally announce the change in a press release that evening. This would end the speculation, and the morning papers would run the story. A one-paragraph statement was released, confirming the change in captaincy. A press conference was arranged for the next morning at 9 a.m. to explain the decision, and both players agreed to face the media with the coach.

That evening Harry, the two players and I worked out a strategy. Both players agreed that there was nothing to hide. As hard as it was for Vos, he wanted Harry to release a statement in which he said that he felt Skinstad was better equipped to do the job, both at No. 8 and as captain. Vos told Harry that he would fight to make the team, and that he could play at No. 6 for the Springboks. Viljoen wanted to believe it more than he actually did at the time. He had enormous respect for Vos, and his admiration only increased as a result of Vos' reaction to his axing as captain. Viljoen promised Vos that he would give him a fair run at No. 6, and provide him with enough playing opportunity to make a success of the position. As a result, Viljoen's relationship with Krige would break down. Viljoen had made a choice between Skinstad and Vos at No. 8. He had chosen Skinstad. Now he had to decide between Vos and Krige. He would go with Vos. Rassie Erasmus, Markgraaff's favourite to succeed Vos, was completely on the outer. Viljoen did not think Rassie fitted into the back-row mix, or that he was performing well enough. Viljoen did not want to select him. There wasn't a place for both Skinstad and Erasmus; it was one or the other.

The next morning the media questioned the captaincy decision, suspecting that something had gone wrong between Vos and Viljoen. It never had. Viljoen had always wanted Skinstad as his captain. It was a rugby decision. But the media refused to believe this. Markgraaff had an 'off-the-record' talk with JJ Harmse, at the time a journalist with the Afrikaans newspaper *Die Burger*, in which he implied that Vos had been dropped as captain because he stuttered. It was the lead story in the Afrikaans daily papers the next morning.

I knew the 'source' quoted was Markgraaff, as I had seen him in deep discussion with Harmse. I called Markgraaff, and asked him how he could tell the journalist that Vos' stutter was the reason for the change in captaincy. Markgraaff defended himself by insisting that it *was* the reason, and that Vos' stutter impeded his ability to make quick line-out calls. It may have been Markgraaff's reason for wanting Vos out, but it certainly was not why Viljoen had axed him.

Viljoen hated confrontation. He would dismiss stories of disruptive or destructive influences within the squad as 'old wives' tales'. This meant that certain issues were never addressed in a coaching structure in which Markgraaff, Lane and Viljoen had started to differ hugely on selections. Italy were predictably thumped 60-14 in Port Elizabeth, but the first forty minutes were a struggle. In the coach's box, Viljoen and Markgraaff disagreed about the approach and performances of certain players, especially when Viljoen suggested substituting Johan Ackermann.

Markgraaff, a huge Ackermann fan, wanted Mark Andrews taken off, feeling the player had done nothing all afternoon. 'I have been watching Andrews specifically,' Markgraaff said, 'and I am telling you Harry, he has made no impact.'

Viljoen, having coached Andrews in the early part of his career, always backed the Sharks lock. He would never substitute his most experienced forward. Viljoen asked Lane for his opinion, and Tim said he would stick with Andrews. Markgraaff was furious, as he was the forwards coach. He felt insulted that Harry had asked the opinion of the backs coach about a forward substitution.

Harry subbed Ackermann. That night Markgraaff asked to see Viljoen in private, and expressed his disapproval about the game plan and the selections, as well as his obvious inability to influence selections or the Boks' playing style.

Markgraaff wanted out, but Viljoen persuaded him to stay. The final straw came a few days later, when Viljoen pushed for the selection of SA under-21 star Joe van Niekerk at the expense of Rassie Erasmus. Viljoen had never seen Van Niekerk play, but supported Jake White's recommendation that a place be found for him.

White never opposed Erasmus' inclusion. He wanted both Van Niekerk and Erasmus in the squad, and Krige dropped. Markgraaff believed in Rassie, and wanted him as captain. Now he was out of the squad. This made Markgraaff mad, because Erasmus had been in the squad prior to the selectors' meeting. It ended the Viljoen–Markgraaff partnership in a coaching marriage that had been destined to fail.

Viljoen had originally opposed any involvement from André Markgraaff in his coaching structure. But in September 2000 he told me that he was interested in appointing Markgraaff as his Springbok assistant. My advice to Harry was that he should not. The two men did not share the same rugby philosophy, and culturally it would be a clash of two different worlds. I also thought Markgraaff carried too much political baggage after his resignation only three years earlier as Bok coach for calling black rugby administrators 'kaffirs'.

Viljoen asked me to list reasons both in favour of and against Markgraaff's appointment. I offered him three reasons why he should appoint him, and sixteen why he should not. He appointed Markgraaff. Viljoen declared that anything was possible, and that he would make the union work. Markgraaff walked away from the partnership after just seven tests.

Markgraaff, in rugby terms, was not good for Viljoen, and it is doubtful Viljoen was any good for Markgraaff. But in 2000, both men made a huge effort to get along and to work together. They tried to understand each other's worlds. It was fun in the beginning, but fatal in the end.

Rian Oberholzer had also warned Viljoen against a coaching liaison with Markgraaff. When Viljoen's name was initially thrown into the hat for Bok coach, SA Rugby board member Keith Parkinson had wanted both Markgraaff and Viljoen to do the job as a package. This was relayed to Viljoen, who refused point-blank. He refused to work with Markgraaff. Oberholzer, dispatched to pull off the sales job, said in that case he would try to do a reverse sales job on the executive before the meeting to determine the Bok coach.

Oberholzer eventually convinced the executive to give Viljoen the job on his own terms, and to allow him to pick his own assistants. Oberholzer called Viljoen, informing him that he did not have to work with Markgraaff, and advising him that he would be wise to align himself with assistants he trusted. Viljoen changed his mind about Markgraaff after a private meeting with Parkinson in Cape Town on the eve of his appointment. Oberholzer was surprised that, after all the fuss, Viljoen now wanted Markgraaff. During the 2000 end-of-year tour, when the Boks beat Ireland in Dublin, I reminded Oberholzer about his reservations, and said he had called it wrong. The partnership was going to blossom. Oberholzer reserved judgement – he had the last laugh.

In the early days, Viljoen insisted that Markgraaff was misunderstood, and after the first tour I was inclined to believe him. Markgraaff was the ideal assistant. He would regale us with tales of South African rugby's political underworld. He told great yarns about coaching, players and behind-the-scenes scheming. He maintained that he had dropped François Pienaar as Bok captain in 1996 because he was no longer good enough as a player. He was adamant that he would do it all over again, because it was the right rugby decision at the time. He also claimed that his decision had met with the approval of everyone in the SARFU executive. It made for fascinating listening.

Viljoen would also occasionally recall a chapter in his provincial coaching or playing career. Mostly, he would talk from a business perspective, usually about the value of building relationships, networking and seeking solutions. Viljoen preached sophistication and reconciliation. He challenged Markgraaff to make peace with Pienaar, among others, and Markgraaff, after a month on tour, agreed to meet him. Viljoen had invited Pienaar to do the jersey presentation on the eve of the England test. Pienaar accepted the invitation to address the team, but refused an audience with Markgraaff. The issue was not forced, and it was the last time Markgraaff and Viljoen spoke of reconciliation. Viljoen was convinced there was another side to Markgraaff, and that all the big man needed was exposure to different views. Chris van Loggerenberg, conditioning coach of the Boks and a man who had worked for a year with Markgraaff during the Cats' 1999 season, cautioned Viljoen about Markgraaff's negative energy.

Van Loggerenberg praised Markgraaff's rugby knowledge, but told Viljoen that the guy was exhausting in a tour environment. It was a polite way of describing

Markgraaff's eternal pessimism. He never saw a half-full glass – it was always half-empty.

When we arrived in Cardiff for the 2000 test against Wales, all Markgraaff could talk about was the weather. 'Harry, it is raining. Harry, the field is going to be heavy and muddy. Harry, we must ensure they close the roof. Harry, it is still raining. Harry, we are in shit.'

The constant pessimism, funny at first, started impacting negatively on Viljoen. If you tell someone who is prone to insecurity often enough that he's in shit, he starts believing it. Viljoen made a public relations mess of wanting the Millennium Stadium's roof closed. It was all the Bok coaches spoke about for five days. The roof wasn't closed, and the Boks won despite the rain and mud.

Up until 2000, my dealings with Markgraaff had been confined to that of journalist and coach. I interviewed him for the first time in 1996. Our most significant conversation occurred in February 1997, when I called him one Sunday afternoon to tell him that I had information about him calling black rugby administrators 'kaffirs', and verbally abusing Pienaar and André Joubert, to name but two players. Markgraaff denied this. He called me back three times that Sunday afternoon, and cautioned me to be careful about writing the story, as he would be forced to take legal action against me.

I wrote the story, which led the *Cape Times* page one on 17 February 1997, and two days later Markgraaff resigned as Bok coach.

We spoke briefly after his press conference. He was distraught, but not bitter towards me. In February 1997, Markgraaff was an outcast. The incident had embarrassed as much as it had infuriated him. The press conference was a further act of public humiliation. Markgraaff's taped tirade in which he racially abused black administrators was deplorable. Nevertheless, I admired him for the way in which he faced the world media and the South African public. I thought he was courageous at the press conference. He admitted his guilt to a nation, and apologised.

Now, three years later, we were sharing a team bus, the team room and many rugby war stories. His 'bedtime' stories were brilliant. Markgraaff has a good sense of humour, a passion for rugby and an appetite for the politics of the game. And he tells a good story. His phone never stopped ringing, and when it did, he was quick to make a call to someone somewhere, who would pass on information in one form or another.

He was assistant coach, coach, selector, CEO, entrepreneur, businessman, player agent and property guru all rolled into one. He is a student of the game, but herein lay the great Markgraaff myth. He is not the 'master', and never will be. Markgraaff is too single-minded in his rugby beliefs for such a sacred elevation in status. His planet does not revolve around an axis of alternatives. His coaching style is limited, and he is deficient in player management.

In the early stages of the 2000 end-of-year tour, Markgraaff and Viljoen so badly wanted to complement each other. Viljoen talked up Markgraaff's knowledge of the game and his value to the Boks. Markgraaff was equally flattering of Viljoen's approach. Markgraaff seemed to show a willingness to change his mindset. On that tour, he appeared to want to break out of his sphere, if only for a peep. He spent time getting to know Percy Montgomery and Robbie Fleck, and admitted to Harry and me that they were two of the nicest blokes you could wish to meet. He told us that it proved how misleading perceptions could be, and that he had prejudged them to be *souties* with big egos and bad attitudes. Nothing, he said, could have been further from the truth. They were true rugby professionals.

Markgraaff seemed to enjoy their madness, and Montgomery, in particular, won him over. After the test match against Wales in Cardiff, Markgraaff spent the evening watching the match tape. He wanted someone to watch the game with him, and Montgomery obliged. Markgraaff could not believe it. He thought Monty would be the first one out on the town. Instead, Montgomery sat in the team room, drank hot chocolate and showed Markgraaff that he took his rugby more seriously than his nightclubbing.

Markgraaff is a conservative person. He likes routine and a particular pattern, be it socially or in rugby. Markgraaff's tour habits are well known to those who have been in his company. He travels light, because he prefers the great indoors of hotel foyers. He absolutely loves a foyer with a big couch, preferably one situated close to the entrance, where he can monitor pedestrian traffic all day. There you'd find him, comfortably ensconced and in conversation with anyone and everyone. It made for captivating viewing, and was always entertaining if you sat down to listen. Nearly every night on tour you would find him in the foyer, usually with a decent audience. He would sign off with a pot of Horlicks and a few more bedtime stories.

Markgraaff does not sleep. He drinks Horlicks to bring the day to an end, but it only starts up his nighttime activity. He is forever on the go, talking to someone on the planet. His phone bill on that trip was R36 000. Markgraaff is a character – more than the average punter will ever know. A lot of the overseas media's character assessment of him was inaccurate. He may appear dull and dusted, but there's a personality that is king in his own world.

Equally, he is not quite the guru the average rugby fan imagines. I found much of Markgraaff's rugby reputation more fable than fact. I was disappointed in his rugby world. There were no inspirational team talks; every match was the 'most important' in the player's career, and too often he contradicted Viljoen when the situation required confirmation of the head coach's intended plan. His theatrics in the coach's box and his running commentary during a game were more Monty Python than Vince Lombardi.

Markgraaff is admired in certain sectors of the South African rugby public and the SARFU executive for being technically without comparison as a coach. Again, the delivery was never as impressive as South African rugby folklore would have one believe. He knows the game, but no more than you would expect from anyone who has coached internationally. He was obsessed with the physical aspect of the game, and believed that South Africans physically intimidated the opposition. Those methods have evolved, and in this regard Markgraaff has not.

He acknowledged that we needed to promote the more skilful players, but was never liberated enough to forgo a conservative approach for an alternative one. He was convinced we could still bully teams, especially England. Viljoen, on the other hand, encouraged a culture in which the players had a voice. Markgraaff agreed in theory, but never accepted the practicalities of such an approach. It irked him that players should question his coaching, be it a philosophy or pattern specifics. He wanted players to do as they were told; he would do the thinking.

Markgraaff had some input in team selection, but did not have a say in the final composition of the team. This he felt to be unfair, as he could not pick his own pack. He was being judged on a unit that he did not necessarily believe was the right one.

Viljoen and Markgraaff were opposites. They spoke different languages, and the only thing they shared was the pressure from mediocre results. Markgraaff wanted a simpler approach at the Plettenberg Bay training camp in 2001 – one where he would talk and the players would listen – but was satisfied with the number of forward sessions allocated to him. When Viljoen asked him if there was enough time to get through restarts, line-outs, scrums, rucks and mauling, Markgraaff said the fourteen sessions were sufficient.

Not a great deal of focus was placed on scrumming. When Viljoen questioned what was going on, Markgraaff told him not to worry. The forwards, keen on the Viljoen approach of self-empowerment, felt Markgraaff's style was antiquated. The team had prepared well for the first test against France, but they were ill prepared in getting the basics right. Viljoen, once Markgraaff had left, would agree with the forwards that the sessions should have consisted of more substance and less theory.

Markgraaff and Viljoen were mature about the split, acknowledging that their worlds could never dovetail. I scripted a pleasant press release in which Viljoen said Markgraaff would play a pivotal role in his capacity as head of the technical committee, and that he would continue to contribute to the well-being of the Boks. Markgraaff never again had anything to do with the Boks. Now, in 2004, he is back in the guise of convener of selectors.

In his autobiography, *Walking Proud*, former SARFU chief Louis Luyt describes Markgraaff as the 'chosen one' to coach the Boks. To some that's as good as a recommendation from God. It has only added to the Markgraaff legend. Markgraaff has the blessing of Luyt, and the support of the conservatives.

In most northern areas of South Africa, he has been awarded a status that has never been earned through results.

Internationally, his record of eight wins in thirteen games is consistent with the failings of most Bok coaches since 1992. His Super 12 record with the Cats in 1999 is even less flattering. The powerful region finished eleventh out of twelve. Statistically, Markgraaff's coaching at the higher levels spells failure. He has knowledge of the game, but not the personality and pedigree that should make up an international coach's package, or, for that matter, that of convener of selectors.

Much has been made of his ability to identify talent, particularly through his involvement with the Potchefstroom Rugby Institute and Griquas. At provincial level, Markgraaff is a pragmatist. He has enjoyed relative Currie Cup success, as the basic formula of a big and brutish pack will still bring you success in South African provincial rugby. Once you move into Super 12 and international territory, an element of risk and innovation has to be introduced. Markgraaff's character does not allow for this. His is a voice that can make a contribution to our game – but it should never be the accepted voice of South African rugby.

Like Viljoen, Markgraaff is sensitive to public pressure and outside influence. He also has many interests in different domains, which could possibly compromise his decision-making. His link with certain players, in his capacity as mentor (read agent), can be interpreted as unhealthy, and his fixation with brawn at the expense of brain (read Dries Scholtz rather than Stuart Abbott) means Bok rugby will continue to mark time and never advance. Politically, Markgraaff *is* a master, and this is why his name is so engrained in the mind of the incumbent SARFU president, Brian van Rooyen. It also explains why the people he once referred to as 'kaffirs' now support him. Markgraaff is a conspiracy theorist who exists on a combination of paranoia and vindication. Spend time in his company, and you might start wondering about things too. He will redefine how you see a hotel foyer or interpret a greeting from a South African rugby administrator.

Markgraaff commands respect from players, but not all of South Africa's players. It is important to highlight the distinction. This respect is cultural rather than rugby-related. More liberal players see him as a relic of the past, someone who symbolises history rather than the future. For many of the Afrikaans-speaking players, he is 'Oom André', master tactician and preacher of the gospel of Springbok rugby.

Markgraaff has been absent from the Springboks since 2001, but somehow he has always been present. His name pops up frequently, always in the capacity of saviour. He is the man the media call for expert analysis and hard-hitting quotes. He is the one many in SA Rugby approach for technical advice. Markgraaff is never backward in volunteering pertinent information or making a contribution he believes will benefit the South African game.

In 2004, Markgraaff announced that he did not want to coach the Boks. His skills, he said, were best utilised in areas such as selection and identifying talent. Then he was nominated for the position, and expounded on how great an honour it was to be on the Bok coaching shortlist. Then he withdrew, citing family bereavement and pressures as the reason. Then he was in again, and finally he opted out to assume the role of convener of selectors. Did he want in or out? Only Markgraaff had the answer. For now he is in, but Markgraaff has been known to change his mind, be it in selection or the style of play. He says it is to keep the opposition guessing, but to tell a player in the tunnel a minute before kick-off that he is no longer in the run-on XV says more about the decision-maker than the decision. Numerous incidents have occurred in which Markgraaff made a call, just to change his mind a few minutes later; or where he only finalised his starting line-up in the change room on match day.

The most bizarre about-face in my time occurred against England at Twickenham in 2000. AJ Venter was sent on with five minutes to go – a decision taken by both Viljoen and Markgraaff. A minute later, Markgraaff, who always took control of the radio communication to the touchline, subbed Venter and sent on Warren Brosnihan.

Venter, his contribution to the test just the one scrum, could not believe it. He walked from the field gesturing to the coach's box. When Viljoen asked Markgraaff what that was all about, he responded: 'Last throw of the dice!'

You can stop laughing now. It is true.

Even before the test, ridiculous incidents took place. Markgraaff convinced Viljoen to put out a false starting team to confuse the English. The team was announced on the Monday, with Stefan Terblanche at fullback and Pieter Rossouw on the wing. Rossouw had already ruled himself out of the test with a hamstring injury.

I told Terblanche to play along with the media, to talk about how exciting it was to start at fullback, and to convince them that it could be his new test position. Rian Oberholzer phoned me about the selection, and wanted to know what was going on. I said it was a false team, and he blew his top. It contravened the International Rugby Board (IRB) regulation, and he told me that we had better rectify the situation.

The next day we put out a team change, saying Rossouw had failed a fitness test and that Terblanche had been moved to the wing. It was the last time Viljoen released a false starting team, but it was not the last of the crazy moments with Markgraaff.

There was the 20-15 win against France in Durban in 2001. The test match kicks off, and Markgraaff tells Viljoen he has a good feeling … that the Boks are going to win … The Boks turn over the ball and the French attack … he tells Viljoen we could be in shit … that the Frogs have come to play rugby … And so the conversation goes all evening. In the final ten minutes, Markgraaff starts giving instructions to technical analyst Jake White down on the sideline.

'Tell Butch James to kick it into the corner and keep them in their 22. We will win the penalty, kick the three points and take this game. I am telling you Harry, we'll win this game.' Viljoen, absolutely gutted that his New-Age game plan had lasted all of seventeen seconds in the first test, is still trying to come to terms with this bumper-car rugby that is proving successful against the French. Markgraaff hasn't stopped talking.

'I am telling you Harry. We will win this game. We will get the penalty, kick the points and win the game.' There is about six minutes to play. I ask him why we need to kick the penalty to win the game. He barks out that a penalty will give us the win 18-17. I mention to him that we are the team leading 17-15.

'Oh, fuck,' he says, laughing. 'Here I am thinking we are 17-15 down.'

Markgraaff has been portrayed as an enigma by the media. But spend a bit of time in his company, tour with him, and be at his side before, during and after a test – there is no mystery, only fables and fallibility. Viljoen had accepted that Markgraaff was more myth than maestro, although it had taken a confrontation, initiated by Markies after the Port Elizabeth test against Italy, to force the issue of his resignation as assistant coach.

The opening three weeks of the international season had produced more commotion than the entire dramatic 2000 season, which saw Nick Mallett booted out of South African rugby.

Now Markgraaff was gone, the test series against France had been drawn, and André Vos had been dumped as Bok captain. Rassie Erasmus was out, replaced by an unknown called Joe van Niekerk. And Robbie Fleck had just been appointed vice-captain. The soap opera was only beginning, because the All Blacks waited in Cape Town, and so did a showdown with the Sports Minister Ngconde Balfour.

4

Shades of grey
Transformation in SA rugby

As a rugby journalist, I devoted a lot of my energy to the progress of black rugby players in the unified South African Rugby Football Union. It was a constant battle. White coaches did not select black players, and after talking to the coaches, I was always left with the impression that they felt black players weakened their line-ups.

Many saw transformation and development as one and the same thing when they were, in fact, separate entities. Transformation, the devil in white South African rugby, is about opportunity. To be given an opportunity, black players had to be rated by the white coaches in South Africa. This was why opportunity was so limited. I was unrelenting in my criticism about the lack of transformation in our rugby, and felt that there were too many people actively linked to effecting transformation on a daily basis who did not understand the reasons why change was necessary.

Black administrators were just as guilty of ignoring the urgency in transformation; it was not only a white disease. I criticised both black and white administrators, took on white coaches, and found myself labelled a 'lover of blacks' among the whites and a racist among the blacks. Harry Viljoen coached Western Province in 1997, and I consistently criticised him in the press for the lack of black representation in the squad – especially his disregard for talents such as Breyton Paulse.

During that season, Viljoen and I would meet often to debate these issues. What impressed me the most about him as coach during that year was his willingness to sit down, listen and argue the point in a mature way. He knew exactly where I stood in forcing the issue of black representation. In 1998 he invited Gcobani Bobo and Johannes (Bolla) Conradie to his Western Stormers pre-season training camp in Hermanus. I had spoken to Viljoen about them in the off-season, sensing that with the right guidance and coaching they could play for South Africa within the next five years.

Viljoen did not pick them for his 1998 Super 12 squad, saying they were too small, which I interpreted as a euphemism for 'too black'. I was very aware of the political situation in rugby and the need to promote quality black talent. Too many talented black schoolboy rugby players were not making it into provincial squads and drifting away from the game. Politicians played numbers games with rugby's administrators, as they were at a loss to explain why so few were making the grade.

SARFU's development programme – as I was to see first hand when I joined the Boks in 2000 – was a big farce. Millions of rands were ploughed into game development, all-star camps were held every year and facilities were improved in black areas. But those responsible for black player development would draw up a different list of black players every year, and provincial, Super 12 and national coaches would rarely communicate with this department. On paper, it looked very impressive. Each time the government asked questions, SARFU's apologists showed them balance sheets, the various Elite training squads, from under-15 through to under-21, presented them with lists of black names, and spoke of change being just around the corner in senior rugby. The practical implementation was not as impressive.

Whatever changes took place would never have been effected without the quota system, which forced white coaches to pick black players at provincial level. But the quota system is a mess at senior level because talented players are not identified, and the implementation of the system has for too many years relied on the selection of two black wings plus thirteen white players. Coaches reveal their agendas in the language they use. Often I would listen, half-stunned, at how white coaches referred to black players. They would use words such as 'non-whites', 'players of colour', 'development players', 'quota players', 'players from previously disadvantaged backgrounds' and 'them'.

I have never heard a white player described as non-black. Call it semantics, but describing a player as non-white is as good as calling him inferior. When I chatted to the black players who would play for the Springboks between 2000 and 2003, this was exactly how they felt about the situation. They couldn't understand why coaches were unable to refer to them as rugby players, or as black rugby players. Every fashionable and misguided euphemism implied weakness. I have attended many meetings, be it with provincial, Super 12 or national coaches, and the level of inherent racism must be seen to be believed. These people are anti-black, and half the time they don't even know it.

Hanyani Shimange, Free State and Cats hooker, told me that the first time he was ever made to feel like a quota or development player in South Africa was when he started playing senior provincial rugby. Shimange, a very good player, captained his schools team and is from a comfortable financial background. At school he was the best hooker, and that is why he played rugby. The moment he reached provincial level, coaches identified him as a quota player from a previously disadvantaged background. They saw black, added one and one together, and came up with three. This type of maths and logic dominated all discussion on transformation within South African rugby.

When Viljoen asked me to join his management team and assist him in an advisory capacity, his main selling point to me was transformation. He said that I had beaten the transformation drum for a decade, and yet very little had changed within. He offered me the opportunity to change things at the highest level, and he would be amenable to black player identification for the Springbok team. He wanted to pick a team fully representative of the country's demographics. Viljoen said that he respected my rugby knowledge and my belief in black talent. He knew that I wanted to see quality black players coming through the system and making it at the highest level, but that I was as quick to dismiss the plodders the development department were flogging as future test players. One only has to go back and look at some of the squads that were identified. The majority of these 'rising stars' never played provincial rugby, many because they should not have been identified in the first place, a situation which gave the white coach the excuse to condemn all black talent as inadequate.

The media accused Harry of 'buying' me in order to avoid confrontation and daily criticism. I was described in the media as having been his most ardent critic. The truth is that I was a huge critic of his, but I was as big a cheerleader. It depended on how I viewed a particular situation. If something warranted criticism, I never held back. If praise was due, I was the first to slip on the pompoms and kick up my heels.

I never asked Harry if his motivation to involve me was an attempt to keep me inside the tent, pissing out, a view most of the media held. It did not concern me if his motive was to remove me from the media while he was Bok coach. He had sold me on the transformation idea, and I was up for the challenge. My ten years of writing rugby had been a brilliant experience; now the opportunity had opened up to do something different, and hopefully effect meaningful change in the game.

Viljoen was walking into a political minefield, and my role was to be that of sweeper. For someone who felt so passionate about the issue of black representation in our rugby, it was a fantastic opportunity. I found a wonderful transformation ally in Jake White, who had coached several quality black rugby players at junior level. Harry had involved Jake, and respected his view on black talent. Together we would push for greater opportunities for black players, but for a purpose. The player had to have the chance of playing test rugby on ability alone. Transformation was about providing the opportunity.

Eight months after Harry's appointment, we were in Cape Town preparing for the Tri-Nations test against the All Blacks, and Sports Minister Ngconde Balfour had called an urgent meeting with Viljoen. He wanted to speak about the lack of black player representation in the Bok squad. Balfour wanted five black players in the match 22, but this was not happening. Balfour wanted to know why. Viljoen agreed to see him at the team hotel.

I did the homework and sat in on the meeting. Oberholzer was also present. Balfour was bullish and fired up. He had come to condemn the situation, but he was ill informed. He made accusations he could not back up, and involved himself in the selection of individual players. Instead of focusing on the issue of transformation, he wanted to know why Deon Kayser was not playing, and why Etienne Fynn had been dropped. He drew a triangle of SA Rugby, with the Boks at the top, the Super 12 in the middle and the Currie Cup at the bottom. He ticked off the Super 12 and Currie Cup, saying that he was happy with their progress. But the Springbok level was not acceptable.

Harry sat there listening. He was getting angry. I could see it in his expression, but he said nothing. I intervened, telling Balfour that I disagreed with him. The problem lay at provincial and Currie Cup level, and it had a knock-on effect at national level. A pool of black players did not exist at Super 12 level to justify inclusion at test level. Viljoen had picked Conrad Jantjes out of the Vodacom Cup to play in his test 22. This he had done on Jake's recommendation, who thought that Jantjes possessed the right qualities to become a very good test player.

Lawrence Sephaka had been identified as a future test prop, and had trained with Viljoen's national squad, yet he could not make Laurie Mains' Cats Super 12 side. I read out the statistics of black player representation in the Super 12. It was appalling. In 2001, only six black players were given regular game time. Viljoen had picked four black players in his test 22 for the 60-14 win against Italy in Port Elizabeth. I argued that it was an incredible return that three out of a Super 12 pool of six had made the test side. I did not include Jantjes, as he did not play Super 12.

Balfour should have been barking at the Super 12 coaches, but that would not have been front-page news. This meeting was a definite page one story, and Balfour was desperate to show that he was on rugby's case. But he had picked the wrong time and the wrong guys, because we had valid answers to every question he posed. Balfour, however, had no answers to our questions. Viljoen was as frank as I'd ever seen him in these kinds of meetings. Usually, he was very diplomatic and steered clear of confrontation. Not this time.

Balfour asked him whether Deon Kayser would be playing against the All Blacks. Viljoen said he would not make the starting XV; he was going to select the uncapped Marius Joubert. Balfour wanted to know why.

'Because Joubert is better,' Viljoen said.

'I think Kayser is better,' Balfour snapped.

'That is why I am the national coach,' replied Viljoen.

Balfour asked why Fynn had been dropped. Viljoen was equally frank. 'Because he is not good enough,' Harry said bluntly. 'Why aren't you questioning why Johan Ackermann has been dropped? I picked Etienne because he did well in the Super 12. Since working with him, I know he is not up to test standard. That is why I have dropped him.'

'Other leading coaches in South Africa tell me he is the best tighthead in South Africa,' Balfour retorted.

'You asked for my opinion,' Viljoen said. 'I don't believe he is.'

Balfour then softened his stance, and the last few minutes of the meeting were less confrontational. Balfour said Viljoen had to understand that he was under huge pressure from government and the black community to improve the situation of black players. Viljoen said he fully supported transformation and was committed to picking black players. But he was not going to select players he felt were not good enough.

The meeting ended, and the media awaited us as we entered the hotel foyer. Viljoen and Balfour were all smiles. Balfour held an impromptu press conference, saying how productive the meeting had been. He endorsed Viljoen and gave him his public support.

It was just another political day in South African rugby. Now Viljoen could focus on trying to beat the All Blacks. The media speculated that Kayser would definitely play, due to political pressure. Viljoen announced the team, and Kayser was on the bench. He picked Joubert because he felt he was the best man for the job. Ironically, Joubert tore knee ligaments nineteen minutes into the test, and Kayser completed the match.

Transformation would be a constant theme in every squad selection during my three years with the Boks. In Harry's time as coach, Jake White was the one who provided video analysis and statistical data on black players who were considered good enough for test rugby. Viljoen was comfortable being guided by Jake and me on these issues. In the process, Harry broke the mould. He picked black players who were not wings. Jake said that the challenge was to reinvent the white winger, who had become a virtually extinct species in South Africa. He was right. If coaches consistently gave black players game time, then the options would be extended beyond selecting two black wingers in every big game. We had to find quality black players in every position.

Fynn was picked as a tighthead to play France. In hindsight, it was probably the worst test for him in which to make his debut. France's scrum is among the best in the game. Their forwards destroyed him. Viljoen gave him another chance against Italy in the final quarter of the game. His impact was minimal. Off the field, his contribution was not great. Fynn is a very likeable guy, but it became obvious at training sessions that he was not the best tighthead in the country.

Fynn had been rewarded with the Bok job for his efforts at Super 12 level, but as Viljoen would discover as the season progressed, test rugby is a different animal from Super 12. Jantjes, Paulse, Kayser and Fynn all played against Italy. It was a significant step in the right direction. And the encouraging aspect was that Viljoen was willing to invest in quality black talent, but was not prepared to window dress and select black players merely to appease politicians.

I monitored the game time of black players in the Super 12, and again later that year in the Currie Cup. The results were disturbing. Wayne van Heerden, identified as a black forward with the potential to play test rugby, was playing for Rudolf Straeuli's Sharks in the Super 12. In the several Super 12 meetings he attended, Viljoen specifically asked Straeuli to give Van Heerden game time. In eleven matches, Van Heerden played a total of thirty-seven minutes. Matters improved marginally for Van Heerden in 2003, but the lack of game time was significant. In two seasons of Super 12, Van Heerden had been involved in nineteen Super 12 matches, for a game time total of 252 minutes out of a possible 1 520 minutes. Picking a player in a match 22 and giving him 16.5 per cent game time over two seasons cannot be interpreted as an opportunity or commitment to transformation.

Van Heerden is an example of Super 12 coaches' attitude towards black representation. Generally, it was awful. The bare minimum of players was selected, and in most cases the players were wingers. Oberholzer and Viljoen worked tirelessly at these meetings to change the mindset. Oberholzer and Straeuli would take on the same fight a year later.

In 2001, Viljoen presented the coaches with a list of possible black Super 12 candidates, which Jake and I had compiled. Each Super 12 coach, in turn, told us why it would not be possible to play them: too small; not well enough conditioned; the player could not speak English or Afrikaans and therefore could not understand the game plan; the game was new to these players and they did not understand the rules; and the most patronising: 'concerns for the player's safety' ... You name it, we heard it.

The coaches wanted an official quota attributed to Super 12 selection. Oberholzer refused, saying they'd use it as a cop-out when they wanted to drop a white player. They used the quota system as the excuse. Oberholzer wanted coaches to pick black players because they were the best in their position. His idealism was to be applauded, but it was unrealistic. I still maintain that there should be a quota system in the Super 12, and it should be a minimum of five black players per match 22. Otherwise we will never break the mould.

Super 12 coaches showed no malice towards black players in our discussions; they simply did not believe there was enough quality black talent. The only exception was Cats coach Tim Lane, and he happened to be Australian. I don't think Viljoen ever anticipated how much resistance there would be from the Super 12 coaches when it came to transformation or co-operation at a national level. South African Currie Cup coaches and their provincial presidents put the provincial team before the region's Super 12 outfit, and the Super 12 coaches advance their cause at the expense of the national team. In 2003, all four Super 12 coaches were rewarded with a financial incentive linked to performance in the competition. This only served to entrench the status quo. The incentive scheme of each Super 12 coach should be coupled to the performance of the Boks as well.

If a Super 12 coach can produce enough players to be selected for the Bok squad and they give the necessary support to the Bok coach, then they should share in the rewards of the Bok team. It is the only way to ensure that the Super 12 coach thinks nationally. Ideally, the four Super 12 coaches should also serve as the conveyor belt to the national job. If the country's best coach is in charge of the Boks, then coaches two to five should be leading the four regional Super 12 campaigns.

Regional teams in South Africa struggle for exactly the same reason the Boks have struggled for the past five years: provincialism.

In 2001, Viljoen was very frustrated at the lack of co-operation from the Super 12 coaches. He tried to arrange regular national squad training sessions, but none of the four Super 12 coaches would agree to a common day. They all had their own schedule, and each one argued it would be to the detriment of the region to sacrifice the player for national training. Once again, national interests came second.

When Straeuli was the Sharks coach in 2001, he was as big an obstacle as the other coaches. When he succeeded Viljoen, he experienced similar frustrations. He would joke about how difficult it was to be the Bok coach. 'We are a fucked-up rugby nation,' he would say. 'If we worked together, it could all be that much easier. But we all work against each other. And it is not going to change. The guy who is screwing me could be the next guy in charge, and then someone else is going to screw him.'

Straeuli later admitted that he had worked against Viljoen at times, and he was realistic enough to know that provincial and regional coaches were working against him. Straeuli had an advantage over Viljoen in that he was willing to board an aeroplane, visit each region, speak to each coach and chief executive, and make every effort to compromise. Viljoen could not be bothered. He did not have the energy or desire to play the political game in South African rugby. Harry found the rugby world ugly, its politics dirty and the people shameless back-stabbers.

In making a success of his business life, Viljoen had moved on to a more sophisticated plane. He quickly realised that any sophistication in South African rugby was viewed as a threat. The conservatives would resort to anything to crush a foreign world invading their precious existence of tradition and old boys' clubs. Straeuli was brought up in this environment. He could relate to the political agendas and clandestine nature of the rugby world. As a player, Viljoen had been appalled by it, and wanted to move beyond it. It was naive of him to believe this possible.

Very little had changed in South African rugby since Viljoen played the game twenty years earlier. Transformation was the most significant development for rugby's homogenous flock. In apartheid South Africa, the selection of black players had not been a consideration. Now, on the surface at least, it was everything. But black players were still scared to complain. Those who expressed their concerns were – and still are – accused of playing the race card trick or trying to secure a place in the team on the basis of their colour.

Coaches and administrators are not prepared to listen to black players' concerns. South African rugby avoids the issue when it should be educating its people to confront the subject and seek solutions. Each Bok coach assures you that there is no racism in his team. 'Go and ask the black guy how he feels,' has been a common response. What is the black guy going to do – tell the media the coach is a racist?

In his book, *Chester, A Biography of Courage*, which I wrote, Chester Williams discussed both the subtle prejudice and blatant racism he had experienced as a Springbok. The response of white players and coaches who had been part of Williams' career was to defend themselves, call Williams a liar and tell the world how disappointed they were in him. I heard so many of Williams' former teammates say: 'And we thought Chester was a good guy.' Obviously he was when he shut up and did not challenge the system. When he spoke out, he was an ungrateful black player.

When it comes to black players, the system stinks in South African rugby, and, as I said earlier, it is not just the fault of whites; the black administrators are just as guilty. In 1996, SARFU established the Elite squad, which consisted of black players deemed to be among South Africa's most talented prospects.

In 1997, the following black players were selected: Nkosinathi Makaleni (flyhalf), Roderique Manuel (centre), Barry McDonald (centre), Godwin Bossr (scrumhalf), Morné Goetham (No. 8), John Camp (wing), William Grey (flyhalf), Dekado Jantjies (prop), Morné Loxton (flyhalf), Henry Magongoma (wing), Phakamani Ngema (hooker), Jason Oliphant (wing), Fernando Penshaw (lock), Mkuseli Jamiso (prop) and Cornel Titus (flyhalf).

Ever seen any of these players in the Super 12?

Sas Bailey, SARFU's former head of game development, challenged me at a rugby indaba for never writing any positive stories about transformation during my days as a journalist. 'Look at the statistics,' he said. 'We have produced seventeen black Springboks since 1992, and all you did was knock us.'

'Yes, let's look at them,' I replied. 'How many of these seventeen black test Boks played regular test rugby? How many did not even make their provincial or Super 12 teams when they returned from international duty? How many are still playing? The statistic of seventeen black Springboks is damning. It is an indictment of the attitude of rugby officials and coaches towards black representation.'

Bailey never raised the subject with me again, but a closer examination reveals the number of black players as inadequate if judged according to Vision 2003, the sport's ideals for the future, of which transformation forms an integral part. It is obvious that the selections lacked conviction. Only coloured wingers Chester Williams and Breyton Paulse have played more than twenty test matches, with Wayne Julies' test experience recorded as ten minutes. Kaya Malotana's test career lasted eighty minutes against Spain; Quinton Davids played in four matches, and was never once allowed to play the full eighty minutes; Adi Jacobs was used mostly as a substitute; Bolla Conradie alternated with other scrumhalves in 2002; Conrad Jantjes played a full season in 2001 and has not had a look-in since; Etienne Fynn was given fifty minutes in two tests; and these days McNeil Hendricks has to settle for Currie Cup rugby after two tests in 1998.

Dale Santon has never started an international; Ricardo Loubscher was picked in 2002 and only played in one test. In 2003 he was dropped after only one test, but won a third cap against Uruguay as a late second-half replacement. Kayser hung around for five years for his thirteen appearances out of a possible sixty tests. Of the black test players, only three are of African extraction, the mass market SA Rugby so enthusiastically wants to lure as a signed-up customer. Between them, this trio of players has been entrusted with going the full eighty minutes only seven times.

Bobo played a full match against Argentina and New Zealand, Malotana was given eighty minutes against Spain, and Sephaka has played four full tests. South African rugby has a way of presenting outstanding paperwork on any subject. They spare no expense to bring in the best consultants, and when you review the figures, it always looks favourable.

But paperwork can never expose mindsets. In order to know how people truly feel about issues such as transformation, you have to work in the environment, be in constant contact with decision-makers and share a few beers with them. Usually, what you hear is frightening. I often told Viljoen, Straeuli and Oberholzer that drawing up the best plans makes no difference when the people we sell them to are the same ones who stuffed up the previous plans.

In SA Rugby, changing the songs was useless if the same cheerleaders were doing the singing. Transformation could only ever succeed if those who had to select players believed in the ability and potential of the black player. When the majority of the Super 12 coaches in 2003 wanted a quota system of four black players in their match 22, it was clear that they did not understand the science of transformation. For them it was just something that could be ticked off the list before they moved on.

White players were also uneducated about transformation – how it was defined within the game and what the consequences of effective transformation would be. White players saw transformation as quotas and the selection of a black player at the expense of a better white player. This was illustrated in a questionnaire I compiled for a national squad of forty-six in 2002, prior to the start of the international season. In order to work effectively with a squad, Straeuli had to know what and how they were thinking. I drew up a list of questions that would provide information on each individual. On transformation, the following questions were asked:

- Do you believe you understand transformation and SA Rugby's Vision 2003? If so, explain in a paragraph what your interpretation is.
- Do you believe that every black player who has played test rugby in the last two years is a merit selection?
- If you are a white player, do you believe you are at a disadvantage in South African rugby? If the answer is yes, please explain why.
- If you are a black player, do you believe you are at a disadvantage in this country? If the answer is yes, please explain why.

The players who participated in the exercise represented the elite in our rugby in 2002. Of the forty-six players, the majority admitted they did not understand either transformation or Vision 2003. The majority of the white players felt that not every black player who had played test rugby in 2000 and 2001 was a merit selection, and half of the black players agreed that there was tokenism in black selections.

The squad was split as to whether being either black or white was a disadvantage. Clearly, the players did not understand transformation, and needed to be educated. The results of the exercise allowed Rudolf some insight into the minds of the players with whom he had to work. Unfortunately, no education programme was ever initiated, either at national or provincial level.

This is the reason why transformation remains so misunderstood in South African rugby. As an issue it is discussed, but never explained. Transformation is incorrectly equated with the number of black players in a test team. The quota system, much maligned, has worked at junior level because of coaches' attempts to select the best possible team. It has not been successful in professional rugby because of the mindsets of the coaches and administrators.

No official black player quota system existed in the 2004 Super 12, despite only ten black players being given more than 50 per cent competition game time in 2003. In 2003, only 25 of the 126 South African players used in the competition were black. Of these, only ten played in more than 50 per cent of the games. Injuries were a contributing factor. Established backs such as Deon Kayser, Conrad Jantjes and Breyton Paulse were sidelined for a great portion of the season. Injuries, though, cannot be used as an excuse that less than 20 per cent of South Africa's Super 12 players in 2003 were black.

If playing opportunity is the basis of transformation, then the state of black representation in 2003 was unacceptable. Ashwin Willemse was the only black player to be involved in every Super 12 match in 2003. It was no coincidence that with this sustained opportunity he excelled. He was also the only black player to be selected for the match 22 in the World Cup quarter-final against the All Blacks. On resigning, SARFU president Silas Nkanunu conceded that he had failed as president in expediting effective transformation, both at national and Super 12 level.

His successor, Brian van Rooyen, is treading a similar path by allowing the Super 12 coaches to make their own selections. Most of those coaches do not have a good track record in picking black players.

The 2003 Super 12 black player game time – over 50 per cent
1. Ashwin Willemse: 90% (790 minutes out of a possible 880)
2. Wylie Human: 81% (713 minutes)
3. Gcobani Bobo: 75% (662 minutes)
4. Dewey Swartbooi: 68% (598 minutes)
5. Egon Seconds: 60% (525 minutes)
6. Edrich Fredericks: 58% (506 minutes)
7. Enrico Januarie: 57% (504 minutes)
8. Lawrence Sephaka: 57% (503 minutes)
9. Quinton Davids: 52% (461 minutes)
10. Bolla Conradie: 50% (440 minutes)

Black player game time – less than 50 per cent
11. Ricardo Loubscher: 49% (435 minutes)
12. John Daniels: 44% (387 minutes)
13. Fabian Juries: 43% (375 minutes)
14. Norman Jordaan: 42% (366 minutes)
15. Etienne Fynn: 38% (332 minutes)
16. Dale Santon: 36% (313 minutes)
17. Hanyani Shimange: 31% (272 minutes)
18. Breyton Paulse: 26% (231 minutes)
19. Wayne van Heerden: 24% (215 minutes)
20. Kennedy Tsimba: 23% (203 minutes)
21. Deon Kayser: 23% (201 minutes)
22. Randall Julies: 16% (140 minutes)
23. Adrian Jacobs: 14% (122 minutes)
24. Eddie Andrews: 8% (74 minutes)
25. Conrad Jantjes: 8% (70 minutes)

In 2004, ten of the regular starting sixty Super 12 players were black, and only twenty-six of the 120 South African tournament totals were black. The situation has not improved.

The belief that black players weaken a team never featured in the early stages of Viljoen and Straeuli's tenures. Both spoke of a 'new South Africa'. They understood transformation, but as the teams struggled and tests were lost, both hinted that they were hamstrung because of transformation. Again, neither truly believed that colour was not an issue.

Viljoen was aware of how closely his team selections would be monitored during his first tour. In the final test against England, he dropped Chester Williams, believing the player was no longer good enough for test rugby. Viljoen informed Williams about his decision, but then made the fatal mistake of including him among the reserves, hoping that he would not have to use him. By picking Williams, it meant that there were two black players in the test 22.

In 2000, no official black player quota existed in the test team, but it was accepted that the Bok coach would never select fewer than two black players in his match-day squad. Viljoen was mindful of this, and tried to cover himself by adding Williams to the list of substitutes. Williams, understandably, was very upset that he was being used as a political pawn five years after helping the Boks win the World Cup. In his biography, he said:

> If he did not think I was good enough, then fine. That was his opinion and I had enough experience of coaches not rating me in my career. He told me I was finished as a player but then he picked me in the squad. It had nothing to do with thinking I could add value. It was political. I would have preferred him to leave me out rather than pick me as a token. I would sit through 80 minutes that symbolised the most heart-breaking reality of my career: I was still being used as a black player making up numbers. Ten years after playing my first match for Western Province League, after a World Cup final and three Currie Cup finals I was simply a black player warming the bench for South Africa. It hurt more than it angered me.

Viljoen had learnt his lesson. Never again would he pick a black player just to appease the politicians. But another dynamic had started to cloud Viljoen's judgement: he perceived his support from the white conservatives to be dwindling. He received information that these people thought him too liberal in his views on transformation, and that he was making the game 'black' by extolling the talents of black players at press conferences. As the pressure mounted, Viljoen did not want to alienate the traditional white support. Rugby forced him to move in conservative circles he had long ago abandoned. Now he was concerned about white people who thought he was making the Boks a 'black team'. We received letters from disgruntled white supporters who yearned for the good old days of Danie Craven and Frik du Preez, accusing us of 'cheapening the Bok jersey' by selecting Black players.

During the 2002 Tri-Nations, Viljoen started asking: 'What will the white supporters think?' This had never been a concern of his during the first eight months of his tenure. After that, I knew that he was picking black players because he felt an obligation to SARFU and the new South Africa. It was something he had to do, but did not necessarily want to do.

Straeuli's mindset would undergo a similar reversal as his test results deteriorated and the pressure mounted. Whenever I briefed Straeuli on the dos and don'ts of transformation speak, he insisted that I shouldn't worry. He stressed that he 'did not see race', and that he picked players purely on merit. His duty was to promote a better South Africa, and in order to prove his commitment, he wanted it entered in his contract that he would select a minimum of six black players for the 2003 World Cup, picking at least four in his match 22.

Oberholzer did not want this clause included in Straeuli's contract. According to him, Straeuli could then use transformation as an excuse should the team fail. Rian asked Straeuli whether he believed that there were four black players who were good enough to make his test match 22. Straeuli said there were. Rian then asked him whether there were six who were capable of making his World Cup squad. Straeuli had no doubt. Oberholzer told him to pick those players, because that is what he believed as a coach.

But Straeuli insisted on signing something to prove his intent, and eventually signed a pledge confirming his commitment to transformation. He did it of his own volition, and it was never part of his official employment contract. In Straeuli's first year as coach, he allowed Tim Lane, who he had kept on as an assistant at the insistence of Oberholzer, to guide him in selection.

Straeuli and Lane had completely different approaches to the game, and in an ideal line-up they chose different players than one another. But in 2002, Straeuli was easing himself into the job, and showed very little stubbornness. He absorbed what Tim had to say, selected the backs Tim felt could do the job, and agreed with Tim that an expansive game was the way forward.

When Tim suggested that Bolla Conradie and Adi Jacobs could play meaningful roles in the Bok set-up, Straeuli backed Tim's opinion by selecting them. Jake White urged Straeuli to pick Ashwin Willemse. He told Straeuli that Willemse was the toughest and most competitive wing in the country. Willemse had yet to play Super 12 rugby, and was still playing under-21. Straeuli wanted to see more of him before making a call. Willemse played for Chester Williams' Sevens team and Jake's World Cup-winning under-21 team. A year later, he would be the star of a very ordinary Bok backline.

In 2002 the Boks played some champagne rugby, and French journalists quizzed Straeuli on his team's style of play. Arnaud David of Le'Quipe wrote that Straeuli's Boks were the complete opposite of Straeuli. He described Straeuli as a serious, conservative and dour character. The team were outrageous in their approach, adventurous in everything they did and full of characters.

'How could this be?' he asked Straeuli at a press conference in Durban.

Straeuli laughed, and said the journalist did not know him well enough to judge his character. The truth was that although Straeuli had an understated and witty sense of humour, he did not have the capacity to develop an adventurous game plan. His rugby personality would be reflected in the Boks' play a year later, after he had given Tim Lane the boot. It is no coincidence that when Lane departed, so too did many of the black inclusions in the match 22. But in 2002 Straeuli was doing everything right, and publicly saying all the right things.

Chester Williams' biography was launched a week before the Boks left for their end-of-year tour. I gave Straeuli a copy, feeling that certain issues within the squad needed to be addressed. I knew that many of the black players were pleased that Williams had finally revealed how it felt to be black in the Bok set-up. I also knew that several white players had taken his comments personally, and were very defensive about the book. Straeuli read it, and was very sympathetic towards Chester. 'You never know,' Straeuli told me, 'because it does not affect you as a white player.' At one team meeting he and manager Gideon Sam spoke about the book, and Straeuli read an extract in which Chester spoke of his desire to play rugby and be recognised not as a black man, but as a rugby player in the Bok team. This moved Straeuli, and he told the players that he saw all of them as rugby players; it was how he hoped they viewed each other. Rudolf wanted to create a forum in which black and white players would feel comfortable talking about race, prejudice and cultural issues. He spoke of racial and cultural diversity and the new South Africa. Then he opened the floor to the squad. Corné Krige broke the ice. He said it would be unfair of any white player to think he knew what it was like to be black and in the minority in the Bok squad. He asked the black players to speak up and let him know when there was any ill feeling.

Krige and Gideon Sam stressed that we had to find solutions to racial problems. Breyton Paulse then stood up and said that for the first time he was comfortable in the Bok set-up. He felt he had a say, and that his value as an experienced test player was appreciated; he felt respected. This was massive coming from someone like Breyton, who was reserved and said very little publicly on the issue of race.

I believed that the meeting had been extremely significant in breaking down race barriers, but I was mistaken if I thought we were now dealing with solutions and not problems. A team environment shapes so much, and the squad that played in the 2002 Tri-Nations was young, energetic and fearless. Tim Lane told them they could do anything, and convinced the backs that Australia and New Zealand were in awe of them.

Straeuli also managed to extract good value out of a forward unit that still had its limitations. But a year later, and Lane and many of the more liberal thinkers were gone. The environment changed, the squad of 2003 resembled a government office of the early 1980s, and Straeuli was a different character. Like Viljoen before him, Straeuli started talking nervously about the 'colour mix' in the squad, despite selections that should have excited him about the prospects of the black players.

Straeuli had initiated a selection system designed to eliminate emotion and provincial prejudice from the equation. Each of the four Super 12 coaches, the two national selectors and Straeuli himself would pick their form 22 after every round of Super 12 matches. They would then tally the votes at the end, which would allow them an objective view of the form team during the competition. When the votes were tallied, six black players had made the tournament form 22. But these votes were discarded, and instead Straeuli and the selectors chose on gut feel. As for black player representation, Straeuli made an issue of it before every selection. He hinted that he would struggle to select six black players in a World Cup squad of thirty. In fact, he did not even know if there were five, and he definitely did not think he could consistently start with three.

The Bulls dominated Straeuli's early 2003 selections. Bulls coach Rudy Joubert was included in the squad a week before the start of the international season after Lane's sudden departure, and the mood and dynamic of the squad was totally different from that of 2002. Straeuli's earlier bravado about black representation had long since been replaced by a belief that very few black players were good enough to play in the big games at the World Cup.

Willemse was the only black player to make the match 22 in the 2003 World Cup quarter-final against the All Blacks. He had consistently been South Africa's best back all season. In 1995, Chester Williams was the only black player in the Bok team in the World Cup final. He played on the wing. In 1999, Breyton Paulse was the only black player in the Bok team in the World Cup play-off for third and fourth. He played on the wing.

South African rugby had certainly not turned itself over to the black man. It was still very much a white man's sport, played and controlled by whites. Ironically, South Africa's best player of 2003 happened to be Willemse. He was also nominated as one of the IRB's rookies of the year.

Yet when the Boks crashed out of the World Cup, some people still claimed that transformation was killing the South African game. I disagree. Transformation will help save South African rugby if applied correctly. The under-19 and under-21 systems have produced outstanding black and white talent, and merged them into world champions in both age groups. They were successful because coaches Eugene Eloff and Jake White embraced the talent of the player, whatever his colour.

On 16 May 2004, White announced his first test 22. He selected six black players. Once again, it was a controversial decision. Whereas Straeuli had been accused of not acknowledging the quality of black players in 2003, White was criticised for selecting too many. It again highlighted the complexity of transformation in South African rugby.

Professional coaches blame grassroots development, and claim that black players are not emerging. They are. Senior white coaches just don't select them. In January 2004, Bulls coach Rudy Joubert omitted SA under-19 centre and hero of the 2003 under-19 World Cup win Earl Rose because he was too small. Joubert 'feared for the player's safety', and suggested that Rose be put on an intensive three-month gym programme.

But what happens? Rose is selected for the national Sevens team, where the activity is of such a nature that all he will do is improve his fitness level and lose weight. Again I ask the question: How serious are our coaches about developing quality black talent?

If Joubert had a genuine interest in Rose, he would have asked that the player be withdrawn from all rugby for three months, sent to the Sports Science Institute with a specific goal in mind, and then reintroduced him into senior rugby. But this only happened when Jake White was appointed Springbok coach.

White met with Rose and his father, and set up a further meeting with a strength consultant, who prepared a programme for Rose. White withdrew the player from the national Sevens, kept him on a Sevens contract, and told him he had three months to prove he wanted to progress in the game. This kind of approach has been sorely lacking in the past. A black player does not weaken a team if the right black player is selected. Politicians don't seem to understand this, nor does rugby's black administration.

They often reveal their true feelings when they say that South African rugby will transform, even if it means losing matches along the way. This sort of statement only adds to the perception that picking a black player weakens a team. In the three years that I was involved in Springbok rugby, no test match was lost because of black representation. But many were won because of the deeds of black players.

5

In the belly of the beast

What goes on in the Springbok camp

In 2001, Harry Viljoen wanted his Springboks to act like the directors of a business. In 2002, Rudolf Straeuli wanted to turn the Springboks into rugby players again. Neither Viljoen nor Straeuli found the right balance. Viljoen failed to understand that, at heart, the Springboks were rugby players and not businessmen. Straeuli ignored the fact that the Springboks were highly paid rugby players who assumed the status of sports professionals. They were not a new intake of students or national servicemen.

In April 2002, I flew to Sydney to spend a few days with Straeuli, who had just been appointed Bok coach. I had to co-ordinate his media interviews and run through everything Viljoen had done in his fifteen months as Bok coach. Rather predictably, Straeuli was not interested in the literature associated with Viljoen. The two had clashed in 2001, when Straeuli was coaching the Sharks.

Viljoen did not enjoy Straeuli, who hardly enthused about Viljoen as Bok coach. This resulted in little co-operation between the two men. The ill feeling between them came to a head in Auckland in 2001, after Straeuli's Sharks had destroyed the Blues in a Super 12 match. Earlier in the week, Straeuli had extended an invitation to Viljoen to visit the Sharks dressing room after the match. Viljoen did not accept the invitation. He was not interested in being two-faced. Earlier in the year, Viljoen had tried to establish a more effective communication system between him and the nationally contracted players, because they had complained to Viljoen that they never knew where they stood with the national coaches. Harry would communicate with each one individually after the week's performance in an e-mail message in order to supply the player with feedback.

Viljoen thought his e-mail system would the best way to improve the situation, but his intentions met with resistance. The players were not ready for this kind of approach, or for the honest reviews. Neither were the Super 12 coaches. Typical of the South African rugby player's mentality, those players struggling with form blamed their ineffectiveness on the national coach, who, they said, gave them different instructions to the regional coaches.

It is not uncommon for a South African rugby player to set the national coach against the regional coach. The regional coaches, with Straeuli and the Cats' Laurie

Mains the most outspoken, objected to what they called Viljoen's 'interference' in their Super 12 campaigns. The e-mails became an issue, the regional chief executives got involved, the media in each region backed the Super 12 coaches, and the attempt to communicate more effectively was killed off after two rounds of the competition.

Viljoen was irritated that everything was such a struggle in South African rugby. He could not even e-mail a player without it becoming a political and media issue. Super 12 conference meetings that involved Viljoen were meaningless. Viljoen told the coaches what his expectations were for the Super 12. He also pleaded for time to spend with a national team, and proposed one-day camps every fortnight. None of this ever came to fruition.

That night in Auckland in 2001, Viljoen did not visit the Sharks dressing room either before or after the game. Instead, Harry, Jake White and I went to dinner with former All Blacks coach John Hart and former All Black Andy Haden. On returning to the team hotel, just after 11.30 in the evening, we bumped into Rudolf and some of the Sharks management. Harry congratulated them on the win. Nothing more. Rudolf asked if he could see Viljoen about a few things, and Viljoen told him to call him in the morning.

But Straeuli wanted to see Viljoen straight away. Viljoen agreed, and Jake and I accompanied the two of them to Harry's room. There was not much idle chitchat. Rudolf expressed his disappointment that Harry, as national coach, had not shown his face after the win against the Blues. He said he picked up a 'funny vibe' from Harry, and asked if it had anything to do with him. This was the trigger for Viljoen, and he let rip. Usually diplomatic, this time Harry went straight for the jugular. Rudolf, he said bluntly, irritated him, because he never listened and always assumed he knew better. He always had the answer without ever listening to what the other person had to say. Straeuli readily agreed that it was a weakness of his, and then talked for the next thirty minutes. Jake and I watched the exchange like a tennis match. The discussion, if you could call it that, confirmed the mutual animosity. It solved nothing.

Viljoen admired the Australian way, while Straeuli felt their influence detracted from South African rugby tradition. Straeuli indirectly had a go at Viljoen in the media during the 2001 Super 12 season. Each time the Sharks beat an Australian team, Straeuli would mention how certain people believed South African rugby had to take lessons from the Australians. In the build-up to the Super 12 final against Eddie Jones' ACT Brumbies, Straeuli was quoted as saying it would be a good experience for his side just to play in the final, and that he hoped the Sharks would learn from the Aussies. The dig was aimed at Viljoen, who knew it. When the Brumbies won 36-6, Viljoen told the South African media he hoped Straeuli had absorbed the lessons from the Australians, because there had been plenty on show.

The two men were complete opposites, and when Straeuli succeeded Viljoen, he was not going to entertain a system or a way of thinking introduced by Viljoen. Straeuli would try to reinvent the wheel instead, assuring the media that he was going to put the 'pride and passion back into the Bok jersey'. Ironically, by the time Straeuli accepted his resignation package, the public was vociferously complaining about the lack of pride and passion in the Bok jersey.

I think the accusation that the Boks lacked pride and passion is rubbish. There is both pride and passion in the green and gold jersey, but at times the Boks simply weren't good enough, as Viljoen and Straeuli discovered. If something needed to be introduced to the Boks – coaches and players alike – it was some rugby intelligence. Viljoen encouraged a businesslike approach. For example, he did not want players calling out numbers in the team bus to ensure that all were present. 'My directors don't scream "number" and act like schoolboys at board meetings,' he told the players. 'Look to your left or right and make sure your roommate is seated. It shouldn't be difficult.' Straeuli had them calling out numbers within a fortnight of taking over.

Viljoen, having acquired a keen fashion sense thanks to the input of his wife Magda, also believed the players should enjoy individuality in the way they dressed when on tour. He hated always being in a Bok tracksuit. He also disliked the schoolboy uniform look. It was difficult to get Harry into anything green; it was impossible to get Rudolf out of it.

Viljoen preached a boardroom culture; Straeuli promoted a 'back-to-basics' theme. He would humble the players publicly, because he believed that was what the rugby supporter wanted to see. He would run them up hills and do everything that had made the Bok and Blue Bulls teams of yesteryear successful. And he reinstated the trial game to prove how serious he was about taking the selection process beyond the Super 12 matches.

Logistically, the trial match of 2002, held in May, was only possible because no South African side made the Super 12 semi-finals. A free weekend thus became available, or the match would not have happened. The trial game was a success. It showcased the country's leading players, and with the Bulls Rugby Union offering free admission, a Sunday crowd in excess of 25 000 turned up. Straeuli had scored with the media. They applauded the trial match, and the public loved it even more. Straeuli scored again when he took his first test squad to the Pretoria Police College for a ten-day camp in June 2002.

When Bob Skinstad and I had suggested a similar training venue to Viljoen at the end of 2001, he dismissed the idea. In Harry's opinion, the players were professionals who deserved to stay in the best accommodation available. He did not think running a camp in a police or military set-up would solve whatever problems existed. Skinstad and I argued that the idea was to strip away all the gloss for a week – no more – for the players to gel as a team. Viljoen told me to investigate the possibilities, and in January 2002 I made calls to various institutions. I also visited the naval base in Simonstown, but they were unable to accommodate the Boks in June 2002.

The police camp exercise, which Straeuli backed, was a good plan, due to the structuring of the training. It was not a military exercise but all about rugby, emphasising the technical aspects of the game. Straeuli wanted privacy in order to get to know the squad. He managed to arrange this, and the media accommodated his request to allow the squad a few days behind closed doors.

The camp was a one-off, and it worked. It would not be managed again, although Straeuli would have liked that kind of environment all the time. He did not enjoy five-star hotels, believing that they made the players 'soft' and encouraged hangers-on to collect around the team.

Straeuli's perception of the Bok player differed a great deal from Viljoen's, and highlighted an area in which South African rugby lacked professionalism. Very often, the national coach did not know much about the psychological profile of the player with whom he would be working until it was sometimes too late. A lot of stories are told about players and coaches at provincial level, and they have a carry-on effect into the national squad. Players arrive either prejudiced or favoured, depending on the gossip.

Before the trial match in May 2002, I mentioned how important it was that we familiarised ourselves with the type of player available to the selectors. I drew up a question-and-answer document aimed at revealing what the player thought of himself, and how he viewed Bok rugby, his teammates, the contractual system, the laws of the game, transformation and world rugby.

All forty-six players invited to the trial match would complete the document, and all would put their names to the answers. We wanted them to speak up and be accountable for what they said. The results were revealing. Of the forty-six, only nine felt that they were the best player in the world in their position. Even more insightful was that only seven of the forty-six identified a South African player as the best in his position.

There was a definite lack of self-belief among our players, and they did not rate each other highly. This was important to know, as later in the year we would be confronted with situations where the Bok player rated the opposition player higher than the guy next to him. Another aspect that emerged from the questionnaire was that very few of the players truly understood transformation. Many felt that as white players they were at a disadvantage because of their interpretation of transformation. The contracting system was another headache. Few could offer a solution, but most recorded it as a serious problem in South African rugby.

Provincialism was mentioned as another negative aspect, but the players listed 'physical presence' and the emerging young talent as the country's strengths.

Players also felt that there would always be incredible support for the Boks, despite poor results and a negative media.

Straeuli was pleased with the honesty of the players. The questionnaire gave him something to work with, and was probably the most informative exercise the Boks undertook in my time with them. It also took perception out of the equation. The players had shared their views after Straeuli promised that nothing divulged in the questionnaire would be held against them.

Quite rightly, Straeuli deduced that our players lacked professionalism and did not take responsibility for their performances. He asked me to surf the Internet for examples of where our players had publicly lacked accountability, and to compare it with a hard-hitting example of accountability in another professional sporting code.

On the eve of the trial match, the forty-six players in Pretoria were presented with the following statement by Manchester United's Ryan Giggs, after the club finished third in the premiership and lost in the semi-finals of the European Cup on the away-goals rule:

> We have let ourselves, the manager and the supporters down. That is unforgivable. There are no excuses for any of us. Any pain we are feeling right now is probably self-pity and we haven't earned the right to that. We have no divine right to win anything. You have to earn success and on that basis we deserve to finish empty-handed this season …

United had won nine trophies in the past seven years (the Premiership five times, the European Cup, the FA Cup twice and the League Cup).

Then the players were shown the following comments made by Springbok players:

> 'You don't win in New Zealand and Australia.' – *a Springbok after losing to the All Blacks*

> 'I hate the Poms. They have already peaked.' – *a Springbok before the English test. England won by a record points*

> 'Even with all my injuries I am better than the fit guys here.' – *a Springbok on the strengths of his teammates*

> 'If we lose to England it won't be a train smash.' – *a Springbok before the England test*

> 'We played too much rugby. We cannot win every test.' – *a Springbok after the test defeat against England*

> 'It happens. It was a bad day at the office.' – *a Springbok after losing to France in Paris*

'The public's expectation is too much.' – *a Springbok on the pressures of test rugby*

'I would love to play for the Springboks, but I need security and English club rugby offers me that.' – *a Springbok on why he quit international rugby. His test-playing record was less than 50 per cent*

'The coach did not have a game plan.' – *a Springbok on why the Boks lost to Australia in the World Cup semi-final in 1999*

'The players won the quarter-final and not the coach.' – *a Springbok on the World Cup quarter-final win against England in 1999*

'SA Rugby does not look after their test players.' – *a Springbok on being paid R3 million over three years*

The Springboks' record during this time: lost to England three times, lost to New Zealand five times, lost to Australia three times, lost to France twice … and lost in the semi-finals of the 1999 World Cup.

The message to the players was that they had to start taking responsibility for being professionals. The 2002 early season catchphrase was, 'We look at ourselves first.'

Viljoen had conducted a similar exercise with the players a year earlier. He had also spoken to them about professionalism, the right attitude and accepting that rugby was now a job, but this was never translated into something tangible. Bok players don't know the meaning of professionalism. The odd individual has cottoned on, but as a group they define professionalism through the salary they earn. Very few are prepared to account for themselves as professional rugby players.

In March 2004, I was asked to write an article for *SA Sports Illustrated* on the Boks' approach to conditioning and their professionalism as paid athletes. This is what I wrote:

There is no substance to the claim that Springbok rugby players are the most physical in the game. It is something we in South Africa live on because of the tough man image of those who played test rugby when it was a sport and not a job. It is why the athletic ability of our top players is so guarded from the public. Everything is left to assumption and perception. The facts are damning. Our senior players are slobs when compared to athletes in other professional codes.

I read a great article in the *New York Times* on American baseball player Barry Bonds, who broke Mark McGwire's record for scoring the most home runs in a season. The author David Grann writes that when Bonds first entered the

National League in 1986, he had a sprinter's build. But, after a few years, he became one of the first of a new generation of players who lifted weights and gradually transformed himself from a 185-pound lead-off hitter into a 230-pound slugger.

Bonds' body fat was lower than anyone else's in the squad – 6.2 per cent at the start of the 2003 season. 'It was too low,' said strength coach Greg Anderson. 'Every month we take his blood and test his mineral levels to make sure they are in line, so that if he is 10 milligrams off in zinc or six off in magnesium or five milligrams off in copper, that is what we replace.'

Americans have turned sport into both a science and a business. England, current holder of the rugby World Cup, has followed a similar journey under Clive Woodward. South Africa has opted for the ox-wagon approach, and the poor old oxen have finally run out of steam. In 2001, Harry Viljoen introduced the Boks to blood testing at the annual training camp that precedes the international season. Every member of the squad was tested. It cost a lot of money, but it was money well spent. The test was revealing. The people who conducted the tests were amazed that half the players were actually going to play test rugby two weeks later.

Blood tests would ensure that every player knew what was good or bad for him. Money well spent in principle was really money wasted, because our players could not justify why the national governing body was spending this kind of cash on them. To be effective, the testing had to be done once a month, and every player had to take charge of what he put into his body. It was simply asking too much. Nothing came of the data, because our players could not appreciate the responsibility of being professional athletes.

I do not know of one player who underwent private testing, or employed a private strength coach. Each one relies on what his province, region or the Boks provide. The players wait for someone to point them in a direction. Rarely is there a unified approach from conditioning and strength coaches in this country. Each has their own view, or, if they share a similar view, then their egos clash. Each coach also has his personal preferences. It doesn't matter what the expert can offer – a coach uses whomever he is comfortable with.

Current Springbok coach Jake White, an assistant to Viljoen in 2000 and the early part of 2001, adopted the most professional approach to conditioning when he took charge of the national under-21s in 2002. White was a constant critic of the poor conditioning of the Boks. He believed our senior players were soft and spoilt by big salaries, were not held accountable, and were not prepared to change their lifestyle to fit in with their profession. Rather, the profession had to fit in with their lifestyle.

Dieticians addressed the players, daily menus were drawn up for use at home and the diet philosophy was explained to each player.

'You eat this because it will ... you don't eat this because it will ...'

But each year a dietician had to explain anew to the players what they should be eating, why, when and in what quantities, which irritated White no end. The players always used the post-Christmas excuse, which further annoyed him.

White offered his under-21s no such escape, combining the skills of conditioning expert Derick Coetzee and strength expert Mark Steele to establish a strength and conditioning programme that every one of his under-21 squad had to pass if they wanted to play in the 2002 World Cup. Failure to do so meant that they would not be considered for selection. White took flak from certain people because of his approach, but he was sick and tired of hearing that a player was 'not a gym kind of person' or that 'he is not that strong but he is a brilliant player'. White believed the player would only be better if he was stronger and better conditioned. No athlete has ever got worse because of better conditioning.

Never shy to ask elsewhere, White was given the Australian Rugby Union model to study. He wanted to gauge the standard requirements set out in each position. A position-specific test on strength, agility or pace had never been conducted on the Boks.

Every region was secretive about testing. Players' results were not released, and the players remained protected and unaccountable. The media was certainly not privy to any information, and even the national set-up had to prize data out of the different regions. Suspicion and distrust were rife, a mindset shared by rugby's head office.

Jake White and national teams general manager Butch Watson Smith pushed for the under-21 model to be applied to the Boks. Naturally, they experienced resistance: the under-21 season was structured differently; the under-21s had not played Super 12 rugby; the under-21s had not been through thirty-odd matches in a season. You name it, there was a reason why there could be no standard entry level established for players wishing to play test rugby.

But Rudolf Straeuli eventually warmed to the idea, and in January 2003 he invited sixty players to Cape Town for testing. The Sports Science Institute of South Africa conducted the tests. There would be no provincial bias, and there would be full disclosure. Players were judged on what they could do physically. Some were abysmal. A minority stood out. On the whole, most of the senior Boks were in a worse physical condition than White's national under-21 squad.

More excuses were made: it was only January, or some players had come off a tour, or others were on the mend after injury. It was the mindset of kids wanting to play sport, and not of professionals wanting to be paid good money to do a job. The Sports Science Institute had tested the Boks in 1999, and many of the problems that emerged then still existed in 2003.

The players' general fitness was good, but their strength and conditioning were below acceptable levels. Many were training with injuries, and had played for some time with injuries that had never properly healed. Sports physicians, orthopaedic surgeons, radiologists, dieticians, psychologists and biokineticists made assessments, and cognitive testing was also done. It was as comprehensive a test as any team in the world could be put through.

It was acceptable for the props to run the 10-metre speed drills in 1.95 seconds, for the locks and hookers to do it in 1.9, and the loose forwards and backline in 1.8 seconds. Half the squad failed the test. In the 40-metre sprint, the following standard was set: props, 5.7 seconds; locks, 5.6; hookers, 5.5; loose forwards, 5.4; inside backs, 5.3; and the speedsters in the back three, 5.2. This is the minimum requirement. A third of the squad failed the test, and back three specialists Pieter Rossouw, Ricardo Loubscher, Stefan Terblanche and Breyton Paulse all ran between 5.32 and 5.21, below the standard.

Friedrich Lombard was the only tested player to break 5 seconds, and loose forward Joe van Niekerk's 5.06-second sprint was the next best. In a later test, Brent Russell would run the 40-metre sprint in 4.75 seconds. Van Niekerk's explosiveness was unmatched, both in the vertical jump and the sprints, but his upper-body strength was alarmingly weak.

In the bench press he could only manage a maximum rep of 125 kilograms, with Roland Bernard and Hendro Scholtz setting the pace among the loose forwards at 150 kilograms. At 110 kilograms, Pedrie Wannenburg's best effort was even worse. It was an indictment of the conditioning of South African rugby's finest talent. Van Niekerk and Wannenburg are two exceptional players. Physically, they did not make the grade when it came to out-and-out power.

White argued that if Van Niekerk could bench press 140 kilograms and run 40 metres in 5.06 seconds, imagine how good he would be then. Why settle for mediocrity when we have players with the raw potential to be brilliant? Players let themselves down. Van Niekerk, already one of the game's best flankers, knew that there were areas in which he had to improve. He had to increase his strength, yet when he was put in rehabilitation for two months in Cape Town, his body fat percentage increased. In an interview he joked about the loneliness of eating spare ribs at a restaurant nearly every night.

It might sound like an innocent remark, but it illustrated how immature our players are as professional sportsmen. Van Niekerk, for all his potential, would have been chopped from an American football squad for not being good enough physically. That is how far behind South African rugby is as a professional code.

We overlook Big Joe's weaknesses because he has other strengths. But we should not be compromising on anything. If he is to be the best the world has ever seen, then the player needs to take responsibility for his body. Equally, those who pay his salary every month must show an iron fist. I mention Van Niekerk specifically, as he is the best we have in this country. But others were in similar situations. The testing blew away false perceptions and confirmed why certain players were not performing. Many of them had not recovered from injury.

Lukas van Biljon suffered because of a neck and shoulder operation. He could manage only 105 kilograms in the bench press, compared to Hanyani Shimange's 150 kilograms. Even scrumhalf Bolla Conradie, with a push of 120 kilograms, showed greater upper-body strength. And then we wonder why Lukas has not been as dynamic in contact in the last year. In the pull-ups, Conradie, Paulse and Russell (with twenty-three consecutive pull-ups) comfortably showed the high standard of their weight-to-strength ratio. Van Niekerk could do only six, compared to Scholtz's nineteen. Van Biljon did nine, as opposed to Shimange's twenty, and among the locks Selborne Boome was the best conditioned in nearly every aspect of testing. Boome managed eighteen, which was double Victor Matfield's nine and triple Bakkies Botha and Quinton Davids' six.

In every discipline, Davids was hopelessly off the pace. Yet he was still picked later in the year. He was not the only one. In 2003, too many professionals were playing test rugby when they should have been in a gymnasium improving their strength. Rugby coaches will rightly dismiss judging a player solely on his testing. But they cannot ignore statistics that show the player to be lacking in strength and conditioning. It shows in our results at international level. And it has shown for some time in northern hemisphere teams that are stronger in the contact and at the breakdown. Physically we don't match them, and you only have to take a look at Wannenburg and Van Niekerk's strength statistics to know why they don't make the hard yards in contact.

White will take testing seriously, as he did at under-21 level. He obtained the right result in the first year he set a standard entry exam – his under-21s won the World Cup in 2002. The Boks can expect a similar attitude from their coach in 2004. It is long overdue.

In 2003 Straeuli was right in wanting to crack the whip, but the implementation fell short of the talking. Straeuli knew the players could not be trusted to do things on their own, and he was right. Very few players were prepared to do additional work, be it to improve strength, speed or skills. The exceptions were André Venter, Robbie Kempson and Louis Koen. These players consistently did more, and were always working on improving themselves in their respective positions.

Straeuli opted for a disciplinarian approach because he felt the players could not make their own decisions and wanted to be shown the way in everything. He often told me that Harry had never understood the animal he was dealing with in the South African rugby player, and that is why all his systems failed. Structure, said Straeuli, was everything. It is what the Springboks of 2002 and 2003 yearned for, and it is what they got.

The strict timetable irked the more adventurous and outspoken players, but they were in the minority. Sadly, most of the Boks wanted the formula spelt out, typed out and handed out as a daily reminder. During my three years with the team, Springbok players wanted discipline and to be led, whether to a video session or in a training run. Only a minority assumed responsibility and led by action rather than intention. Corné Krige matched his words with his deeds, and in 2003 the coaches considered John Smit to be the obvious successor to Krige.

Joost van der Westhuizen commanded respect, especially among the Bulls players, who were in awe of his achievements, his ability to fight back, and his doggedness to rise above his critics and defy them time and again. Van der Westhuizen led from the front. He possessed a lot of bravado, but he lacked the acumen of a thinking leader. Joost was not skilled or refined enough in the reading of the game. Players from other regions had respect for his achievements as a player, but there were plenty who could not stand him as a person.

Bob Skinstad was a great motivator and full of ideas, but his weakness was that he was both preacher and sinner. You can't have it both ways and be taken seriously as a leader. Skinstad talked a lot about professionalism, but his actions did not always match up. His words therefore lost their impact. An excess of leadership did not exist in the squad that was selected for the 2003 World Cup. Selborne Boome, Neil de Kock and Victor Matfield are strong individuals, but their leadership abilities are secondary to their value as players. The same applies to Joe van Niekerk and Werner Greeff.

Louis Koen is a rugby thinker and his work ethic in the squad was incomparable, but as a test player he was never good enough. The motivators in the 2003 World Cup squad were Krige, Smit and Van der Westhuizen. But Joost always had to be in the starting XV to be effective, or he would sulk and not contribute much. Straeuli was very aware of this, and regularly stroked Van der Westhuizen's ego. Straeuli accepted that leadership was limited, which was why structure was so important to this particular squad.

'Professionalism' and 'pursuing excellence' were words easily uttered within the squad. Their meaning, though, was not always understood, and this ignorance impacted negatively on performance. The vague definition of professionalism frustrated coaches and support staff, and explained the structured work ethic of the squad. They trained hard and did whatever was required of them – some even a little more. But they wanted to be told what to do, and then do as they were told.

Most of the players rarely asked questions. They did not have the confidence to challenge coaches for fear of their opinions being misinterpreted as a sign of disrespect. To be fair to the players, during video sessions the coaches were not always able to cope with an introspective and challenging South African player. Confrontation makes both player and coach uncomfortable. Nick Mallett was the exception. His post-match video sessions are the stuff of Bok folklore. Although Mallett probably never intentionally meant to humiliate anyone, the abrasive and hard-hitting video sessions humbled those he criticised.

Both Straeuli and Viljoen were very aware of the Mallett legend and the fragile nature of the South African player's psyche. Tim Lane likened the Boks to the French, whom he had coached. The mentality of the French and South Africans was the opposite of the Australians. Australian players, said Lane, would hammer each other in post-match video sessions. They reviewed the position and not the individual. They demanded accountability from each player in every position. South African and French players take criticism personally; they withdraw and retreat. Friendship means more to them than ruthless professional evaluation. Criticism that occurred in front of teammates had to be qualified with a positive spin, which would accentuate the good, rather than focus on individual mistakes or negative issues. Video sessions under Straeuli were constructive, although some would rightly argue that they should have been more penetrating, given some of the underperformances during his spell as coach. Early on, Straeuli took no nonsense during the video sessions, but his attitude did not last long, as he did not want to alienate the players.

When the Boks were in Cape Town preparing for the second test against Wales in 2002, Straeuli set a tone in his first video analysis that he never matched again. The Boks had won the first test 34-19, but had not been convincing. Early on in the video session, Bob Skinstad congratulated Warren Britz for competing effectively at the kick-off and winning back the ball. 'Why are you applauding him?' Straeuli fumed. Skinstad replied that Britz had won back the ball. Straeuli wanted to know where the ball had gone once Britz had won it back, pointing out that it had been flicked back five metres to no one, which had put the Boks under pressure.

'There was no plan to what he did,' Straeuli continued. 'It was done out of desperation. How can you say "well done"? Stop pissing in each other's pockets. It is going to get us nowhere. Let's be honest with ourselves.' It was an impressive outburst, but it was not heard often enough. In that particular week it became obvious that our players lacked professionalism. Straeuli instructed video analyst Dale McDermott to work through the night after the test in order to have twenty-two individual match tapes available for each squad member. Each tape would include only one particular player's contribution to the game. It was the first time during my association with the Boks that this level of analysis would be available to the player in video format.

By the Monday evening, two days later, only three of the twenty-two players had bothered to collect their match tapes to view them. Straeuli lost it. He felt that the players did not really care. They played the game, but lacked the introspection to improve the next week. This was an attitude Straeuli would try to improve in 2002 and 2003. Video analysis took up a huge part of the weekly schedule in those years. Straeuli and his assistants all played a role in presenting individual and team analyses, but I often suspected that little was actually being absorbed.

One of the challenges was to encourage our players to own up to their mistakes.

Players such as Skinstad and Krige had no problem with this. They would even take the blame for something that was not their own fault to see if another player would own up. Few players ever did. It was quite an achievement for a player to say 'sorry', but often he did not even know why he was apologising. An apology acted as a defence mechanism, as the player did not want to be singled out by the coaching staff. Stefan Terblanche's defensive game was particularly weak. He struggled to understand the defensive pattern, and in match situations would commit suicide defensively. One aspect all the coaches discussed with the wingers was to be careful about being suckered into straying off their wing on defence.

'Stay on your wing and don't commit yourself unnecessarily,' Tim Lane preached on a weekly basis. 'Don't take yourself out of the game. Read the play, communicate to the guy on your inside and then make a calculated decision.'

In Brisbane in 2002, Stefan came off his wing again. Afterwards, Lane asked him why this had happened. Stefan said that it was the way he was told to play by his regional coach. 'Well,' Lane said, 'you are with the Boks now and not your regional side or your regional coach.'

For a moment Terblanche had forgotten that his regional coach was now the national coach. Straeuli just smiled. He liked Stefan and would not embarrass him publicly, but it exposed the average Bok psyche and technical inadequacies that made them so vulnerable against technically adept teams. In 2002 and 2003, Straeuli concentrated on individual tutorship, and the packhorse in the technical team was McDermott, who had the unenviable task of spending more than ten hours a day cutting clips and putting together video packages for the coaches and players. He also videotaped every session, whether it took place on the field or in the team room.

But he would often mention to me how many times he taped sessions and cut the clips for the coaches, and then they were never used. McDermott, logistics manager Mac Hendricks and kit steward Philip Malakoane were the unsung heroes of the 2003 World Cup campaign. Their hours could not be measured for reward. All of them made mistakes in the course of a week, but they put in the hard slog.

Hendricks, in particular, battled the apathy of Nike South Africa before every test, as well as the deliberate obstructions of provincial unions in South Africa. Nike, for all their good intentions, was a nightmare to deal with. Jerseys would arrive late and the sizes were invariably wrong. After four years of test rugby, they still could not get Breyton Paulse's size right.

Hendricks was a nervous wreck most Fridays before a test as he scanned every jersey to make sure the size was correct and the match inscription had been done correctly. When we played the United States in Houston, Nike representative Mark Pollard sent the jerseys to Dallas to have the names stitched on. That was the last Pollard ever saw of the jerseys. The Friday evening team photo was a joke.

We managed to find twenty-two jerseys from the previous tests among the squad, and players put on whatever jersey they could lay their hands on. A player making his first appearance for the Boks would have thought he was on *Candid Camera*. This was Bok rugby, but because of the ongoing failings of Nike South Africa, the situation was more like a club fourth-team get-together on a Saturday morning.

'Anyone got a jersey?'

The replacement test jerseys only arrived on the Saturday morning of the game.

The players never knew what a guy like Hendricks actually did on tour, and many didn't give a hoot. Hendricks would have to listen to the players' whining all the time, while trying to combat the provincial unions' pettiness. When Viljoen was coach, playing in Durban was like playing away from home. The visitors were treated better. When Straeuli took over, playing at Newlands was like an away game. The only two unions that made the Boks feel like the number-one priority were the Bulls and Lions, with the Bulls in particular offering superb hospitality and support.

Straeuli acknowledged Hendricks' contribution, and was not afraid to point it out to players who did not always appreciate the role of the support staff. They did not always understand the mechanics of each member's portfolio. Straeuli once said that he would love to give each player his own budget and see whether they all made it to Australia in time for the first practice session. He was sure it would be a disaster.

Springbok rugby players are treated like royalty by sponsors and hotel staff, and live a charmed life on tour. They operate in a cocoon that is not the real world. Everything is paid for. Everything is pre-arranged, from flights to accommodation to food to entertainment. Everything is provided on request, at times even without request. Anne Lee Murray, public relations manager of SA Rugby, was like a mother to all the players. If they could not get hold of their agent to do something, then Anne Lee would do it. Anne Lee or the agent would always act as a crutch; it wasn't healthy.

The mere concept of applying for a visa was foreign to most of the players who had never travelled in their private capacity. On tour, the player gave his passport to Mac Hendricks, who did the rest. Hendricks and Malakoane would arrive at the airport four hours before the squad to ensure that the check-in was completed timeously. On occasion, British Airways, sponsor to the Boks, even arranged the check-in from the team hotel. The Boks are spoilt by the unconditional support they enjoy. Because of it, they don't have to think for themselves, and often act in a manner that suggests they are incapable of thinking.

On the 2001 end-of-year tour, six of the players packed their passports in the luggage that would be transported by truck from Paris to Genoa. The truck left on Saturday night, and on the Sunday morning six players had no passports. They hadn't realised that you needed a passport to get from France to Italy.

This type of incident always jolted management and made them appreciate the limited headspace of the average Springbok player. Straeuli never wanted fingers pointed at management, but he did not excuse their fallibility. Gideon Sam would reprimand management and support staff who slipped up in front of the players, in order to show them that no exceptions were made when someone was inefficient in their job.

The system of fines, applied within the Bok team for any disciplinary failing, was applicable also to management, although the management member would pay R150 as opposed to the player's R800. This caused unhappiness among management, who felt they were not being paid R100 000 each Saturday. R150 was a big sacrifice for some; for the players, R800 was merely an irritation.

Under Straeuli and Sam, weekly management meetings were conducted in a formal environment. Viljoen was more relaxed in his approach to management meetings, but this wasn't ideal either, as each unit head operated in a vacuum. Viljoen could be accused of not having enough meetings; Straeuli and Sam were guilty of having too many.

However, I preferred Straeuli's approach, although a lot of time was unnecessarily wasted. Straeuli seemed to believe that the longer a meeting lasted, the greater its significance. The more hours the coaches put in, the bigger the sacrifice. Everything was measured in length, and not quality of time.

Straeuli and Sam allowed each management member to have a say at these meetings. Everyone produced a written report: technical, medical, logistics and media. In the latter part of 2003, Corné Krige, as captain, represented the players at these meetings. In most respects, Bok management was very professional. Coaching deficiencies, security paranoia and questionable leadership decisions in 2003 should not detract from the logistical, medical and technical input.

Everything about the Boks under Straeuli could be likened to a high school operation. Straeuli treated the Boks as his pupils. He and Sam were the headmasters. There was a weekly timetable, and a daily reminder of the weekly timetable. There were copious amounts of paperwork … every day. Initially, the timetable did not change. As 2003 unfolded and then unravelled, Straeuli tampered with and tweaked the daily schedule erratically and without warning. Players, reliant on the structure, felt uncomfortable with the changes. They aired their grievances to management through Krige and the players' committee.

Among their demands was that the starting XV should be announced on the Monday morning for the players' peace of mind. They wanted better communication and the occasional laugh, such as recreation in the form of a game of pool or table tennis, and a complete break from the team environment on at least one day a week. The requests were granted. The players also questioned the point of the daily dress code, which ruled that everyone wear the Bok tracksuit and the same colour T-shirt. Straeuli was non-negotiable on these minor disciplines.

The Boks, he told the players, are a unit in which the family bond is applauded. Individualism is not promoted, nor is individual preference at the expense of team discipline. Straeuli wanted to instil in his players the belief that every morning was the start of a working day. Each player had to show his teammates respect – and that meant being seated at the same time in 'work' attire and looking presentable. In private, the players criticised the imbalance in the squad's daily schedule. There was no time for escape, and no time for themselves. The players, unconfident in a professional world, wanted structure, but they also yearned for the freedom of a long school break.

School used to consist of four morning periods, a short break, three mid-morning periods, a decent lunch break, two afternoon periods, one last bell and, finally, recreation. The Springboks' daily schedule read much the same. Structure dulled the enthusiasm, especially when players were away from home. The days of being a tourist on a rugby tour were long gone.

Viljoen had tried to change this attitude by instilling enthusiasm in the players to leave the hotel foyer and see the sights. In 2001 the squad went for dinner at a restaurant in Paris, and then attended a show at the world famous Lido. The show was spectacular. Tim Lane had arranged the evening through a business contact. Tickets would have cost each squad member US$100, but instead it was complimentary, and Moët & Chandon supplied two bottles of their famous champagne for every table of four. It was a fantastic evening, and players raved about the experience in press interviews. The evening changed their perspective on touring France, traditionally the tour from hell for any Bok team. Our players could not speak the language and hated the food, craving traditional home cooking.

Viljoen said the players should get out of the hotel and use the free time to enrich themselves culturally. When France beat the Boks 20-10 on the Saturday evening, the media blamed the wining and dining in Paris for the defeat. Coaches and former players in South Africa were also sarcastic about the way the Boks dressed, and hammered Viljoen for focusing too much on image and not enough on rugby.

Straeuli was one of the critics at the time, and wanted to avoid giving the media the same ammunition while he was in charge of the Boks. Team dinners under Straeuli were standard events, normally at a steakhouse, where everyone had a meal and left soon afterwards: in at 7.30 p.m. and back at the hotel by 10.30 p.m. The exception had been in Brisbane in 2002, when Straeuli turned the team dinner into a team activity to gauge how the players would cope with an unexpected event. When they arrived in the team room fifteen minutes before they were to leave for dinner, Straeuli told them there was no bus. He gave them an address and the time they had to arrive at the restaurant, and threw in a prize for showing the most originality for the manner in which they arrived. It was a fun evening, and indicative of the easy sporting mood of the 2002 Tri-Nations campaign.

This would not happen again in 2003.

Many myths and too few truths exist about life as a Bok. Among the myths between 2000 and 2003 were: senior players are excused as duty boys; no cellphones are allowed; alcohol is banned; socialising is banned; players have to speak English to the media; all team talks are conducted exclusively in Afrikaans; video reviews are a humiliation session; the Boks care more about the cash than the jersey; they lose because of a lack of effort; every Bok is the other's mate; sex is banned before matches and partners cannot stay at the team hotel; a selection panel picks the test match 22; the Boks are superheroes – no, they are as vulnerable as any South African; the Boks are machines – no, they tire as easily as the next person.

In 2003, the cellphone issue was blown out of proportion and was misrepresented in the media. Despite numerous calls to journalists to explain what had happened, the accurate version made for boring reading and was never released. Straeuli only had nine days to work with the squad before the first test against Scotland in June 2003. He had to unify a team quickly, but in the first few hours noticed how preoccupied the players were. Every player, in his spare time or between meetings, was on his cellphone. At every meal, most of the players talked on their phones. You couldn't have a conversation without a cellphone interruption.

On the Friday night, Straeuli told the players that he wanted them to talk to one another for the next two days in order to get to know each other. They only had a week before playing Scotland. Straeuli put his cellphone in a box, and said he expected every player's phone to be in there by the end of the evening. Sharks centre Trevor Halstead jokingly asked Straeuli how he expected the players to make contact with their families without their cellphones. Straeuli told him to use a landline.

By the following day, Halstead and André Snyman had not handed in their phones. Straeuli called them out after training, and asked them whether they were part of a team, or did they just do 'their own thing'. He then made the team run while the two centres watched. The cellphones were returned to the players by the Sunday evening.

Prior to the World Cup, Krige again raised the cellphone issue. As captain, he found it disturbing that players were always on their phones in the bus, at team dinners and, in one instance, forty minutes before a test match kick-off. Krige wanted cellphones to be used with discretion. The squad backed him.

Straeuli asked the players what sacrifices they were prepared to make to ensure that the World Cup campaign was a success. As always, the players said they would not drink. Straeuli thought that was unpractical. He suggested that they enjoy occasions where they drank alcohol, but as professionals accepted that there were times when you did not drink. The players agreed to this.

The senior players also wanted the initiation changed, and replaced with a formal ritual in which the new cap was honoured and not humiliated. No booze would be allowed at the new initiation ceremony. In the past, players had been mocked, hit with a cane and generally made to look like fools. A lot of alcohol was consumed, and the initiation would degenerate into chaos. Now, players would unwind with drinks and a bit of fun only after the ceremony.

The players also preferred their wives or partners to move into the hotel only after the match. This arrangement was upheld all year. Partners would always stay with the players on the Saturday evening, as it was part of team protocol for the players to spend the Friday evening together as a squad, staying at the team hotel.

But all of a sudden a story was circulating that the players were not allowed cellphones, alcohol or sex. This was nonsense. Straeuli can rightfully be accused of poor management, more so in 2003 than in 2002, but there were times when he acted in the interests of the team. Sometimes, players used the coach's good intentions to promote their own agenda.

When the Boks played Scotland at Murrayfield in 2002 and lost 21-6, Straeuli and most of the squad were at their lowest emotional ebb. At the team meeting after the match, Straeuli told the players that there were a lot of happy Scottish people in Edinburgh, and far too many furious South Africans. Nearly 20 000 South Africans had travelled from London to watch the game. The booing during the game had been an indication of the prevailing mood.

Straeuli warned that people would be drunk and aggressive. He urged the team to stay in, and said he would arrange for beer to be delivered to the team room. It made sense to bring partners, family and friends to the team room to spend the evening there. He was afraid that the Boks might get involved in fights because of the mood in the streets.

Straeuli and the squad discussed his suggestion, and the players were given the final say. They decided to go out. Straeuli advised them to travel in groups. He had every reason to be worried. That night a local picked a fight with Robbie Fleck. The players stopped it before anything happened, but Lukas van Biljon went outside and gave the person a reminder of why the Boks were not to be taunted in public. James Dalton intervened, and the incident was limited to one flat hand from Van Biljon.

This was exactly what Straeuli had wanted to avoid. On the Boks' return home, stories started to circulate about Straeuli's draconian attitude after the game because he did not want the players to go out. It was a lie. Myths about the Boks will always exist, as legends have an appeal of their own. Often, the truth goes unnoticed or is distorted. Among the distortions was that there was no planning for the 2003 season. The truth is, planning was detailed, but the application was inconsistent. The last few months' activities did not resemble the pre-season documentation.

As for provincialism, it is a strong factor in the Bok team, and some players will avoid others from rival provinces. They may play for the same country and make a living out of the same game, but that is often where the connection ends.

The only booze restriction on players is that no alcohol is consumed until two hours after a game, for medical reasons. Team initiations only occur at specific times, and were refined to honour and not humiliate the player. A player is still caned as part of the initiation, but it is a symbolic act rather than a physical assault.

Security was obsessive in 2003, and game plans were guarded as if they were the crown jewels and burnt afterwards. No player ever laid a hand on one outside of the team room. Security was way over the top, and Straeuli was to blame for the overkill.

Finally, the truth about Bok selection: between 2000 and 2003, the coach made the call on the test 22. He selected the team. He got whomever he wanted.

Typical test match week for the Springboks when playing a night test

Monday
08.00: Physio, as per appointment
09.00: Breakfast
09.45: Meet in team room for briefing
10.00: To the gym for weight training
12.30: Lunch
13.00: Media conference with captain and coach
14.00: Individual video sessions and individual skill sessions. Physio, as per appointment
17.00: In physio room for strapping
17.30: Meet in team room
17.45: Bus to training
18.00: Training under lights
19.30: Training finishes
20.00: Ice baths and jacuzzis
20.30: Dinner
21.30: Individual video analysis (optional). Physio, as per appointment

Tuesday
08.00: Physio as per appointment
09.00: Breakfast
09.45: Briefing in team room where details of field session are discussed
10.00: On the bus for field session specific to forwards (scrums, line-outs) and backs (moves, tactical kicking)
12.00: Training finishes
12.30: Ice baths and jacuzzis
13.00: Lunch
13.15: Media (selected players)

14.00: Team unit theory session, tight five, loose forwards and backs.

15.00: Physio, as per appointment

17.00: In physio room for strapping

17.30: Meet in team room for field session briefing

17.45: On bus to training

18.00: Team training, with emphasis on defence

19.30: Training finishes

20.00: Ice baths and jacuzzis

20.30: Dinner

21.30: Physio as per appointment. Individual video analysis (optional). Player briefing for media one-on-ones

Wednesday

08.00: Physio as per appointment

09.00: Breakfast

10.00: Swim session

11.30: Physio, as per appointment. Player media briefings, where relevant

12.30: Lunch

13.00: Media hour (one-on-one interviews with media)

14.15: Theory session (be it team defence or forwards with forward coach and backs with backline coach)

16.30: Team video session (specifics on opposition at a review of previous evening's training session)

17.45: Leave for training

18.00: Training under lights

19.30: Training finishes

20.00: Ice baths and jacuzzis

21.00: Team dinner at restaurant

Thursday

08.30: Match 22 confirmed to media

09.00: Breakfast

Players have rest of day to themselves

18.30: Meet in team room

19.00: Video session with focus specific to opposition

20.00: Dinner

20.30: Massages available (optional). Physio, by appointment

Friday

09.00: Breakfast

10.00: Press conference with captain, coach and manager

11.00: Theory session with focus on attack and defensive drills and set-piece play, be it line-outs or scrums

12.30: Lunch

13.30: Individual skills (optional)

18.00: Meet in team room for match-day photo

18.30: Leave for light training run at match venue

19.00: Captain's run, where the captain controls the 45-minute session as a dress rehearsal for match day

20.00: Team dinner at hotel

Evening free. Movies optional

Saturday

Match-day schedule is specific to kick-off time

In the event of a late kick-off, players can eat between 8 a.m. and 11 a.m.

11.15: Fun with ball skills, racquet sports and a walk around as a squad

14.00: Lunch and afternoon to themselves

17.00: Strapping in physio room

17.30: Meet in team room for final pre-match coach's talk

17.45: On the bus to ground

18.00: At the ground

18.25: Warm-up starts

18.55: Onto the field for anthems

19.00: Kick-off

20.30: Post-match recovery. Ice-baths and swim if facilities available

21.00: Media conference with captain, coach and players

21.30: Post-match function

22.30: At the hotel for dinner

23.00: Informal team gathering. If the Sunday is a travel day, then all luggage must be packed and put in team room by 1 a.m.

Sunday

Usually a travel day

6

Hit and miss

Selection and training

Rudolf Straeuli's master plan for winning the World Cup was non-existent. There were plans, but they changed every week. The ideal Bok team, identified by Straeuli at the start of 2003, never played against either England or New Zealand. When Straeuli disclosed his team preparation philosophy to his employer and the South African media early in 2003, he identified scientific selection, conditioning, black player representation and game plan strategy as the key elements in his grand plan. In none of the departments did the end result match the original idea.

Selections were certainly not based on a scientific approach, and the physical conditioning schedule, drawn up by the Sports Science Institute in Cape Town and approved by the national coaching staff, was never implemented. In my first two years in the set-up, team selection relied very little on science. There was no methodology on how a player was to be either selected or axed. No position-specific template existed. Harry Viljoen and Rudolf Straeuli, the two Bok coaches with whom I worked, could not articulate the attributes required to be a Bok in each position. They relied on gut feel, their own player preferences, and the input of national selectors Wynand Claassen and François Davids.

At times, test squad selections were made in the heat of the moment, and sorely lacked the professionalism you would normally associate with a business. Selection is a player's livelihood, and in a corporate environment you assume each position is defined by a job description and a performance review. As an outsider, I imagined selection to be different, especially with the advances in modern technology. I pictured a situation where the wise men of Bok rugby gathered together for a few days, studied individual player tapes and specific match plays, and discussed in detail the merits and deficiencies of each player.

I assumed that a selector would have a file on each player, and whatever you needed to know about the player could be answered by referring to the folder: How much game time has he had? How many games has he played in the season? Has he been injured and, if so, how long was he out of the game? Were his injuries of a serious or niggling nature? How had he fared each week during active competition? How did his individual performance measure up to the team he was playing in, and was his performance of the required standard when compared to his opposing player? What were the player's match statistics, and how did his graph show up over a period of twelve weeks in a competition such as the Super 12?

In January 2003, South Africa's Springbok selectors could not provide you with those answers, because they did not have the data. Attempting to advance the cause of the technical department within SA Rugby was one of the most frustrating political fights for any Bok coach, as well as for Rian Oberholzer, the MD of SA Rugby. There was simply too much resistance. When I arrived, existing structures included a technical committee, headed by André Markgraaff. The committee met at least once a month, but very little of what they discussed was ever carried over to the national set-up. Viljoen did not care much for the technical committee, as he did not respect the rugby knowledge of those who served on it for the comfortable fee of R30 000 a month. A strong technical department, operated on a day-to-day basis by technical experts, was non-existent in South African rugby.

Viljoen spoke about it. Straeuli took it further, and in his final year desperately tried to advance its cause. Oberholzer recognised the need for such a department, which would be headed by a director of rugby. Alan Solomons was Oberholzer's ideal candidate for the job. His work ethic was unequalled, and his success with the Springboks, in South African rugby and with Ulster in Ireland could not be disputed. He also enjoyed international respect.

Straeuli was willing to work with Solomons, and by all accounts Solomons was prepared to return to South Africa after a successful stint with Ulster. But bringing back Solomons found no favour with board members or provincial presidents, who disliked him personally. His credentials were never questioned; they simply did not like him. The position was put on hold.

Oberholzer lost that battle with the board, some of whose members felt qualified to be appointed to the position themselves. It placed unfair pressure on Straeuli. He was operating within a system in which he had to play the dual roles of director of rugby and Bok coach. He had to do all the negotiating with provincial coaches, Super 12 coaches and their chief executives. It was an endless exercise that resulted in numerous aeroplane trips and meetings, and much paperwork. And he still had to prepare for an international season and coach the Boks.

The marketing, media and commercial divisions of Springbok rugby were strong. Resources were plentiful, and what could not be done in-house was outsourced. Cost was rarely a factor. The Boks as a brand were brilliantly marketed, sponsorships were healthy despite dismal test results since the 1999 World Cup, and the public relations department, led by Anne Lee Murray, always made a huge effort. The Springboks' marketing campaigns – a combination of outsourced expertise and internal concepts – compared favourably with any in international sport. But when it came to a rugby department, the Boks lagged behind.

Jake White was appointed to run SA Rugby's technical team, which included Dale McDermott, in 2002. They had to service the Boks and SA under-21s, as well as lend whatever assistance they could to the Super 12 coaches and national Sevens coach Chester Williams. England had more than forty technical experts working on their opposition, and six dedicated exclusively to South African rugby. The Boks had Jake. An added problem was that Straeuli and Jake rarely spoke. They tolerated each other, but no more than that. If Jake presented Rudolf with information, it was apprehensively received because it came from Jake. The reverse was also true. Jake knew that whatever he gave Straeuli would not necessarily be taken to heart.

There was no trust within the national set-up, and very little trust between the Super 12 coaches and the Springbok set-up. Personalities dominated the game and affected decision-making. Paranoia was rife, as was illustrated when Sevens coach Chester Williams and Stormers assistant coach Jerome Paarwater attended what was supposed to be a closed Bok training session in Cape Town before the 2003 Tri-Nations test against the Wallabies. Straeuli wanted Williams and Paarwater removed. He trusted no one, not even them. Adriaan Heijns had to tell the two men, who were seated in their car at the Bishops school grounds, to leave. Needless to say, Williams and Paarwater were furious, and leaked the story to the press. Bok management merely dismissed it as a 'misunderstanding'. The truth was that Straeuli did not want anyone there, not even Williams.

Oberholzer was aware of the insecurities of each coach, and how much they distrusted each other. He tried to find a balanced solution that would benefit everyone. For three years, all I ever heard was the slogan: 'National team first'. Practically, it rarely worked. The provinces run South African rugby, and provincial interests take priority, which is what Oberholzer fought to change. He never succeeded, but it was not through a lack of effort, be it from Oberholzer, Viljoen or Straeuli. Provincial presidents in South African rugby put their province first, and only then consider the requirements of the Springboks.

Each Super 12 coach operated in isolation, and none of his data was made available to the national coach. Even a player's medical records were only reluctantly released. Conditioning statistics were also a well-guarded secret. Nothing was transparent. At national level, the coach relied on hearsay, gut feel and, occasionally, a little science based on the odd statistic gathered on the way to a selection meeting.

Viljoen, in his fifteen months as Bok coach, and Straeuli, in his first year, would not have been able to tell you a player's medical history or his career graph. If you had asked them who the most consistent and effective line-out ball winner was, the answer would vary, as no statistics existed. Viljoen, Straeuli and the two national selectors would not have known who kicked the ball the furthest out of hand, who could kick with both left and right foot, who passed comfortably on both sides, who made the most tackles, took the ball up the most and had the ability to offload effectively in the tackle.

The information was simply not available. Selection was a hit-and-miss affair. They got some right, but too many wrong. Player weaknesses would only be discovered when it was too late. One example was Deon de Kock's selection for the 2001 end-of-year tour to Europe and the USA. Viljoen had watched a highlights package of the Falcons match against Western Province. De Kock's play had been robust in the face of the Province defence, and was rewarded with a few tries. Viljoen liked what he saw, and De Kock's name was added to the selection mix. The incumbent Springbok scrumhalves were Joost van der Westhuizen and Neil de Kock. In the season's first seven tests, Neil de Kock had only had one start, in which he neither excelled nor failed. It was assumed that Joost and Neil would go on tour. Harry thought differently, and told me that Deon de Kock had impressed him. I made a few phone calls and obtained some information on the player, and reported back to Viljoen.

Heyneke Meyer, the Bulls Super 12 coach, had not picked Deon de Kock because he found the player's service too slow, and he had a poor pass. He was a good athlete, but lacked the basic strengths of a quality scrumhalf. I mentioned this to Viljoen, whose response was that Meyer might have had a personal problem with the player. Harry still liked what he saw. The selectors met immediately after the Currie Cup semi-finals in October 2001. Knowing how emotional these meetings can be, I arranged with SuperSport for a two-hour window for the finalisation of the touring squad.

Viljoen would then address SuperSport viewers live at 7.30 p.m. As was customary, the team list would be given to SuperSport at least an hour before-hand so that graphics could be designed to accompany the announcement. The media usually also receive an embargoed squad prior to the official announcement, to assist them with deadlines. Touring squads are finalised on a Saturday, because the Sunday print media is the biggest forum for rugby exposure.

With this particular selection, I thought two hours would suffice. Viljoen seemed content that the squad had been finalised during the course of the week after telephonic discussions with the two selectors. The role of the selectors between 2000 and 2003 was to advise and offer alternatives. It never came down to a vote. The coach had the final say, although coaches would conveniently use the selectors as their fall guy if they did not know how to break bad news to a player. They would say something along the lines of: 'I pushed for you, but the other two wouldn't budge.'

Viljoen had given me a provisional squad, and the second scrumhalf's name was listed as De Kock. There was no initial. I asked him whether it meant Deon or Neil, and he said they would decide at the meeting. The clock ticked, and still there was no answer. The media were getting anxious. They thought

I was being a prick, trying to make their lives difficult by not releasing the squad. But there was no squad. I interrupted the meeting and said we needed to release the names to SuperSport. Claassen said they could wait. I said they could not. Contractually, the squad announcement was theirs exclusively, and advertisements had been sold around the timing of the announcement. I needed an answer.

Viljoen wanted Deon de Kock. Claassen agreed with him. François Davids said Neil de Kock had done nothing wrong all season, but had enjoyed very little opportunity. It made no sense to axe him. The three debated the issue for another few minutes. I left the room. Now it was close to 7.25 in the evening. I went in again, and said a final decision had to be made. 'D' or 'N'? Davids eventually relented, but wanted it placed on record that he felt Neil should not be dropped. Deon de Kock was selected. The media initially thought Harry had read the name out incorrectly.

De Kock, out of his depth on tour, struggled even in training. Joost was not playing particularly well, and lacked the insight to orchestrate the kind of game Tim Lane proposed. Lane wanted to try something different during the tour. He recommended starting Deon against England. Harry said the player was not up to it. He told Lane that the player's pass was not good enough, and he was too sluggish with his service. Ironically, he was agreeing with Heyneke Meyer's assessment, but it was a little late in the day. De Kock's lot on tour was game time against Italy and a start in the final tour match against the United States. Deon de Kock has never played for the Boks again, and cannot make a Super 12 squad. But he is a test Springbok!

Other selections during Viljoen's era similarly bordered on the bizarre, in particular his fascination with Joe van Niekerk. Yet Harry refused to back him with an eighty-minute start in any test. Viljoen selected Van Niekerk on Jake White's recommendation, but then dismissed White's suggestion that Van Niekerk should play in the away test against Australia in 2001.

Jake told Viljoen how good Van Niekerk was, while conditioning coach Chris van Loggerenberg told him that the player was not up to test level in terms of his conditioning. Viljoen made the decision to select Corné Krige as the reserve loose forward against the Wallabies, and never gave Van Niekerk game time. The next week, against the All Blacks, he replaced Krige with Van Niekerk. It was a coach's call; there was no science to the selection. Later in the year, Viljoen again told the media he was going to unleash Van Niekerk on the world during the European tour. He sent him on against France in Paris after seventy-seven minutes, with the Boks trailing 20-10. A few days later we were travelling in the bus to training in Genoa, Italy. Viljoen told Tim and me what his match 22 would be against Italy. Van Niekerk had not made it. Lane and I questioned his exclusion, especially after all the pre-tour hype. Viljoen's explanation was that the player had not made an impression against France. We said: 'Harry, he only played the last three minutes.' Harry replied: 'I thought it was six.'

Before training started, Viljoen called the squad together to announce the test 22. Lane came over to me and asked if I had said anything further to Harry. I said I hadn't, and wanted to know why he asked. 'Well, he's just picked Joe,' said Lane.

Mark Andrews was not playing in the Italy test, and Viljoen picked AJ Venter at lock. Venter played the best test of his career, but prior to the match, Viljoen had assured Andrews that he would start against England. Venter's effort was in vain. Van Niekerk was dropped for the test against England when Viljoen announced the match 22 at training. Lane, Skinstad and I asked Viljoen if he had explained the omission to Van Niekerk. He said he didn't need to, and that Joe needed to learn that things don't always come easily in life. I said: 'Harry, you picked him. He never selected himself.'

On different occasions that week, Skinstad, Lane and I took Van Niekerk for a drink to cheer him up, encouraging him to learn from the experience and be a better player for it. He was twenty-one years old, and we told him he would be the best in the world. Skinstad gave him a lot of guidance on that tour.

The incident with Van Niekerk was not the first time Viljoen had changed his mind on a selection in the space of a few minutes. After Percy Montgomery's kicking failure against New Zealand at Newlands in July 2001, Viljoen indicated that he was going to drop Montgomery for the Pretoria test against Australia, and start with Conrad Jantjes at fullback. We were in Durban preparing and having a few drinks in the pub. Tim, Butch Watson Smith, Chris van Loggerenberg, Jake White, Harry and I were present. During our conversation, Harry said that he had changed his mind. He felt Montgomery should be given another chance. Later in the evening he thought of playing Thinus Delport, and then settled on Montgomery again before going to bed.

When he announced the team the next morning, Jantjes was at fullback. Jake and I had urged him to pick Jantjes, but to play Montgomery at flyhalf, at centre or on the wing.

When I asked Harry what Jantjes had done overnight to make the team, he laughed and said he had only been winding us up the night before. His answer did not convince me, because he had said the same thing to Lane and Butch Watson Smith, who had no reason to want to see Jantjes in the team other than on merit. Jake and I also believed Jantjes was good enough, but we had a soft spot for him because we felt he had never been given a fair chance.

Harry's strength did not lie in making selection decisions, and it would have been better for all concerned had he been able to tap into statistical data on each player. For example, he picked Trevor Halstead at outside centre against England, and Halstead is one of the slowest midfielders in the country. He is powerful, but pace is not his weapon. It was another of those gut-feel calls.

I told Straeuli the story of Deon de Kock and Joe van Niekerk, if only as motivation for establishing an essential, detailed player database. Straeuli was very amenable to making selection more scientific. He had been through enough selection meetings to know how fallible the process was, and had been its victim as a player. He also agreed that so much more was now at stake for professional players, especially financially. A selector now held a man's career and livelihood in his hands. The game was no longer just a sport.

Because of his late appointment in 2002, Straeuli did not have the preparation time available to influence the permanent establishment of such systems. Technically, the Boks were lacking in resources from 2000 to 2002.

As the Wallabies assistant coach when they won the World Cup in 1999, Tim Lane could not believe how far behind the Boks were in their technical preparation. He told Harry about the Wallabies system and how technologically advanced they were. The Wallaby players would each receive individual tapes and CDs on their performance within twenty-four hours of a test's completion. The information on the opposition was as detailed, both in print form and on video.

In 2002, Straeuli advanced the production of video analysis and individual analysis within the Bok set-up. Dale McDermott was added to the Bok squad as a video analyst, and his primary job was to cut videos for analysis, both in a team context and in a private capacity for the players. He would also video the opposition, and hand the tapes to the coaches to present to the players. Jake White, through an association with the Council for Scientific and Industrial Research (CSIR) in Pretoria, initiated a more detailed analytical system, but it was still ordinary when compared to England, Australia, New Zealand and France's equipment. And it was also less effective because of the resources England had compared to us.

England uses a system called Prozone for all their analyses. Operated by sensor, the system was installed at Twickenham and Northampton, where they play their home 'A' internationals. Technologically, England was on another planet, and this was borne out when a representative of Prozone flew to South Africa for a presentation.

I attended the Prozone presentation with Straeuli and one of his technical advisors, Dr Gerrit Pool. We were all blown away by the match detail and breakdown in player performance offered by Prozone. The sensor tracks every player's movements for eighty minutes. The depth of analysis was something Straeuli and I had never seen before. One of the elements new to us was the specific tracking of a player's movements. If players were not involved in the game for a sustained period of five minutes, they would be circled on the match graph and their clock would start at zero again.

We were told that Clive Woodward used this technology religiously to determine his players' work rate. They were constantly aware of being involved in play because there was a clock on them all the time. During the presentation, the 2002 test between the Boks and England was used as an illustration of what Prozone could offer. Straeuli was asked whether he thought the Boks had ever been in the game after being beaten 53-3. Straeuli replied that the teams were evenly matched in the first twenty minutes, when England led 3-0 and playing numbers were equal. He argued that the turning point in the match occurred when Jannes Labuschagne was sent off for late-charging Jonny Wilkinson. 'At that stage, it was a 50-50 game,' Straeuli said.

Prozone proved otherwise. In the first twenty minutes, not one of the England pack was circled for non-activity over five minutes. Four players in the Bok pack were circled.

'Even then you were playing with a few men short when it came to effort,' the Prozone representative explained. There was no counter to the presentation. The sensors had picked up every movement of each player – things we could not see on the match video. The sensor tracked a player's off-the-ball movement: what he did before receiving the ball or making the tackle and, most importantly, what he did after completing an action.

It showed how lazy our players were in turning and getting back. Too many of them were guilty of walking when they should have been jogging or running. The statistics were damning. Prozone was prohibitively expensive at more than R10 million. It was also not practical in South Africa, where the Boks play their home tests between five or seven stadiums every year. England plays every home test at Twickenham.

Oberholzer tried to effect an arrangement with the four main regional stadiums, as Prozone would also benefit the Super 12 squads. It was to no avail. Straeuli had to make do with whatever White and the CSIR could formulate, and what SA Rugby could afford. When White took charge of the under-21s, he used more detailed statistics on player conditioning. He based these profiles on a model first used by the world-champion Wallabies in 1999.

The Super 12 coaches showed no enthusiasm for this model either, as they felt it was antiquated. Inevitably in South African rugby, everyone will tell you why something won't work instead of trying to see if it can work. During his travels to Australia, England and New Zealand, Harry Viljoen also recognised the necessity of detailed player databases. However, neither Viljoen nor Straeuli had the time to pursue the issue. They needed a dedicated director of rugby for the job, as both were forced to waste time and energy putting out political and provincial fires, and sidestepping political sensitivities and provincial differences. And after one test loss, the best-intended plans usually ended up in the wastepaper bin. In 2003, Straeuli wanted a professional selection system that would eradicate provincial bias and personal prejudice.

He had learnt a big lesson from the 2002 end-of-year tour to France, England

and Scotland. The final squad selections were made half an hour after the Blue Bulls beat the Lions in the Currie Cup final, and as many as six changes were made to the intended touring squad based on the match. Straeuli, as caught up in the emotion of the occasion as the other two selectors, reviewed the situation after the tour. He felt that a more scientific approach would have counteracted the emotional element in the selection.

Straeuli aimed to fix the inconsistencies in selection. Two independent consultants, Bruce Becker and Rob Benadie, were assigned to Straeuli at a cost of R100 000 a month. I was also seconded onto the special projects team, and paid an additional R10 000 a month. Our job was to establish a system that would give Straeuli the assurance that the best players would be picked to play test rugby. Becker and Benadie, previously of Accenture, the independent consultants who had been hired to investigate the state of the professional game in South Africa, had extensive knowledge of South African rugby's failings, as they had been at the heart of the audit.

Both are bright and very enthusiastic guys with a strong corporate background, but their knowledge of the game is limited. Not satisfied that Butch Watson Smith was the right person to be involved, Straeuli used Becker and Benadie for work ordinarily assigned to the general manager. A system whereby all four Super 12 coaches, the two national selectors and Straeuli would each select a form team on a weekly basis was agreed upon. Each Super 12 coach would also present a short overview of players. The rationale behind the arrangement was that the national coach too often selected a player in isolation, without consulting the person who had been coaching him for the last six months.

Each player's discipline would be monitored on a weekly basis. Every one of us had a different perspective on who the biggest offenders were, but we needed data to confirm the habitual trespassers. This would also allow us to spot trends that may be developing in different types of offences. We would be able to ascertain whether South African players had a specific problem with the interpretation of the law, or whether they were simply ill disciplined because they did not know or understand the laws.

The goal kickers' accuracy would be monitored, and their kicking over twelve weeks would be depicted in a graph to establish trends such as form, and home-and-away strike rate. The same applied to line-out jumpers. Who was our best line-out forward? Over a period of twelve weeks, we would know. Whose work rate was the best? Who peaked early in the season, and who were the late starters? In theory it all looked wonderful. Straeuli presented the plan to Rian Oberholzer and the board. They were thrilled. On top of this, Straeuli had identified individuals in Europe, Australasia and South Africa who would study patterns, game plans and players on a weekly basis. These analysts would file a report twice a month, and Straeuli would sift through the data and make his findings.

Straeuli asked South African referee Tappe Henning to assist with the Boks' training sessions during the 2002 Tri-Nations. Henning's assistance had a massive impact, with the team penalty count per game reduced from an average of twenty to ten. Henning was outstanding with the players. He is a passionate Bok supporter, which helped. Players wrote law exams so that Henning would know which players struggled with which areas of the game.

The Boks were very heavily penalised in the tackle situation, and the players admitted that they did not understand the law. Henning worked to improve their knowledge in theory sessions and on the practice field. During mealtimes, he would casually engage with the players about the laws. Tappe encouraged them to talk about interpretations, to good effect, especially at training. For the first time our players were thinking actively about why they were doing things on the field. Henning emphasised the importance of being street smart, understanding the referee and knowing the laws. He challenged the players to play referee and put themselves in the referee's position.

Straeuli knew he had to take it a step further in 2003. Referees were asked for general input in the build-up to the international season, and the four South African Super 12 referees reported trends on a weekly basis. They provided us with feedback on our own players' strengths and weaknesses regarding the application of the law.

'Too many Bok teams have been selected on emotion,' Straeuli told a media information session. 'Too many players are picked or dropped on the last ten minutes of the season. A system has to be established in which the player will be judged over a period of time.'

Oberholzer and the board were never shown the consistent workings of the system. Occasionally Straeuli would discuss it with Oberholzer, but Rian made it clear that he did not want to influence decision-making on selections, and left the project to Straeuli. He trusted Straeuli to adhere to the formula he had created. But the system was flawed. It could not be properly implemented. In the first five weeks of the competition, Bulls coach Rudy Joubert and Stormers coach Gert Smal did not take part. Both said it was impossible to communicate the information from Australia and New Zealand, where their Super 12 teams were playing.

It was a feeble excuse, and Butch Watson Smith had to remind them in writing of their responsibility to the project. Watson Smith's memos were meaningless. A failure to deliver the weekly feedback held no consequences. However, the Sharks' Kevin Putt was the most impressive of the Super 12 coaches in his approach to the selection process. Putt applied himself, and was both honest and unbiased about the players. He never favoured his own players, and his insights into the weekly performance of the Sharks players were sincere and objective. Unfortunately, his reports were not always what Straeuli wanted to read, which was another failing in the system. Coaches use statistics to support their own argument, but will invariably dismiss any data that contradicts their own views on a player.

By week six everyone was contributing, and form teams were being selected. Some of the selections exposed the national selectors' inadequacies. In some cases, a selector would write: 'Did not see the entire match, but heard player x was not good.' In the same report, the selector would add that another player had been very good. How did he know if he had not seen the match? Again, weekly selections were being based on hearsay, which was a problem. As the person tasked with compiling and formatting all the selections, I pointed this out to Straeuli, who said he would address the situation. He wanted to avoid a confrontation, and advised me to stay out of it. Other selection problems also emerged. Keith Parkinson, a member of the board, sent Straeuli a letter expressing his thoughts on the composition of the test team for the season's first international against Scotland. Parkinson sarcastically referred to Straeuli's 'advisors', saying that he felt qualified to offer advice as someone who had actually watched most of the Super 12 matches.

Parkinson included his match squad 22, but mistakenly called Quinton Davids, the Stormers lock, Quinton Daniels. Straeuli chuckled about this, as Quinton Daniels had played rugby as a flyhalf/inside centre for Western Province League and Boland in the early 1990s. Straeuli showed the letter to Oberholzer, who said he would take it up with Silas Nkanunu, as it was unacceptable for a board member to try to influence national selection. Straeuli did not confront Parkinson on the issue. Instead, he sent him a letter acknowledging his view, and met with him as a courtesy. Straeuli was aware of Parkinson's political influence, and did not want to get on his wrong side. He humoured him when he should have told him to stay out of the selection process.

At the conclusion of the Super 12 the votes were tallied, and they were to be used as the yardstick for selection. But this never happened. Straeuli selected on gut feel and emotion, which was exactly what he had previously told the board and media he wanted to avoid. Gcobani Bobo (41 votes) and Robbie Fleck (33 votes) lost out to Trevor Halstead (7 votes). Straeuli's explanation: 'Coach's call.'

Dale Santon (3 votes) also got the nod as back-up to Danie Coetzee (58 votes), when other hookers such as Hanyani Shimange, Lukas van Biljon and Gary Botha had accumulated more votes.

Bolla Conradie (27) also received more votes than Joost van der Westhuizen (23). Their game time was similar, but Conradie was never invited to one Bok training session in 2003. In 2002 he had played in every test. These are just three examples to illustrate how a concept was sold to the board and media, but proved to be a smokescreen to buy time for a World Cup plan that had no constancy. It also explains the inconsistency in selection, the failure to pick black players, the disregard for the information supplied by the Sports Science Institute and a game plan strategy that completely changed from that which was presented to the board. Addressing the board, Straeuli identified the following black players as World Cup selections midway through the 2003 Super 12: Deon Kayser, Gcobani Bobo, Bolla Conradie, Hanyani Shimange, Lawrence Sephaka and Quinton Davids.

Straeuli established a game time monitoring system for black players and predetermined game time goals during the Super 12. Only half of the goals were met, and Kayser, Conradie, Shimange and Davids never made it to the World Cup. Straeuli ended up selecting players who had never featured in the 'scientific' selection process aimed at eradicating provincial bias and sentiment, as promoted by Straeuli himself.

Scientific conditioning was another plan that impressed in Powerpoint presentations, but was ignored in the final month's preparations. The Sports Science Institute had been employed as consultants to guide the conditioning preparation and to calculate optimal player conditioning. Professor Tim Noakes was consulted, and his team suggested a course of action that Straeuli accepted as his guideline to ensure that the Boks would peak from the play-offs onwards. This included three training camps of eight, nine and twelve days respectively, with the players at home for six and four days' rest before departure. A four-day bush camp – or *Kamp Staaldraad*, as it became known – had not been part of the original World Cup conditioning plan. The players were supposed to have gone home for those four days. At the first camp in Pretoria, Straeuli suddenly changed his mind and kept the players together for more than thirty days. He would not allow them to go home for fear of being negatively influenced by family, friends or the media.

The recommended mental conditioning programme, piloted by twelve players, team physiotherapist Matime Diali and me, only made it as far as management. The official World Cup squad of thirty was supposed to complete the programme, but instead Straeuli took them to the bush for a quick fix in bonding and team spirit. Straeuli presented the board and the media with information, theories and ideas, which he flogged as his World Cup 'plan', but which in the World Cup proved inconsistent with team strategy and team selection.

Werner Greeff's unceremonious fall from grace at the World Cup exposed the inconsistency and obscurity of Straeuli's selections and strategy. It also confirmed Straeuli's inability to make a decision and stick to it – a weakness described by former Bok coach André Markgraaff as Straeuli's greatest vulnerability. Throughout the World Cup planning, Greeff was earmarked as the number one fullback to play against England. Greeff's role was pivotal to the implementation of two game plans. He was to play fullback but alternate at flyhalf on defence, and in certain structured plays on attack. Greeff's ability to attack the gain line at flyhalf would be an element of surprise against England.

The initial plan involved Greeff at fullback and André Pretorius at flyhalf. When fitness concerns cast Pretorius' involvement at the World Cup in doubt, Louis Koen was slotted into the No. 10 jersey. Depending on his fitness, Pretorius would then be used as an impact player. When Greeff fractured his ankle midway through the Super 12, great care was taken to ensure his fitness for the game against England. Greeff was part of Straeuli's rehabilitation squad in Cape Town, and his recovery was monitored on a weekly basis. Straeuli picked Greeff despite the player not having completed a first-class game in six months. He was so highly rated and his role at the World Cup considered so important that all he had to do was prove his fitness in the week before the World Cup squad announcement.

Greeff completed the fitness tests and was selected. Regular 2003 fullback Jaco van der Westhuyzen was passed over. Everything went according to plan in the Boks' World Cup opener against Uruguay, but the playmaking ploy was not used at all. Ironically, Greeff scored with his last touch of the ball. He would not play fullback again in the tournament.

Straeuli picked Van der Westhuyzen to play England. This was definitely not part of the plan, as Van der Westhuyzen had been omitted from the original squad. Straeuli never explained Greeff's World Cup demise or why the coaching staff had lost faith in him. Other selections were equally inconsistent with Straeuli's original World Cup strategy. Jorrie Muller was axed for the World Cup opening game despite showing good form in the last two Tri-Nations tests. Muller's provincial colleague Jaque Fourie was picked at outside centre. Fourie's fitness had been in doubt until a fortnight before the World Cup training camp in Pretoria.

Fourie, sensational against the South American minnows, hurt his knee in the latter stages. He made a speedy recovery, but never started in the midfield again in the first XV. Like Muller, Fourie had not been included in the original World Cup selection plan. Neither was young flyhalf sensation Derick Hougaard, who had played very little Super 12 rugby, and managed only one vote during the eleven rounds of the competition. He was also not picked in any of the seven internationals leading into the World Cup.

On the day before the World Cup squad announcement, Hougaard was still not guaranteed a place. He was only selected when Pretorius' fitness concerns ruled him out.

This explains why Koen started against England. Yet Hougaard played in the crucial No. 10 jersey against the All Blacks in a World Cup quarter-final. This was never in the initial plan. Danie Rossouw would also not have been at the World Cup, but Straeuli had been instructed not to select Bulls lock Geo Cronjé following his refusal to room with black teammate Quinton Davids.

Dale Santon, at thirty-four the oldest member of the squad, never featured in any World Cup plan prior to the 2003 international season. Santon's selection would make up the black numbers in the squad. His World Cup contribution of twelve minutes against Georgia supports this assumption. In May, Thinus Delport was playing for Gloucester. A release had to be negotiated between his club and SA Rugby. He, too, had not been part of the original plan. Straeuli spoke of a World Cup plan throughout the first eighteen months of his tenure, and justified the constant chopping and changing of the team on the basis that he 'knew who his World Cup XV' were; he just didn't want to reveal his hand. With each poor performance, Straeuli asked the media and public not to overreact, but to judge him on the World Cup.

When you analyse his weekly selections, Straeuli stumbled from one combination to another. There was no consistency in his approach towards a player or a style of play.

He did not back Stormers scrumhalf Conradie in 2003, despite picking him in ten tests in 2002. He was unsure about Brent Russell's mental toughness, and when the Sharks fullback failed once against New Zealand, it was enough to convince him that Russell should not be selected for the World Cup.

Russell's ankle injury at the World Cup camp in August was not the reason he was omitted. He could have been given time to recover and nursed through the opening two or three pool matches in much the same way the New Zealanders did with Aaron Mauger and Ali Williams. Trevor Halstead was a coach's call at inside centre, and André Snyman was picked despite reservations from the backline and defensive coaches. This combination proved incapable of taking the step up at international level.

Straeuli bemoaned the loss of the brilliant Jean de Villiers through injury, but he never selected him when he had the chance. He sent him home from the World Cup camp, only for De Villiers to be voted man of the match in three of his next four provincial outings. Only when Gcobani Bobo was ruled out of the tournament was De Villiers drafted in, and, in turn, his injury opened the way for Jaco Van der Westhuyzen. Bulls' utility forward Pedrie Wannenburg played in every test match in 2003, only to be booted out on the eve of the World Cup selection. Wannenburg was one of the highlights in the otherwise pitiful 2002 end-of-year tour.

Subsequent to the Springboks' World Cup quarter-final defeat, Straeuli spoke of the need to keep the squad together. He blamed the World Cup defeats to England and New Zealand on inexperience and youth. It is a common perception that the Boks were boys playing in a man's tournament. Yet in the quarter-final against the All Blacks, the average age of both starting XVs was twenty-five. In test experience, the All Blacks totalled an average of twenty-three test caps per position to South Africa's eighteen. New Zealand's run-on XV included five players in their first international season; South Africa only had one more player in his debut test season.

The All Blacks were as youthful and inexperienced as the Boks. The difference was that New Zealand coach John Mitchell had identified twenty-six players for his first seven tests as coach, and he picked the same twenty-six for the World Cup, adding four players who had been part of an extended training squad of forty earlier in the year. For the last five months of 2003, Mitchell worked with the same squad. When Mitchell took charge, the All Blacks started producing a consistent brand of attacking rugby.

In eighteen months, Straeuli used in excess of seventy players, and never once in twenty-three tests fielded the same starting XV in successive tests. Straeuli did not discover a new breed of Springbok at the World Cup. Hougaard, Muller, Schalk Burger and Ashwin Willemse all emerged from a very successful under-21 national set-up, while Fourie was outstanding in the 2003 Super 12.

Straeuli spoke of the youthfulness of his squad, but he played a quarter-final against the All Blacks with a captain who has since retired from international rugby, a scrumhalf who had already announced his retirement, a fullback who had joined Leicester and a wing who had always planned on returning to club rugby in England. He also selected the French-bound Koen as one of his seven substitutes. When the All Blacks announced their starting XV for the quarter-final, it included fourteen players from the 52-16 win against the Boks in Pretoria. The only change was forced through the injury of centre Tana Umaga. Straeuli's Boks showed eight changes.

Inexperience did not cost the Boks the chance of World Cup success. The inability of the coach to identify a squad and stick with it and a defective selection system were to blame. The area that most exposed these flaws was in the midfield, where thirty-five different midfield partnerships were used between 2000 and 2003. And at the 2003 World Cup, Straeuli and his selectors chose five fullbacks and one specialist centre. Even England boasted more specialist South African centres at the 2003 World Cup than the Springboks: Port Elizabeth's Mike Catt and Cape Town's Stuart Abbott versus Stormers and Western Province midfielder De Wet Barry. Lions utility back Jorrie Muller had been selected – and listed – as a specialist centre, but he had played fullback in the 2002 under-21 World Championship. Jaque Fourie was also picked as an outside centre, but he had played fullback in the 2003 Super 12, while Werner Greeff, the Boks' best fullback, was used as a back-up centre. Jaco van der Westhuyzen's test experience as a centre was four minutes, against New Zealand in 2000.

In forty-six tests between the 1999 World Cup and the 2003 World Cup, three Springbok coaches used thirty-five different midfield combinations, whether they started the test, played in the test or finished the eighty minutes. Among these combinations have been twelve outside centres and thirteen inside centres – nineteen different players in total. Such has been the uncertainty as to who or what constitutes an inside or outside centre that the majority of the nineteen players used have been tried at both No.12 and No. 13. No midfield combination has succeeded in playing five successive tests, with Barry (wearing 12) and Fleck (wearing 13) starting three on the trot in 2000, and Barry and Joubert starting in all four Tri-Nations matches in 2002.

Even then, neither combination could start and finish each test. Fleck got yellow-carded in the 2000 opener against Canada, and Barry did not finish the match. In the next test, against England, both players left the field injured. Barry and Joubert's partnership in 2002 saw Joubert receive a yellow card against New Zealand in Wellington, and a red card against Australia at Ellis Park. Earlier in the Ellis Park test, Barry had also spent ten minutes in the sin bin on a yellow-card offence. The uncertainty in the South African midfield is obvious, which has only been compounded by the different views and strategies of the three national coaches (Nick Mallett, Harry Viljoen and Rudolf Straeuli) and four different backline coaches (Alan Solomons, Jake White, Tim Lane and Rudy Joubert).

Injury, too, has exhausted the search for continuity, with Barry, Joubert, Fleck, André Snyman, Jean de Villiers, Trevor Halstead, Gcobani Bobo, Japie Mulder, Adrian Jacobs, Grant Esterhuizen and Deon Kayser all missing test selection at some point because of serious injury. The statistics of South Africa's midfielders since 2000 are alarming. If a player is said to have lost the plot, it begs the question: Did the selectors and coaches ever know the plot?

Teams taken seriously at any level usually have a settled midfield. It is not always spectacular, but it sure is efficient. Australia had Tim Horan and Jason Little for a decade; the All Blacks relied on Walter Little and Frank Bunce; and South Africa were world class in 1995 with Hennie le Roux and Japie Mulder. In the last four years, England has developed a midfield as effective as any in Mike Tindall and Will Greenwood. South Africans Catt and Abbott provide capable back-up. Since the 1999 World Cup, the Boks could not claim anything that resembled building or developing a midfield combination. Injury has influenced choices, but even when there has been no injury there has been no commitment from the selectors.

Barry is the classic example of a centre who should, by now, have played forty tests, when he has just passed twenty. All three national coaches since 1999 have identified Barry, as they did Fleck. None found it in their respective selections to invest in this midfield identification. Instead, each flirted with a different attraction, almost on a weekly basis.

In May 2004, incumbent Springbok coach Jake White also entrusted De Wet Barry with the No. 12 jersey in his first test selection. However, White's selections seemed to be as hit and miss as any of his predecessors. He picked Joe van Niekerk, who had played only forty minutes of club rugby in a seven-month layoff, to play Ireland in June 2004; Faan Rautenbach, who had not played rugby in three months; and Pedrie Wannenburg at No. 8, when he had played the entire Super 12 as a lock or flank.

Luke Watson, the form open-side flank in 2003/04, was not even selected for the SA 'A' squad. Watson's omission was not the result of a scientific selection process. White simply does not rate him. In 2003, White told me that Watson would never make a side he coached. He also had not picked Watson for his under-21 side in 2002/03.

When I asked White whether he and his selectors had kept a statistical database on the players, he said no. The selection reflected this. The coach of the Boks may be new to the job, but the flaws in selection are very familiar.

Different Bok 12/13 midfield combinations since 2000 – used as a starting combination or changed during the match

1. Barry/Fleck
2. Mulder/Fleck
3. Rossouw/Montgomery
4. Mulder/Barry
5. Barry/Esterhuizen
6. Fleck/Esterhuizen
7. Vd Westhuyzen/Esterhuizen
8. Van Straaten/Fleck
9. Barry/Montgomery
10. Fleck/Kayser
11. Fleck/Joubert
12. Van Straaten/Kayser
13. Van Straaten/Snyman
14. Halstead/Snyman
15. Halstead/Montgomery
16. Van Straaten/Halstead
17. Jacobs/Halstead
18. Jacobs/Snyman
19. Halstead/Barry
20. Snyman/Joubert
21. Jacobs/Joubert
22. Barry/Joubert
23. Barry/Jacobs
24. Greeff/Joubert
25. Jacobs/De Villiers
26. Fleck/Jacobs
27. James/Fleck
28. Halstead/Joubert
29. Bobo/Joubert
30. Barry/Bobo
31. Barry/Snyman
32. Barry/Muller
33. Bobo/Muller

34. Barry/Fourie
35. Greeff/Fourie

Midfield combinations – 12/13 – used in 2003

1. Halstead/Snyman (v Scotland)
2. Halstead/Joubert (v Scotland)
3. Bobo/Joubert (v Scotland, 2nd half; and against Argentina)
4. Barry/Joubert (v Australia)
5. Barry/Bobo (2nd half v Australia)
6. Barry/Snyman (v NZ)
7. Barry/Muller (v Australia)
8. Bobo/Muller (v NZ)
9. Barry/Fourie
10. Barry/Muller
11. Greeff/Fourie
12. Barry/Muller
13. Barry/Muller

No. 12s used since 2000

1. Barry
2. Mulder
3. Rossouw
4. Fleck
5. Vd Westhuyzen
6. Van Straaten
7. Halstead
8. Jacobs
9. Snyman
10. Greeff
11. James
12. Bobo

No. 13s used since 2000

1. Fleck
2. Montgomery
3. Barry
4. Esterhuizen
5. Kayser
6. Joubert
7. Snyman
8. Halstead
9. Jacobs
10. De Villiers
11. Bobo
12. Muller
13. Fourie

Total numbers of centres since 2000 (in no particular order)

1. Barry
2. Mulder
3. Rossouw
4. Fleck
5. Vd Westhuyzen
6. Van Straaten
7. Halstead
8. Jacobs
9. Snyman
10. Greeff
11. James
12. Bobo
13. Montgomery
14. Esterhuizen
15. Kayser
16. Joubert
17. De Villiers
18. Muller
19. Fourie

7

Cashing in on chaos
Contracting and remuneration

The Springboks are among the best-paid rugby players in the world. Given their poor performance since 1998, they are definitely the best-rewarded under-achievers in the game. Players will tell you otherwise, but any sportsman earning between R1 million and R3 million a year in South Africa has no right to plead poverty.

I don't begrudge any player his hard-earned money, as I have seen first hand how these guys punish their bodies. By all means pay them well, but demand excellence. If they are not capable of delivering, boot them out. Professional sport is a cutthroat industry where only the great survive the ruthless nature of the business. In South African rugby, too many mediocre players have cashed in on a contracting system that rewards making the team rather than excelling in the team.

The contracting of a player is a topic that resurfaces all the time. I had many informal discussions with players on the subject, and none will accept that they are anything other than victims. They believe the financial risk should lie with the employer, and they rely far too heavily on the argument that their career spans only five to ten years. When negotiating contracts, the players seem to forget that they made the choice to play professional rugby. They could have been accountants, lawyers, bricklayers … whatever. But they wanted to be professional rugby players. No one forced them to take up the game as a career. This is a very pertinent point in the debate, because when you make a choice, you accept the consequences.

The Bok players did not want to face any consequences, unless they were financially beneficial. When the Boks won, they argued that they attracted the crowds and were entitled to a portion of the gate revenue. When they lost, no one suggested that they should not get paid, or that they be held accountable for failing to sell out the next week's test. In times of struggle, the player sees rugby as a sport. In good times, when the scoreboard reads favourably, it is a business that should operate on winning incentives.

Since the advent of professionalism, South African rugby has never managed to perfect an incentive scheme. Players are rewarded for becoming Springboks.

They are given financial guarantees simply to play. This formula does not inspire winning, and is one reason why results have been so poor since 1998.

Harry Viljoen and Rudolf Straeuli both held strong opinions on the contracting of national players and the poor returns on expenditure. When Viljoen succeeded Nick Mallett, he inherited a contracted group of players. The structure, as discussed in Chapter 2, was basic, and the point is that there was no financial incentive to win, but huge financial kickbacks just to play. Viljoen wanted to introduce a new system in which he would identify a group of players that he felt would always be assured of selection in his squad, unless they were injured. They would receive a relatively small retainer of R200 000 or R300 000. The player would then be available for any commercial activities on behalf of the national team. Match day would be the big payday. Viljoen envisaged every player receiving in excess of R100 000 a test, with a R50 000 win bonus. His plan could not be implemented in 2001, as Nick Mallett had already contracted a squad, and their agreements were binding.

Viljoen spoke to the players about excellence and reward, and how the two complemented each other in the business world. He asked them how they would view the situation if they were the ones paying the salaries. The players did not even want to go there. At the first review, Viljoen's temporary solution was to pay the better players more by cutting back on the retainers of the average players. Many of the Springboks were overpaid. Some of them were not playing more than two tests a year and were still being paid.

An analysis I conducted on player earnings between 2001 and 2002 revealed that close to R10 million was being paid in retainers to contracted players who could not make the test 22 on a regular basis. It was a ridiculous situation: in 2000, Corné Krige played in eleven tests and was paid R600 000; a few other players earned the same, but for making the squad in two tests. This example was put to the players. Good players could either demand that performance should motivate salary, or they could accept always being on a similar reward package as the plodder. It made no business sense.

If players wanted to be paid like top businessmen, they had to act the part. Viljoen would not pay sub-standard performers simply to keep everyone happy. He told the squad very firmly that every average player pocketing a Bok salary was taking potential earnings away from the quality player. The wastage between 1999 and 2001 could not be ignored. Kaya Malotana played one test, but was paid R1.2 million. Brendan Venter took part in three tests, of which he finished one; he was paid more than R1 million. André Snyman, ravaged by injury, earned R1.4 million for four tests. Wayne Julies, a ten-minute Bok in the 1999 World Cup group match against Spain, was paid R957 500 for his effort.

Both Viljoen and Straeuli desperately wanted to avoid this sort of situation. But when Straeuli left in December 2003, he had managed to create a similar set-up. Rian Oberholzer also wanted the system changed. He did not want the coach to have too much input in salary negotiations, because in the past players had accused coaches of 'playing God' with their lives.

Oberholzer aspired to an arrangement in which a coach advised a contracting specialist of the players he wanted contracted, and the specialist then put the deal together. The players' salaries would have nothing to do with the coach. The plan was never implemented because Viljoen, and later Straeuli, insisted on being part of the contracting, as they were the ones selecting the players. As such, they both felt that they should be determining the player's value. The counter-argument was that as coaches, they should not be involved in establishing a player's financial value; a financial expert should work on the contracts. The issue was never resolved.

Player sensitivities, length of service and various other sentimental attachments influenced the contracting. Some of the senior players were given contracts based on previous performance, even when it was obvious that they were not going to make the squad. Players also used the overseas option to pressure coaches. Players would complain how hard it was to earn a living playing rugby in South Africa.

In South Africa in 2001, a good Bok player was on more or less R600 000 with his province, which included his Super 12 involvement. On top of that, he was paid match fees, win bonuses and for individual endorsements. Conservatively, you could add at least R200 000 to the initial R600 000. In addition, the Bok contract came into play. A player in the B-category would be paid R600 000, excluding his match fees and win bonuses.

The annual earning potential was in excess of R1 million. South African players who had made the Bok squad the year before always factored in a Bok contract as part of their annual package. This should not have been the case. The Bok contract should be a bonus. If you play well enough, then you are rewarded accordingly. The standard retainer is what the province is prepared to pay for a player. Viljoen wanted players to understand this. He did not make much of an impression.

Players still felt that they could be given better deals and find more security overseas. I fully agree on the security factor. If an overseas club contracts you for two years, you know what your earnings will be. No national team can offer such a guarantee, and in the professional environment it would be unreasonable to expect that they could.

Springbok players still want the security of a one-year retainer, regardless of results or form during the international season. If complications arise in the negotiation, then they follow the overseas route. Invariably the players who wanted to go overseas were those who felt they had achieved everything at test level, acknowledged that their best days were over and wanted to cash in on the

European pension fund – a two-year club contract. But there were also quality players at the pinnacle of their career who were keen to experience a different culture, and who backed themselves to return to South Africa and be selected for the Boks in a World Cup year.

Joost van der Westhuizen, however, was in a category of his own. He used the overseas market to ensure that he would be awarded a contract with the Boks. His intention was to go to Newport only if no financial guarantees were forthcoming at national level. Harry Viljoen felt that Joost had played his best rugby by the middle of 2001. Harry was prepared to release Joost, but then the player indicated that he was about to sign with Newport. The financial haggling began, and somehow Van der Westhuizen convinced Viljoen of his value to the Boks until the 2003 World Cup. Harry went to extreme measures to offer Joost a financial package close to what he would have received overseas.

The player accepted the deal, as he never really wanted to leave South Africa. He then claimed that he had decided to stay because of his loyalty to the game in South Africa. That was not strictly correct. He stayed because he was offered enough money in this country.

Braam van Straaten was another player who was shrewd in his contractual dealings. And in this particular instance, his actions disappointed Viljoen. Braam is one of the most genuine and likeable guys, a real team man who loves the Boks and South African rugby. When he signed for Leeds, Viljoen asked to meet with him. Harry, who originally had not selected Braam in 2001, now regarded him as a crucial part of his plans. I attended the meeting between the two of them at Viljoen's offices at the Victoria & Alfred Waterfront.

Viljoen had increased the A-category annual retainer to R800 000, which was the maximum he could offer Braam. He said he appreciated Harry's offer, but that he would only be in a position to make a decision once he knew what Western Province was prepared to pay him. Province had refused to extend Van Straaten's contact, which had influenced his decision to sign with Leeds. Now that Viljoen had made a new offer, Braam was going to see Western Province chief executive Rob Wagner after our meeting. The following day Braam called me, and rejected Harry's offer. Financially, the Leeds deal was still better. Harry accepted his decision, and told Braam he would still select him for the end-of-year tour. Viljoen was going to play Braam until the last available opportunity.

In a subsequent interview with Stephen Nell of the *Cape Times*, Braam claimed that he would never have gone back on his word, and that he owed it to Leeds to honour his commitment. He told Nell that straight after the meeting with Harry, he had called Leeds' Phil Davies and told him the Boks had tried to re-sign him, but that he had never been interested. It was a moral decision, he said, and one he had to see through on behalf of South African players after Joost had reneged on his Newport contract.

Nell climbed into Harry in the *Cape Times*, and backed up his indignation with strong comments from Phil Davies, who accused Bok management of unethical conduct with his newly signed import. Harry was disappointed in Braam, who had not told Phil Davies or the media that he had investigated the possibility of both a national and provincial offer, had added two and two together, and had only then opted to stay with the Leeds offer because it was still better. It had been a financial and not a moral decision.

If Braam felt so strongly about the Leeds agreement, why did he not tell me he was not interested in discussing Harry's offer? I was the one who had phoned Braam to set up the meeting and told him what it would be about, and he agreed to see Harry.

I urged Harry to take Braam on about the matter, but he said he would deal with it privately. I don't know if he ever did, but Harry still selected Braam for the end-of-year tour, and showed him no malice.

When a player leaves this country, the South African media always argue the case of the player. As a rugby writer, I did it for a decade. The player phones you, he is your source of information and you take his side. You accuse SA Rugby of being unprofessional and neglecting their players, and you wonder, what's an additional R300 000 or R500 000 between friends? It's easy when it isn't your money. Where contracts are involved, players in South Africa manipulate the media beautifully, and every rugby writer I know in this country, myself included, has fallen for players' heartbreak stories.

After a year of working with the players, I hardened in my opinion about who was getting the raw financial deal. It certainly was not them. If a player is good enough, he could go overseas for two years in the prime of his career and return in a World Cup year. Such a player would back his own ability to make the team. In this way he would get the best of both worlds. In the past three years, Selborne Boome and Robbie Kempson have followed this path. Before them, Jannie de Beer, Fritz van Heerden and Brendan Venter made a similar decision, and it worked out for them.

When I last counted, at the beginning of 2004, there were around eighty South Africans playing club rugby in Europe. New Zealand was the only other country to challenge the South African figure, and if you include Japan, then the Kiwis dominate the world circuit as player exporters. Player exodus is a reality in the evolution of professional rugby. Players will go where they can make more money and find the security of a two-year contract. The lure of playing only club rugby must also not be underestimated for those players exposed to the pressures of test rugby over a sustained period.

Players also leave when they are disillusioned with a coach. Joost signed with Newport when he thought Mallett would remain coach. Percy Montgomery and Pieter Rossouw signed overseas because both assumed Harry would remain coach, and he had indicated that he was not going to select either. Corné Krige was about to sign in Europe when Harry resigned. Harry had lost faith in Corné's ability, and did not believe he was good enough to play test rugby. Corné, in turn, thought Harry's coaching had set South African rugby back a few years. On hearing that Harry had packed in the Bok job, Corné also changed course. He stayed in South Africa.

Mark Andrews and Warren Britz left primarily because Rudolf Straeuli told both of them that they would not be selected. Robbie Fleck fell into a similar category. Straeuli had told Robbie that he was not among the top ten centres in the country. Stuart Abbott left because of a lack of opportunity, but still wanted to come back. Only when Straeuli failed to offer him a selection guarantee did he set aside any Bok aspirations. In Abbott's case, the media had reason to attack the contractual decision-makers. Abbott was playing superb rugby in England and had, through his agent Jason Smith, expressed a desire to return to South Africa to play for the Springboks.

Straeuli was not interested. He did not believe Abbott was the solution to the Bok midfield wobbles. A year earlier, Viljoen had also not rated Abbott highly enough to invest in him. He thought that Abbott lacked the size to be an international midfield factor. In Straeuli's case, he was also convinced that Butch Watson Smith, as national teams general manager, was only pushing for Abbott because the player was from Cape Town and had a strong association with the likes of Watson Smith and Cape Town-based Basil Bey, an institution as a schools coach at Bishops and a respected talent-spotter. Straeuli was sent tapes of Abbott's performances. He was not too enthusiastic. The media started putting pressure on Straeuli about Abbott, and Butch Watson Smith questioned his negativity towards the player. Abbott's agent, Jason Smith, was persistent in arguing the claims of his client. Then the media in England started writing up Abbott as a candidate for England's World Cup campaign. Straeuli was in a corner, as word was circulating that for Abbott first prize was the Springbok and not the England jersey.

Eventually Straeuli agreed to phone Abbott. He spoke to the player, offered him an incentive scheme that would net him the same he was earning at London Wasps, and promised him a place in the SA 'A' squad. He said he could not select him for the Bok squad based solely on his performance in England. He had to see him play in South Africa. Straeuli expected an answer from Abbott in a few days.

The flaw in Straeuli's offer was that the only game for which he could select Abbott was against Namibia. It made no sense to judge a player against Namibia but not on an entire season in England's Zurich Premiership. Understandably, Abbott felt that there was too much uncertainty in the offer, and he threw in his lot with England, was picked for the World Cup, and today has a winner's medal to justify his decision.

We had to save face in the media, and put out a release stating that we had pursued Abbott, but that he chose to play for England. Straeuli exploited the fact that he wanted guys who were 'passionate' about the green and gold jersey and who dreamt of playing for the Boks – not England. The media bought the story and softened their stance. The truth was, Straeuli had never been enthusiastic about Abbott.

Jake Boer is another player who has performed brilliantly in England, captaining Gloucester and producing consistently fine performances. Jason Smith also represents Boer, and the player indicated that he was desperate to make the Bok team.

Boer, a Capetonian, had bought a holiday home in Cape Town, and wanted to return to South Africa on a permanent basis after five seasons playing English club rugby. Straeuli tried to negotiate a Super 12 contract for Boer with Oberholzer, and hinted that he may be interested in picking him for the Boks. Oberholzer had already brought back Kempson and Thinus Delport at a considerable price, and before he would consider spending more money on another player, he wanted to know that Straeuli would definitely select him.

Straeuli was unable to make a firm commitment, and Oberholzer said he was not prepared to invest huge amounts of money to buy Boer out of his contract, only for Straeuli not to pick him. It became a rather messy and embarrassing affair. I had sent a message to Boer to contact Straeuli, as the player was going to be in South Africa and Straeuli wanted to meet with him. Straeuli asked me to set up a meeting either in Durban or Johannesburg before the first Scotland test in 2003. But Straeuli was not convinced enough of Boer's worth to fight for him. Oberholzer said he would not pay for Boer's flights because he could not justify the cost to the board, or offer the board members a valid reason why the national coach was meeting with an overseas-based player. They would want to know why Straeuli was flying in players he was not even sure he wanted to pick. As Straeuli could not offer a definite selection decision, there would be no free flight for the player. Boer would have to pay for his own flight. I thought that insulting. Straeuli shared my opinion, and we sought an alternative arrangement. Jason Smith told me that Boer would remain in Cape Town for another fortnight, and Straeuli decided to see him there. The poor Boer was told to wait and not to speak to the media. Straeuli had Boer on standby to meet with him, and then never did. Straeuli eventually phoned Boer after five in the afternoon while driving to the airport, explaining that he had been unable to obtain the financial backing.

I did not give up the fight for Boer. I asked a few players about his abilities, and Krige, in particular, was very flattering about him. He thought Boer could make a positive contribution to the team in terms of attitude and mentality. He had played some excellent rugby in England. I urged Krige to 'sell' Boer to Straeuli. Krige tried, but Straeuli would not budge. Boer was never contacted again.

Percy Montgomery's decision to go overseas was a different matter altogether. Montgomery kept us in the dark about his plans. We had heard that he'd signed with a Welsh club. Straeuli rated Montgomery very highly and respected his value as a utility back. He thought Monty was the best fullback in the country in 2002. A day before we were due to release the 2002 national trial squads, Montgomery's agent, Craig Livingstone, called to inform Straeuli that Monty had opted to go overseas. He would not be available for the trial match. Livingstone said Montgomery was concerned about transformation in South African rugby, and felt that he might be a victim of the system because there would be pressure to select coloured fullbacks Conrad Jantjes and Ricardo Loubscher. Livingstone said Montgomery would call Straeuli. While Livingstone spoke to Straeuli, Montgomery called, and left a message saying he was unavailable for selection. He was going overseas, and it was a financial decision based on a need for financial security.

Straeuli returned Montgomery's call and asked him to reconsider. Straeuli assured Percy that he was his number one fullback, but that he had to play in the trial game to be picked for the first test. Montgomery said he wanted security. Straeuli replied that he, too, desired security, but in rugby that was a luxury. He told Montgomery to think about his offer, and if he changed his mind, Straeuli would select him without holding anything against him. I was in on the conversation. 'You know where my office is,' Straeuli said. 'Think about it and come up and see me.'

When the conversation ended, Straeuli and I discussed a plan of action. Straeuli backed Montgomery, but was annoyed that he thought transformation might harm him. If he was the best, argued Straeuli, why should he worry about other players? I recommended releasing a statement explaining the situation, as I thought it necessary before we announced the trial teams. It would give us an opportunity to explain why Straeuli had not picked Monty, and also allow us to state our case before the player told his sob story about why he was forced to go overseas.

Straeuli and I had no other agenda. I think Montgomery is one of the best talents to have played for South Africa, and I remain one of his biggest rugby supporters. He is a class act who should be playing in South Africa and not for the Gwent Dragons, but I make no apologies for the statement. Straeuli cannot be accused of not supporting Montgomery. In fact, had Montgomery not been suspended for six months in 2003, he would have been selected for the World Cup. Straeuli wanted to buy him back for both the Tri-Nations and the World Cup. Informal discussions had started with his agent, as Straeuli saw Montgomery's left boot as a necessity at fullback. There was no fullback in South Africa with a strong kicking game.

Montgomery's versatility at flyhalf, wing and in the midfield would also have provided the squad with additional depth, and allowed Straeuli to select one less backline player and one additional forward for the World Cup. But then Montgomery shoved a touch judge in a club match and was banned for six months. All negotiations broke down. In March 2004, under new coach Jake White, talks were resumed with Monty, and he was selected for White's first test 22.

Kempson's progress at Ulster was closely monitored. He is a player who epitomises professionalism. His work ethic is top class, but when he left South Africa to play for Ulster, I thought it was unfair of him to say that South African players were given a raw deal. I responded through the media, stating that Kempson had been well looked after financially for the six months he had been out of the game because of injury. I fought the fight for SA Rugby against Kempson in the media.

In Kempson's case, I could understand why the media accused us of losing a class player and questioning why SA Rugby allowed this to happen. It was unacceptable that a player of his calibre should leave, but there are two sides to the story. Kempson wanted to go. I thought this should be made clear, or it would turn into another one-sided contract story. Kempson had wanted a new challenge, and would be paid a lot more than had he stayed in South Africa. He was also very keen to work with Alan Solomons. When Kempson returned to play a few tests in 2003, we chatted about the past and cleared the air.

The contracting issue is complex. It is never as simple as identifying a player and paying him what he is worth. Every year, South African players raise national contracts with the South African Rugby Players' Association (SARPA), which in turn exhausts the situation by calling numerous meetings, without ever providing a practical, objective solution. In 2002, an annual budget of around R30 million was set aside for the contracting of Bok players, and close to R40 million was budgeted in 2003. This included match fees, win bonuses and management salaries.

Straeuli felt the money was sufficiently competitive with other sports codes, as South Africa still offered the player quality of lifestyle. Straeuli wanted to use the money wisely. He did not believe in a big retainer, decent match fee or small win bonus, but advocated a big match fee and no retainer.

Oberholzer removed himself from the contracting of players with the appointment of Butch Watson Smith as national teams general manager. Butch would control the purse strings, and he was careful to show total transparency in his dealings with the players. Derick Minnie, an independent board member, chaired the remuneration committee. Player salaries also had to meet with his approval. The system was expanded to include team manager Gideon Sam, player agents and representatives from SARPA.

Straeuli, however, still wanted to be a part of the negotiations to determine what each player should be offered. A compromise was reached, and Straeuli would still have a say. In the end, he would have the only say.

Craig Livingstone, considered the best of the South African agents, represents most of the Bok team. He was always approachable, and in discussions with Harry and Rudolf he was prepared to listen and not just make demands. In 2002, Livingstone proposed that the captain receive an additional annual R50 000, which Straeuli and Watson Smith agreed was fair. The captain had many more individual responsibilities. The majority of the players were opposed to a big match fee, for fear of missing the match. But Straeuli argued that it was important for SA Rugby to spend their money on players who actually played.

Straeuli's only compromise was the introduction of a lesser annual retainer, which ranged between R200 000 and R400 000. The exceptions were the senior players Skinstad and Krige, who were on R600 000, plus the new match scheme of R75 000 a test, with a win bonus of between R10 000 and R25 000, depending on the opposition. Joost was also on a different contract, which guaranteed him a minimum annual retainer of R500 000 until the end of 2003. If contracted Bok players were injured, the standard injury clause would come into effect. The clause ensured players a minimum of R25 000 a month for six months. If they did not play during the six-month period, their contract was reviewed.

In my three years, not one player was cut from his contract without warning or gradually being phased out. Some were demoted from one category to another over a period of a year. Others knew well in advance that their form did not warrant an extension of their contract. The big match fee meant that money would be spent more wisely, because it could at least be attributed to a player who was actively involved in a test match. But the system was flawed on two counts: the match fee instead of the win bonus was the player's incentive; and Straeuli's erratic selection policy created uncertainty among the players.

When the forty-six players who attended the 2002 national trial match in Pretoria were asked which contracting system they preferred, the majority said that it was fair to both the employer and the player to settle on a one-year contract. Straeuli's interpretation was that they chose this option as none of them were prepared to back themselves. For the 2002 home tests and Tri-Nations, some players were on retainer and the old match fee of R25 000 a test and R10 000 for a win. A minority, including youngster Joe van Niekerk, chose the R75 000 a match option.

By the end of 2002, everyone was on the big match fee. The deal for an annual retainer with a bare minimum of R200 000 had been confirmed. But Straeuli's selection dilemma killed the effectiveness of the big match fee concept, and exposed the vulnerability in the system. The Bok coach picked more than seventy test players in his two seasons as coach. He rotated and alternated players, and in twenty-three tests never once selected the same starting XV in successive test matches. Naturally, this concerned the players, and they had every reason to feel aggrieved. Straeuli would rest a player, who effectively lost R75 000.

On away tours, a compromise was reached. The entire squad, irrespective of how many players were selected, would receive the match fee of R75 000. The match 22 would qualify for the win bonus. Performance never featured prominently. It was all about pay for play.

In the 2002 end-of-year tour, players who survived the three weeks were guaranteed R225 000, regardless of the result. As an example, Bakkies Botha played for sixty minutes for his R225 000. Bolla Conradie played for only ninety minutes. For Straeuli, contracting players was a serious problem because he never knew who his best players were. In 2003 he contracted nineteen players, and only seven ended up going to the World Cup. Marius Joubert was the only one who was ruled out of the tournament because of serious injury. All the others could have played in the tournament – Brent Russell and Bob Skinstad included – if Straeuli had backed them in selection as much as he did when he offered them contracts.

Nor did the contracts reward the best or the most valuable players. Viljoen and Straeuli were both swayed by seniority and the need to please these players. Krige, Skinstad, John Smit and Joost were identified as key to ensuring unity among the players. Straeuli and Oberholzer needed the entire squad to sign the World Cup incentive contracts without fuss. If the four senior players were on board, they would help convince the rest of the squad to sign.

A lot of debate revolved around the World Cup contract, which was said to favour the IRB and not the players. Oberholzer, a director of the World Cup, pronounced the agreements fair. He addressed the squad, and fielded any questions about a contract he had helped draw up. Oberholzer was adamant that the players would not be prejudiced for sacrificing their individual commercial rights because of the World Cup participation agreement. He convinced Straeuli, who in turn convinced Krige and the senior players. Krige's task was then to convince the squad to sign. Krige raised a few concerns, which were taken into account, and the odd amendment was made. All the Boks signed the World Cup participation agreement.

Because of the IRB contract, certain countries threatened that they would unite in defiance and withdraw from the World Cup. Once the Boks had signed, most of the other countries followed soon after. The Bok incentive to win the World Cup was more than R1 million per player, as well as the promise of a 2004 national contract for every squad member. Management would receive around R300 000 per person, but the head coach and his assistants were also part of another structure, which would reward them for a successful campaign.

Oberholzer was chuffed that the Boks had signed, and when the Tri-Nations representatives met for a SANZAR meeting in Brisbane in August, the All Blacks were still in negotiation. Oberholzer mentioned how quickly the Boks had agreed to their incentive scheme, to which his New Zealand counterpart responded that

Oberholzer could have offered each Bok a billion, he knew his money was safe. The New Zealand bosses were certain they would be paying out win bonuses.

Straeuli's poor national squad contracting was the equivalent of a R4-million waste in 2003, as he did not pick several of the players he had contracted. It did not affect the Bok budget massively, as annual projections always included win bonuses in all four Tri-Nations tests. In 2001, 2002 and 2003, the saving because of the Boks' Tri-Nations defeats in eight of the twelve tests was close to R5 million. In 2003, Skinstad, Krige and Van der Westhuizen were the biggest winners financially. Skinstad's national contract amounted to R800 000. He played only seven minutes against Argentina, and was paid the R75 000 match fee and R10 000 win bonus. When you break down Bob's 2003 test year, he was paid R885 000 for seven minutes of rugby, with SA Rugby coughing up R126 428 a minute for actual playing time.

Skinstad would argue that he was also paid for commercial work, and that training sessions and emotional uncertainty are work-related factors. He would have a point. However, Straeuli was probably guilty of paying a player in order to shut him up. Skinstad had been very frustrated in the Springbok system, but as long as he was on contract, Straeuli knew he could not criticise or complain about Bok issues.

In 2004, Skinstad signed a short-term contract with Newport. I still believe he could play for the Boks at the 2007 World Cup. He has moved on because he was given a better deal financially. There are no hard feelings, nor should there be. Players change colours in professional sport, and they play in different countries to earn a better living.

The contracting issue would be less of a headache if South African rugby bosses accommodated the selection of foreign-based South African players. SARFU, through its spokespeople, has always argued that by allowing foreign-based players to represent the Boks, there would be a mass player exodus. As a result, the domestic competitions – the Currie Cup and Super 12 – would be weakened. The argument is without substance and out of touch with the demands of a professional code. If a player leaves to go overseas, he is creating a playing opportunity for the player still in South Africa. The conveyor belt keeps on moving. It can only be healthy for player exposure and development at a higher level. The domestic competition won't be weakened. We saw a thrilling Currie Cup competition in 2003. Quality matches were played and more than 50 000 spectators attended the final; all this, despite the fact that the World Cup squad of thirty players did not participate in the Currie Cup. Other players simply stepped into the arena and made a name for themselves.

Our players are going overseas and playing some of their best rugby in the northern hemisphere when aged between twenty-six and thirty-two, a period when most players are at their peak. Because of SARFU's ridiculous ruling and the petty notion that the professional player is being 'disloyal' to his country by playing overseas, these players operate in isolation, and their efforts are derided in South African rugby when they should be applauded.

SA Rugby was only shooting itself in the foot by refusing to pick players who are the best in their positions but happen to be playing overseas. It is a fact that the majority of our players who go overseas are improved players after their European stint. They are exposed to a different culture, are forced to adapt to foreign conditions and mature very quickly as professional sportspeople.

I am by no means suggesting that every South African player abroad is good enough to play for the Boks, but at least let's give Jake White the option to decide for himself. He can't be expected to take on the world, conquer the best teams and restore the pride in our game when there may be first-choice players he wants to select but can't because of a narrow-minded regulation. Stuart Abbott may well have opted to make himself available for South Africa if he could have stayed at Wasps. Abbott left Cape Town to further his career and prospered at his new club. Then we told him to forget it, because he was playing overseas. It is ludicrous how SA Rugby strangled itself because petty politicians, who parade as provincial presidents, insisted that to play *for* South Africa, you had to play *in* South Africa.

An internal regulation should never have been allowed to cause so much damage to our rugby. Those who thought they were doing SA Rugby a favour by drafting the regulation were wrong. The time has come for the new regime to do what is right for the Boks, and that means making every contender eligible for Bok selection. We lost Garry Pagel and Joel Stransky to English club rugby after the 1995 World Cup, and for two years they were the best prop and flyhalf respectively in England. Gary Teichmann played two great seasons for Newport, and Adrian Garvey was still good enough to play test rugby for two years when he went to Wales.

In April 2004, after much debate, SA Rugby offered the players a package deal that would earn each player close to R2 million a year if they played in all thirteen tests and won the majority of them.

They would not be given a national contract, but the compromise was a R400 000 annual incentive if the player featured in 50 per cent of the team's tests. An additional R200 000 would also be paid to the player in the guise of a provincial contract. In effect, the principle of a retainer remained; the difference now was that the player had to play for it. In the past, he was paid the amount upfront.

The deal seemed to be fair, as employer and employee now shared the risk, but the lack of trust between the two ensured ongoing discontent. The story, sadly, is never-ending.

SARFU conceded on the issue of overseas-based players in April 2004, compromising on an allocation of up to three overseas players in a squad of 22.

Currently, playing overseas remains an issue. Skinstad was the most recent Bok to forfeit his national contract, which meant that for the first six months of 2004, the only South African player with a national contract was Marius Joubert. Jake White rightfully argued that he could not contract any player until he had picked his first squad, which would only happen in June. The only certainty on the issue of national squad contracting is the uncertainty. Understandably, it does not inspire confidence in the system, and only entrenches the philosophy of 'them against us' – a belief further enhanced when Brian van Rooyen, in *Rapport*, accused players of being greedy. Van Rooyen told the players to first restore respect for the Bok jersey before making claims for money. He then released all the players' salaries to the media.

The players' association, SARPA, hit back, and accused Van Rooyen of misleading the public with ill-informed financial statistics. The New Year had heralded the arrival of a new president and a new national structure, but while many things have changed in South African rugby in 2004, the contracting of players remains as contentious as ever.

8

Laager mentality
Foreigners and SA rugby

By the time the Springbok squad returned home from their 2000 end-of-year tour, Harry Viljoen was convinced that the knowledge to improve Springbok rugby was not to be found in South Africa. He looked overseas for ideas, expertise and innovation. In my research into the factors that made top teams successful, a few points stood out. The San Francisco 49ers, an NFL club, valued the trust between players and administrators. Player welfare featured prominently in all their literature, as did identifying inspirational players and creative individuals who thought differently and refused to be stereotyped.

Viljoen felt South African rugby could learn from them. We had to treat our players with more respect, and treat them like professionals, with all the responsibility that entails. We had to teach them that being professional did not merely mean cashing a bigger pay cheque at the end of the month. More than anything, Viljoen craved a South African player who could think.

Australian Women's Hockey had redefined the game through a minor adjustment in the pass. Their players were trained to hit the ball harder in the pass, which upped the tempo of the game and allowed them to dominate. It seems a minute adjustment, but it radically changed the way they played hockey. The Australian cricketers' goal to score at four runs an over in test cricket was another example of how a good sports team did not try to reinvent the wheel, but rather paid attention to detail that no one else had ever considered. The difference between scoring at four runs to the over instead of three was the equivalent of gaining a sixth day in a five-day test.

Viljoen looked to Australia for most of his inspiration. He did not focus exclusively on rugby union. I arranged a meeting with Kevin Sheedy, the Essendon Aussie Rules club coach. Sheedy has coached Essendon for twenty-odd years, and is a living legend. One of his strengths is his ability to change, to move with the times and to track down ideas that would give his squad the edge. The meeting with Sheedy was a highlight for me. He told us how he travels to meet coaches from other codes every year, be it netball, ice hockey, hockey, soccer or American football. They would discuss success formulas, but not specifically in their own codes.

'You will be surprised what you learn,' he told Harry.

Sheedy explained what they had done at Essendon, and he thought Aussie Rules skills could benefit rugby union players. The obvious skills were catching and kicking out of hand, the improvement of peripheral vision, and a general approach to professionalism. The work he had done with his squad was revolutionary. Sheedy was a trendsetter. He had brought in sports conditioning expert Dr John Quinn, who had only ever watched a few Aussie Rules games in his life. Sheedy wanted objectivity, not someone who would be influenced by personalities or player profiles. He and Quinn discussed the way Sheedy wanted to play the game, which was an approach based on greater pace and agility. They then worked out what player strengths were required for this to happen. Only then did Quinn compare that profile with the existing squad. The result was that more than half the squad was axed. 'If you are serious about wanting to change the game,' Sheedy said to Harry, 'then you must be prepared to make the player changes.'

Viljoen and Sheedy also discussed professionalism, and Sheedy said the code did not determine professionalism – the individuals made up the code. He shared a great yarn with us. One night in the cold and wet, his team had an awful training session. Everything went wrong. Sheedy eventually called off the session after an hour, and the players found some relief under the hot showers.

He entered the change room, furious, and the players tried to assure him that the next training session would be better.

'Do you really think so?' he asked. 'Yes,' they said. He asked again whether they truly believed they could improve if given the chance to redo the session. They insisted that they could, and said they would show him the next day. He waited until all the players had showered, dried themselves, dressed and applied the finishing touches to their hair. Then he told them to put on their wet and muddy training gear. They had asked for another chance, and he was going to give them one. Not tomorrow, but now. As professionals they had no choice but to obey. They put on the gear, went back out into the rain and trained.

'It is one thing to say something,' Sheedy told us. 'I needed to know they were prepared to do it. It is their job. I needed confirmation of their attitude and not their good intentions.'

We spent much of the day at Essendon. Their marketing staff showed us around, Sheedy allowed us to watch a training session, we were invited to attend a video session, and the following day we would meet their conditioning specialist, Dr John Quinn, a sports scientist who had also worked with the Australian Olympic athletes. The kicking aspect of Aussie Rules is the one area where rugby union can learn from this code. All the players in Rules have to be equally competent kicking with either foot. In a standard kicking drill the squad is lined up opposite each other, only a few metres apart. Player one, using his right foot, kicks the ball to player two, who expects the ball to come to him with pinpoint accuracy. Player two kicks the ball with his right foot, and player two returns it with his left. And so it alternates. After each round the players move further apart, until they are 40 to 50 metres away, and still finding each other with unerring accuracy.

We introduced the drill to our kickers at the Bok training camp in Plettenberg Bay in 2001. The only kicker who was comfortable and effective on both left and right foot was the late François Swart. None of the others could manage consistent accuracy from fifteen metres apart.

When Viljoen discussed the kicking aspect with other rugby union coaches in Australia, he was surprised to learn how much they encouraged tapping into the strengths of other codes. They had no problem admitting that rugby union did not know everything, nor were they insecure about it. The coaches wanted to improve their product, and were willing to accept help from anyone.

Viljoen considered it essential to employ a full-time kicking coach. I recommended that this coach work with every Super 12 team, spend time with all fourteen provincial sides, and be seconded to the Boks during the international season, and to the national under-21 and under-19 teams when they played their World Cups. Viljoen liked the idea, and the obvious candidate was Michael Byrne, who had successfully made the coaching transition from Aussie Rules to rugby union. Byrne worked out of Manly, and had enjoyed success with the ACT Brumbies, the Wallabies and the Manly Sea Eagles rugby league team. He also worked with the Sydney Swans Aussie Rules squad.

We met with Byrne and watched him conduct his kicking sessions. The attention to detail on a specific skill, such as kicking and catching out of the air, was new to us. Byrne was brilliant. Harry told him he wanted him to be with the Boks. Harry made this sort of decision, and then the fight would start to obtain approval from SA Rugby. In Byrne's case it was to be one of the most frustrating times, exposing our lack of professionalism.

Byrne attended the training camp in Plettenberg Bay in June 2001, and stayed for the first two tests against France. The plan was for him to return at the end of the year on a permanent basis and be employed by SA Rugby. He would then put together a team of South African coaches, empower them over the next three years and build up the portfolio in South African rugby. Obviously, this would come at a cost. SA Rugby was hesitant to pay for Byrne's services, even though Harry had given Byrne verbal guarantees. I had to convince Rian Oberholzer in a proposal of the necessity of a full-time kicking and catching coach.

Oberholzer initially resisted, but gradually warmed to the idea. It was an expensive exercise, and he wanted to know from Harry whether it was really necessary, or if it was just a luxury. Oberholzer still had to convince the board that the cost was worth it. Harry did not put forward a convincing argument, and Oberholzer, quite rightly, felt that if the coach was not totally convinced of the full-time need for a kicking coach, why should he be? The proposal was scrapped, and I had to break the news to Byrne. He was subsequently employed by Scotland, and has spent the past two years developing their kickers at all national levels. Yet another opportunity missed by South African rugby.

Harry's sales pitch to justify employing Byrne lacked substance, partly because he was under pressure for bringing in another foreigner. The media suggested that Harry should appoint Bok kicking guru Naas Botha as his kicking consultant.

Harry readily acknowledged that Botha was a great kicker, but it was not his profession to coach kickers. He cited the example of golf coach David Leadbetter. Top pros did not go to Jack Nicklaus for coaching because that was not what he did all day and every day of the week. They employed Leadbetter. We subsequently used Naas on occasions, and you couldn't compare his contribution to what Byrne offered, simply because Byrne made a living out of coaching kickers. For Naas, giving a bit of advice and guidance was a hobby. He had other interests.

But Harry and I also made a mistake. By pushing the Australian influence, we never explored options available in South Africa. In so doing, we alienated many potential supporters in South African rugby. We pushed so hard for the skills of Australian experts that we made ourselves very unpopular with a lot of decision-makers in the South African game. We should have been more politically astute and certainly more streetwise, but to be honest, we didn't care for the provincial presidents. We saw them as dead wood, and did not feel threatened by them at all. But when the Boks started losing, the dead wood rose as one, and exhibited enough life to put a sword into many of Harry's ambitions.

Rugby league's influence was permeating rugby union in Australia, England and France, and, to a lesser degree, New Zealand. Harry was negotiating with Tim Lane to join the Boks as backs coach, and he pointed us in the direction of Frank Ponissi, a rugby league and former Kangaroos defensive coach. On several occasions, Ponissi and I had chatted telephonically, and I knew he could make a contribution to South African rugby. South Africans had never heard of his ideas in terms of defensive systems, and he was very eager to be associated with South African rugby and the Springboks.

Contractual obligations in Australia prevented Ponissi from attending the Plettenberg Bay camp, but he recommended that Les Kiss join us in the meantime. We had met Les in Sydney earlier in the year, when he and Ponissi presented a workshop on defence to Harry, Jake White, the Bok conditioning coach of 2001, Chris van Loggerenberg, and me. The workshop was very impressive, and Ponissi had already conducted a study on some of the South African players.

Our players lacked the defensive mentality of a league player, because they had never been exposed to the kind of structure found in league. Ponissi and Kiss impressed Viljoen, but both became frustrated during their respective spells in South Africa, as they felt the national team should be a finishing school and not a learning school.

A defensive coach, like a kicking and catching coach, should have been introduced across the board in South African rugby. It should have been a full-time post, with the coaches spending time with the provincial, Super 12 and junior national squads.

This never happened, because the board of SA Rugby (Pty) Ltd would not establish a strong rugby division headed up by a director of rugby. Instead, the board was comfortable with the existing technical committee, even though there was no link between the committee and the national coach. Through Oberholzer, Viljoen convinced the board to pay for the services of defensive coaches in a consultant's capacity. However, this would only ever provide our rugby with short-term relief.

Foreigners scare the incompetents within South African rugby, who suffer from an inferiority complex. The situation has not changed with the new leadership of Brian van Rooyen, who has made a point of dismissing any foreign involvement in the Bok coaching structure. Van Rooyen's xenophobia is symptomatic of why South African rugby has fallen behind the rest of the world and continues to struggle. Other rugby teams, such as France, Australia and England, appoint whomever necessary to get the job done, and adapt the information to service their own needs.

South African rugby fears foreign influence. It spurns the knowledge of outsiders, as superior knowledge exposes inadequacies, demands thought and forces change. South African rugby, battered yet belligerent, has all the answers, yet no silverware. Then we have that uniquely South African plague: north versus south, and white Afrikaners versus everyone else. Diversity, which should be South Africa's strength, has never been developed. Black, coloured, English and Afrikaner still operate within the individual stereotypes associated with 100 years of playing the game in this country.

Our rugby philosophy can be summed up as follows: Afrikaners are the big, strong enforcers in our game; the English bring intelligence to the mix; the coloureds have the flair; and the black player is only there because of a quota system and a political peace treaty. In insular South Africa, this kind of thinking drains the potential vibrancy and success. The thought of a foreigner adding value to our rugby is dismissed out of hand. Please don't bring a New Zealander into the laager, and the closest we allow anything French or English is in the form of a croissant or pork pie.

Eight years into professionalism, and South African rugby has chased away the good, the experienced and the proudly South African. Players, coaches and some very good men have simply given up. We had Nick Mallett and Alan

Solomons as coaches. We had François Pienaar, Joel Stransky, Garry Pagel, Naka Drotske, Mark Andrews, Dion O'Cuinneagain, André Vos, Stuart Abbott, Mike Catt, Pieter de Villiers, Dan Vickerman and Brendan Venter as players.

Each one of these individuals left South Africa, introduced a foreign element to the English, Irish, Australian or French set-up, and added value. The Irish did not become South African because O'Cuinneagain captained the side. France did not turn into South Africa because De Villiers propped up their scrum, and England certainly has not emulated South Africa because Catt and Abbott are good enough to play international rugby.

Each of those who have left has been cast aside as turncoats. With five years of experience in coaching and administration in England, Pienaar was viewed as a non-entity in South African rugby on his return to this country. Venter, hugely successful in his first year as coach at London Irish, has returned to South Africa. In the year he has been home, he has not received one phone call inviting him to add his expertise to South African rugby.

Solomons, outstanding at Ulster and now with English club Northampton Saints, has too many enemies in the corridors of South African rugby, and Mallett, victorious in his first season at Stade Français, has offended too many in South African rugby with his outspoken opinions. All remain very good coaches and very good players. All have this in common: they challenged a system internally, found that insularity carried more credibility in South African rugby than intelligence, and have subsequently advanced their careers elsewhere.

All the while, South African rugby slips from one in the world to six. In addition, a generation of rugby followers has now grown up knowing only the misery of the Springboks and South African rugby; not the all-conquering exploits of the past that the old-timers cling to as the reason why South African rugby should still command respect internationally. Brendan Venter has strong views, but he is passionate about the potential strength of South African rugby, and favours any influence that can benefit the South African game.

In a recent interview for *SA Sports Illustrated*, he told me the following:

Our rugby would be enriched with new ideas and strong personalities who speak with experience of having succeeded and failed. You look at England. Trace their upward curve and it coincides with the mass influx of foreign-based coaches and very influential players from the southern hemisphere and France.

John Mitchell [former All Blacks coach], as the England assistant coach a few years ago, added immense value to Clive Woodward's success. In the Zurich Premiership English players have for the past five years been exposed to the thinking of top New Zealand, Australian, South African and French coaches, as well as the introduction of Rugby League coaches.

Ireland has benefited as well in having a guy like Solly coaching Ulster. Players, like Pienaar, Stransky, Pagel, Drotske, Vos, Andrews, [Tim] Horan, [Zinzan] Brooke, [Philippe] Sella and [Philippe] St André, to name ten, have made an enormous contribution to the strength of English rugby.

For all this, England remain England and play like England.

Ask the fourteen provincial coaches and their presidents, the four Super 12 coaches and the national coaches what defines South African rugby, and be prepared for twenty different interpretations.

Is South African rugby white, Afrikaans, conservative, bullish, New Age, diverse, intelligent? There is no definitive style of player or style of play. To label South African players as physically the 'tough' men of world rugby, but equally the 'dumb' men of the international game, is an insult to the likes of John Smit, Victor Matfield, Jean de Villiers, Breyton Paulse, Jaco van der Westhuyzen, Brent Russell, Bob Skinstad, André Pretorius, Neil de Kock, Gcobani Bobo, Pieter Rossouw ...

South African players have skills. Tim Lane proved that with the Bok back division in 2002 and the emergence of very skilled Cats backs in 2003. Western Province and former Springbok coach Carel du Plessis, more mature as a coach than he was in 1997 and more refined in his thinking, produces ample evidence of the degree of talent every week. And Kevin Putt is slowly reintroducing balance and poise to the identity of the Sharks. Foreign input can only be of value, especially in areas where South African rugby is at a disadvantage, as in rugby league and Aussie Rules. Those codes are not played in this country; we don't have local expertise in these disciplines.

Viljoen's great strength was his ability to recognise the need for foreign input. Viljoen, Jake White and I spent an evening at the house of John Hart, the former New Zealand national coach. Hart spoke openly about the resistance to evolution in traditional rugby countries such as New Zealand and South Africa. That was why a country such as Australia has moved ahead – they were willing to embrace anything that could improve the team. Not so New Zealand and South Africa.

Hart seemed excited about the prospect of Tim Lane's contribution to South African rugby. 'He is the best backline coach in the game,' said Hart. 'You could win the Cup with him involved.' Viljoen felt vindicated that he had pursued Lane so vigorously. Rod Macqueen had also told Viljoen that Lane's strength lay in identifying game breakers, and then extracting the maximum out of them through his understanding of the game. Viljoen let himself down when he bought into the Lane philosophy but did not select the players Lane had identified as capable of redefining South African back play.

Lane was forthright in his assessment of Braam van Straaten and Joost van der Westhuizen. Van Straaten, he said, was not an international flyhalf, and he did not think the player was capable of dictating a game. Lane respected Van Straaten's doggedness and goal kicking, but told Viljoen that Van Straaten did not have the tactical appreciation to be a test No. 10.

According to Lane, Van der Westhuizen did not understand phase play, and his option-taking let him down. But Viljoen was not prepared to drop Van der Westhuizen, and said he could change the player's mindset on the field. He accepted Van Straaten's limitations, but when Percy Montgomery missed three penalties against the All Blacks and goal kicking was seen as the reason the Boks lost, Viljoen rushed Van Straaten back into the test team.

Lane did not believe it was the right move, but gave Viljoen his support. He felt that the Boks could 'get by' with Van Straaten at inside centre, but not at flyhalf. Van Straaten was picked at inside centre, although Viljoen again selected him at flyhalf for the end-of-year tour in 2001. On that tour, after the opening test against France, Van Straaten spoke to Viljoen and told him he could not play at flyhalf, as he could not come to terms with Lane's phase-play tactics. Instead of dropping Van Straaten, Viljoen picked him at inside centre, and Louis Koen at flyhalf. As backline coach, Lane was opposed to both selections, but publicly gave the head coach his backing and tried to coach the two players.

Lane is not the confrontational type. He made his feelings known and left it at that, and got on with trying to coach whoever was selected. If you are prepared to invest in a foreigner, then you have to back the foreigner's expertise. Lane never received Harry's full backing. Straeuli backed Lane in the first year, which was borne out in the selections and approach of the Boks in 2002. Lane believed that South Africa's backline players were as good as any in the world, but he felt that conservative attitudes in the South African game meant that these players were never selected. He doubted whether Wallabies such as Stephen Larkham and George Gregan would ever have been given a game in South African rugby, especially Larkham, who was a very unconventional flyhalf.

'The talent is there,' Lane said. 'Somebody has to be bold enough to pick them.' His approach was never better illustrated than on the morning of the test match against Australia in Johannesburg in 2002. André Pretorius had twisted his right knee playing golf on the Thursday. He told no one about it, and started the Friday evening captain's run in obvious pain. He did not last long. He failed a fitness test on the Saturday morning, and Straeuli and Lane debated who would replace him. Lane was adamant that it had to be Brent Russell. Straeuli felt it would be too radical a move, and proposed that a kicking flyhalf be drafted into the squad.

Lane argued that Russell had been with the squad the entire tournament and had to be given a chance. He told Straeuli that the Boks should not think about kicking penalties; they now had to score tries to beat Australia. Straeuli, open to discussion despite being laid low with a viral infection, conceded, and confirmed that Russell would start the test.

Russell had never played a match at Ellis Park. He turned in a magnificent performance that afternoon, and the Boks won a thriller 33-31. Had it not been for the 'foreign influence', Brent Russell would not have played in the match. Lane is also a huge admirer of Jaque Fourie, Jean de Villiers and Marius Joubert, rating them as good as any player he coached in the Wallabies. The foreigners brought a different mindset, an attitude that reinforced confidence and a worldly view of professionalism to the national set-up. The players responded positively to this breath of fresh air.

During the 2002 Tri-Nations test in Brisbane, Lane was the focus of a lot of media attention. Brisbane was his hometown, and there was animosity towards him for joining the Boks. Lane appeared on the popular Australian news programme *60 Minutes*, and spoke about life in South Africa. He boosted the Bok players, spoke highly of their potential and attitude, and was very flattering about living in South Africa. The players made a point of thanking Lane. During a team meeting they said that they admired him for sticking up for South Africa in such difficult circumstances.

The foreigners who formed part of the Bok squad during my time carried no provincial baggage or hidden agenda. All they wanted to do was improve the condition of Springbok rugby. They were easily accepted within the squad, but outside they were the victims of provincial insecurities, cultural inadequacies and paranoia. The media fuelled the paranoia by blaming the Australian influence for every stumble. For this, they used the voices of disgruntled former players and administrators. Some of their fiercest critics among the former players were those who had approached Viljoen to be a part of his coaching team. When Viljoen declined their offer, they turned on him through the media. The media never revealed the agenda of these players.

The foreigners had no agenda outside of wanting to coach within the South African system. Their objectivity was revealing, especially when Byrne worked with the kickers in Plettenberg Bay. He was unfamiliar with the background of the men, and declared the late François Swart as the best student after day one, and Conrad Jantjes as the most natural kicker of the ball. When he mentioned this to the coaches, some of them questioned the absence of Gaffie du Toit, who had been one of the kickers at Plett.

'Mate, I am judging on what I saw out there,' said Byrne.

The political phenomenon within South African rugby left the foreigners in the Bok squad dumbstruck. They had never experienced a mix where racial, cultural and language affiliation was the cause of such division and debate, when it should have been South Africa's strength.

The way in which these foreigners were treated by South African rugby's political underworld has convinced me that a foreign coach could not succeed with the Boks, as too many conservative elements within the game would be plotting the overthrow of anyone who put national interest ahead of a provincial agenda. Blood is thicker than water. This I found out very quickly.

Let me take you back to the end-of-year European tour of 2002. The Boks got smashed in all three tests, and the most chilling aspect of the tour was that our forwards were murdered in every game, both in the tight phases and at the breakdown. Physically, France, Scotland and England were all superior in the contact situation. They muscled our boys off the ball. The Bok forwards were a negative factor on that tour, and Straeuli's value as a head coach and forwards specialist was suddenly in doubt within the corridors of South African rugby.

Straeuli realised that he needed help with the pack, and I arranged, through a French contact, for Straeuli to meet up with a former French international who was regarded as one of the best scrumming specialists. He was keen to come to South Africa, and believed he could make the Bok pack the best in the world. Straeuli duly met the Frenchman in London in the week of the England versus France test, and was impressed. However, he told me he would be isolating himself in South Africa if he introduced another foreigner into the squad. According to Straeuli, the traditional South African rugby supporter was getting fed up with being reminded that the expertise was not available in this country. He embarked on a very South African drive in which everything about the World Cup campaign had to be South African. It was all huff and puff.

Straeuli started talking to the media about playing 'the South African way' and creating a 'unique South African game plan'. He never explained what constituted the South African way, but he was speaking the right language for the Afrikaans market. He wanted South Africans in the squad who were passionate about this country. He was starting to prepare the way for the exit of Tim Lane. In the middle rounds of the Super 12, Lane, coaching the Cats, and Gert Smal, coaching the Stormers, were taking a beating from the media because of their teams' performances.

After a lot of prompting, Straeuli backed both coaches at media information sessions. He had told the media at an earlier session that he might want to involve Smal in the Bok squad, and Lane was already part of the set-up. Straeuli defended both coaches, saying they did not become bad coaches just because of a bad run in the Super 12. He had been in the same situation the year before, when his Sharks team lost four on the trot just before he took up the Bok coaching position. He listed the qualities of Lane and Smal.

In the final two rounds of the competition, I scripted a media information release for Straeuli in which he again defended Lane. He read the release beforehand and approved it, but instructed me to omit Lane's name. 'Just talk about coaches; don't be specific,' he said. I thought nothing of it, until he fired Lane a fortnight later.

Rudy Joubert was enjoying reasonable success with the Bulls, and Rian

Oberholzer felt he should be involved in the World Cup campaign. He suggested that Joubert could assist in a technical capacity or with the forwards, and mentioned this to Straeuli, who became very nervous. He knew Joubert had supporters on the board, and even though the Bulls would win only six in eleven games and finish sixth, it was still six games more than before. Joubert was flavour of the month, and Straeuli knew that it would be safer to have him in his coaching set-up than outside waiting to take over should the Tri-Nations prove a failure.

Initially, Straeuli was very unflattering of Joubert. However, he was more critical of Joubert's personality than his rugby knowledge. Straeuli thought Joubert would be a destructive influence in the squad, and was concerned that his ego would take priority over team issues. I agreed with Straeuli. Joubert also had ambitions to coach South Africa. Because of the regulation that prohibits a foreigner from coaching the Boks, Lane was never a contender to take over from Straeuli. Lane and Straeuli had enjoyed a decent working relationship in 2002, and Straeuli had committed himself to Lane until the completion of the World Cup. But the threat of Joubert was too big, and Straeuli suddenly fell in love with the suggestion of bringing him on board, at the expense of Lane.

It was a low blow, as Lane had endured such unfair criticism and upheaval in South Africa, merely through his association with the Boks. He had left Montferrand after a very successful season in which the club reached the French club final, and he had relocated his entire family to South Africa – a wife, two young boys and a teenage daughter. He was committed to the Boks, and after a year in the country was told to prove his worth after Harry Viljoen walked away from the Bok job. He had the opportunity to go to Saracens for a very lucrative sum of money. He turned it down because Oberholzer had convinced Straeuli of Lane's value.

Montferrand had again approached Lane with an offer during the 2003 Super 12 season, but he turned them down because of the World Cup campaign and Straeuli's commitment to him. A fortnight later, with no warning whatsoever, Straeuli told Lane that he did not believe the Australian would fit into the South African way of playing at the World Cup. We have since seen what that way was, and in hindsight Lane is probably relieved he will never be associated with the campaign.

Straeuli also told Lane that he was making the decision out of respect for Lane's rugby philosophy. He knew Lane could not coach the kind of players he would select, especially the halfbacks Joost van der Westhuizen and Louis Koen.

I discussed the matter with Lane. Naturally he was annoyed, and felt that he had been stabbed in the back. I said it was more a case of being stabbed in the stomach. Lane was very disillusioned with South African rugby. He could not believe the crassness of the political world and people's ability to smile at you while sticking in the knife. And then Straeuli, to make himself feel better, tried to say that the decision was made out of concern for Lane.

Oberholzer was surprised by the decision to sack Lane, but approved it nevertheless. He asked me if I knew why Straeuli wanted Lane out, and I told him it was because Straeuli believed that Joubert was being lined up as his successor. Oberholzer, by promoting Joubert's cause, had given Straeuli a fright. I believe Oberholzer could have kept Lane in the mix if he had wanted to, but at this stage Oberholzer was fighting his own political battle within South African rugby. He could ill afford having another coach fail who had been appointed under his leadership. Oberholzer was also the type of managing director to give the national coach total support and backing. He did not want to be accused of forcing Lane on Straeuli.

The 'South African way' of doing things that Straeuli was now suddenly promoting appealed to the board, the SARFU executive and the Afrikaans media. Many in the executive had never wanted Lane involved, so they jumped at the chance to support Straeuli on this matter. Straeuli tried to defend his decision to me, which I was not particularly interested in hearing. Lane and I had enjoyed a very good professional relationship, which Straeuli interpreted as a personal friendship. In Lane's two years in Cape Town, I had two lunches at his place and he visited my house once ... hardly the stuff of close mates.

Professionally, we had a good understanding and respected each other. I know his worth as a rugby coach, and when on tour we got on famously. The fact that we could share a beer and not have to talk about rugby all night made others jittery. When we played table tennis, shared a laugh and enjoyed each other's company, it did not mean that we were conspiring against the coach or South Africa.

There was a lot of laughter in the Boks' 2002 Tri-Nations campaign, largely thanks to Tim Lane. In 2003, there was very little laughter. Tim's absence was a contributing factor. Tim Lane is a very good rugby coach. But in South African rugby he will always be viewed as a foreigner and a failure because of the Cats' poor results in 2003 and 2004. It is no surprise he is now gone. Ask Ashwin Willemse, Gcobani Bobo, André Pretorius, Jaque Fourie and Neil de Kock about Lane. They were some of the guys he coached. They will tell you why his removal is a loss to South African rugby. Lane's crime was that he did not care for the politics of the game. He dismissed warnings from me, among others, about the underhanded manner in which decisions are made in this game. Lane was told to watch out and to form alliances, especially at board level. He laughed it off.

'I am a rugby coach and not a politician,' he said.

In this country, that's simply not enough.

9

Knocking ourselves out
The Springboks and dirty play

Rudolf Straeuli never advocated playing the man off the ball. Straeuli was from the school that played hard but not dirty. He took responsibility for any player who overstepped the mark, but in this he failed his players and himself. He never followed through on his threats, and a player who brought the game into disrepute was never disciplined.

Transparency was non-existent on disciplinary issues, and the media were never given definite answers. The public, therefore, were ill informed and left to wonder and decide for themselves. The skeletons were left in the cupboard; all Straeuli did was lock the door. With the agreement of the players, Straeuli introduced a system of fines, in which a yellow card cost a player R5 000, and a red card R7 500. These were negligible amounts for players who were paid R75 000 to play a test, not counting the win bonus, which ranged from R10 000 to R25 000.

The discipline blueprint of 2003, presented to the SA Rugby (Pty) Ltd board, the SARFU executive and the media at several information sessions, made for wonderful reading. It promised a new approach to discipline. In the 2003 Super 12 season, the players were monitored nationally for the first time. I was part of the special projects team, which included consultants Rob Benadie and Bruce Becker. All three of us favoured an extensive database to assist the coaches in their identification of trends, and player weaknesses and strengths.

Discipline was critical, as the Boks had an awful reputation internationally. Perception was stronger than fact with the Boks, as no accurate statistic was available to indicate who the biggest offenders were and in which areas they fell foul of the law. Certain players gained a bad reputation because of one incident only, and others, despite constant infringements, continued to offend without censure from the media.

The focus on discipline followed the deplorable scenes in the 2002 test against England at Twickenham, which the Boks lost by a record 53-3 margin. The blatant foul play infuriated Rian Oberholzer. He wanted answers, and Rudolf knew he would have to submit a detailed report of every incident on our return to South Africa. England's governing body, the Rugby Football Union (RFU), sent

Oberholzer a letter demanding an explanation of every incident that involved a South African player. The IRB also put pressure on Oberholzer, who spent several days behind the scenes convincing the IRB why the matter should be dealt with internally. I don't think Corné Krige will ever realise how hard Oberholzer fought for him. Had the IRB charged Krige on the footage supplied by Sky Television, he could have faced a lengthy ban from the game.

Incidents had also occurred in the Scotland test the week before, and official correspondence was received from the Scots as well. There was some explaining to do. Initially, Straeuli and I tried to defend the dirty on-field antics of the Boks to Oberholzer. We said they had happened in the 'heat of the moment'. I defended the players' behaviour because I was far too close to the action. When you stand in a change room after a 50-point defeat at Twickenham and some players are in tears and others are vomiting, it is difficult not to be overwhelmed.

I felt for Krige, and my early reaction was to defend him. Straeuli felt the same way. We told Oberholzer that there had not been a premeditated plan, but as the match lost its shape and we were reduced to fourteen men, some players felt the only way to respond was through aggression. We tried to justify their behaviour when it was inexcusable. Oberholzer would have none of it. He wanted explanations, and an investigation into the incidents. In my three years with the Boks, violent on-the-field scenes marred four matches. But it was four too many if you wanted to be a top-three team in the world.

Three of those four matches had involved Australia, but the most infamous of the four was the 53-3 defeat against England at Twickenham in 2002. On all these occasions, players took it upon themselves to climb into the opposition with fists, heads, elbows and fingers. The coach and senior management failed in not punishing the offenders. Straeuli had impressed on the players that ill discipline would not be tolerated, but these proved hollow words. Individuals who were guilty of bad behaviour were still selected.

Australian coach Eddie Jones described the Boks as a disgrace to international rugby because of such incidents. Jones lamented the lack of consequences as much as the actions of the players. England coach Clive Woodward responded similarly after the Twickenham debacle. Since 1992, the Boks have done themselves no favours when it comes to being branded the thugs of test rugby. The facts are damning. In the decade since re-admission, the Boks have been involved in at least one match a year marred by fighting or ill discipline. During this time, Bok players have been sent off, cited and suspended for indiscretions ranging from punching to biting to kicking to swearing at the referee. Add the period between 1992 and 1995 when a few players tested positive for steroid use, and it is no wonder the world frowns on the Boks.

The Boks are not necessarily dirtier than any other side, but they must be a lot dumber, as they always seem to get caught. Officially, they are therefore the holders of the unwanted crown of dirty play. Statistics from 2000 to 2003 attest to Bok brutality. In forty-one tests leading into the 2003 World Cup, the Boks had twenty players yellow-carded and two red-carded for ill discipline. The opposition in these forty-one tests lost ten players to yellow cards. In the five World Cup matches, Hendro Scholtz added another yellow card to this list. The Boks are their own worst enemies, too often adding fuel to the fire before kick-off by talking about how 'physical' they will be and how 'hard' they will play the game.

Opposition teams have dined out on Bok pre-match hype in the past decade, and very little seems to have been learnt since re-admission. On his departure from South Africa to the World Cup, Springbok captain Corné Krige branded his England counterpart Martin Johnson the 'dirtiest captain' in world rugby. He also boasted about the Boks' physical approach, considered one of the strengths of the South African game, which people were 'guaranteed' to see at the World Cup. His words were like a five-course meal for the British media. They fed on it for a week. On arrival in Australia, Krige apologised for his comment, but the damage was done.

It was not the first time Krige had to apologise to the English. In the 53-3 humiliation of the Boks at Twickenham, a frustrated and desperate Krige climbed into the English. He headbutted, punched and elbowed. The English media described it as a captain's 'few minutes of madness'. Matt Dawson, Jason Robinson and Martin Johnson felt the full force of Krige's presence in that match. Video evidence supported Clive Woodward's claims that the Boks had been dirty and malicious. The tale of the tape made for awful reading. I know, because Rudolf and I had to analyse the tape in an attempt to build a defence against the RFU and IRB.

But there was to be no defence – only Straeuli's sincerest apologies to Oberholzer, the RFU and IRB. Initially, Straeuli and I had been defiant. At the immediate post-match press conference, the English media had a full go at the Bok tactics. Clive Woodward, speaking first, was highly critical of the Boks' thuggery. We would later learn that Woodward had access to video footage we had not seen. He attacked the Boks, knowing he had the ammunition. Straeuli defended his team, unaware that the opposition were fighting with tanks when he thought they only had rifles.

'We play the game hard and not dirty,' Straeuli snapped back at journalists. 'It was a test match. How do you explain my change room? I have two players concussed. Do you think we knock ourselves out?'

It was to prove a very embarrassing moment for Straeuli. Sky Televison produced footage showing Krige doing precisely that. Krige had aimed a stiff arm at Matt Dawson, but the England scrumhalf ducked and André Pretorius, about to make the tackle on Dawson, ran straight into Krige's first. Pretorius' nose was broken and he was knocked out. His test was over. It pretty much summed up the chaos that reigned at Twickenham on that November day. The RFU sent a letter detailing the following incidents:

3rd minute: Robinson punched by Krige after late tackle.

10th minute: Dalton punches Dawson.

12th minute: Fleck punches Cohen.

20th minute: Robinson hit off the ball by James.

21st minute: Dawson complains to ref of Bok cheap shots.

23rd minute: Labuschagne sent off for late shoulder charge on Wilkinson.

35th minute: Krige is penalised for late hit on Hill.

40th minute: James punches Dawson.

41st minute: Wilkinson out of game after James shoulder charge.

50th minute: Greeff knees Back from the side.

55th minute: Krige headbutts Dawson.

58th minute: Krige knocks out Pretorius in charging for Dawson, who ducks a stiff arm.

61st minute: Greeff concedes penalty try with dangerous tackle on Christophers.

69th minute: Krige elbows Johnson in retaliation after being throttled in an elbow lock.

74th minute: Venter headbutts Hill in face.

Once back in South Africa, Krige acknowledged his misdemeanours, apologised to the South African rugby bosses, the South African rugby public and the English. The apology was commendable, but the damage could not be repaired with words. In the next few tests, the Springboks would never get the benefit of the doubt in a 50-50 situation. Straeuli called Krige in, but instead of making an example of him, he merely talked to him. Straeuli was concerned that we, as South Africans, always sold out our own players, when the rest of the world laughed at us for taking a principled stand. He believed that other countries would have settled the matter internally and not exposed their captain to public ridicule, a suspension or fine.

Straeuli informed the media that Krige had been punished 'internally', and that measures would be taken in the 2003 Super 12 to monitor him and other players perceived to be the bad boys of South African rugby. Any player conceding more than two penalties on average in a Super 12 match would not be selected for test rugby in 2003. Krige stayed out of harm's way in 2003. He did his utmost to control his temper in all the matches he played. In the Super 12 he conceded only four penalties, at an average of 0.8 per eighty minutes. He was penalised only once for a late tackle, and never for foul play. In 2004, the situation changed dramatically. Krige was cited for two mindless headbutts on Chiefs centre Derek Maisey, and banned for eight weeks. The ban ended his Super 12 career.

Other perceived offenders proved very disciplined. Robbie Fleck was penalised four times in the competition, at an average of 0.5 per match, Werner Greeff gave away five penalties at 1.1 per eighty minutes, and Butch James was on his best behaviour, penalised only three times at 0.3 per eighty minutes. But perception was fact in the case of AJ Venter. He was penalised thirteen times at an average of 1.9 per eighty minutes, and suspended for four weeks for headbutting Robbie Fleck in the Sharks' opening match in Cape Town. Straeuli would use this incident and the match statistic to drop Venter in the international season, judging him to be too high-risk.

Cobus Visagie was a liability at scrum time, penalised eight times for illegal binding. This was more than double any other South African tighthead prop in the competition. Straeuli believed that Visagie was getting a raw deal, but the referees were not going to change their interpretation. Visagie was too set in his ways to change, and played only one test in 2003. The technical disciplines could be worked on, but Straeuli warned the players that he would not stand for any foul play. Krige backed him up at every team meeting.

Krige often spoke to the team about 'being clever' in a physical confrontation. Punches get thrown at the breakdown all the time; it is an accepted part of the package. But there was no excuse for blatant off-the-ball stupidity. Krige, more than most, knew what went on at the tackle situation and in the breakdown. He could dish it out, but he also took it on the nose, eye, chin and mouth in every match. In Brisbane in 2002, Australian wing Ben Tune split open Krige's eye during a free-for-all. Tune boasted about the punch in the Australian media.

When the Boks played the Wallabies in Johannesburg a few weeks later, a lot of pre-match talk circulated about the Tune punch in Brisbane. Prior to kick-off, New Zealand referee Paddy O'Brien told Krige not to do anything stupid – he would be watching. He also told both touch judges to watch carefully when Tune took the ball into contact. Within a few minutes of the kick-off, Tune was caught in possession, a ruck formed and O'Brien quickly blew his whistle. Tune emerged from the ruck bleeding. Krige had clobbered him. O'Brien asked the touch judge if he had seen anything. He hadn't. Afterwards, O'Brien asked Krige if he had hit Tune, and Krige said he had, but now they were even. O'Brien was amazed that Krige had managed it without anyone noticing. Tune told the Australian media the same story: 'We're even.'

A year later, and the Boks were once again in Brisbane. The Australian media zoomed in on the violence of the 2002 match. I had briefed our players to avoid the topic and to talk up the Australian players. We could not afford to carry baggage into this match. The players were on their best behaviour. Joost backed George Gregan, who had been under tremendous pressure in the Australian media. Joost described Gregan as one of the game's best No. 9s, a superb captain and a challenge to oppose in play. De Wet Barry, who had put a premature end to Steve Kefu's international aspirations with his crunching tackles in Cape Town, praised the Australian backs' class. He played down any suggestion of him being an aggressor or enforcer. Then Jim Tucker, a seasoned pro from the Brisbane *Courier Mail*, asked Joe van Niekerk, set to start for the first time in the international season, how it felt to be back from injury. Van Niekerk replied that he couldn't wait to get 'stuck into' the Wallabies. All Big Joe wanted to do was play test rugby. It was an innocent comment, as he had meant to say how keen he was to actually run onto the field again. Too late!

Jimmy had the line he'd wanted, and the next day he put the Boks away. According to press reports, Van Niekerk was fired up to have a go at the Wallabies. His comment allowed the media to refocus on the ill-tempered match the year before. It also convinced Wallabies coach Eddie Jones that a plan was in place to play the Wallabies off the ball. It was never the case. Incidents against Australia in Brisbane were isolated, but they happened. Bakkies Botha was cited for all sorts of illegalities, and suspended from the game for two months. Robbie Kempson was cited for a late tackle on Toutai Kefu. Again, the damage was done.

Management were caught unawares at the post-match press conference. I take full responsibility for our lack of preparation. I should have attended the Wallabies press conference in order to know what had been talked about. Instead, I remained in our dressing room to discuss with Straeuli how to put a positive spin on another twenty-point defeat. The public were growing tired of 'we are a lot better than the scoreboard shows, and, but for a decision here and there, things could have been different'. We had to show them that we were accountable for the result.

As it was, the media did not want to talk rugby.

We walked into the press conference, and both coach and captain were ill prepared for what was to come. A South African journalist warned me in Afrikaans that there was 'big shit', and that Australia had accused us of thuggery and biting.

Jones specifically accused Krige of lacking integrity, blaming him for spitting blood at a Wallaby player. Krige explained that he had spat out blood from a split lip, and that some had accidentally spattered on Phil Waugh. He had immediately apologised to the player, who accepted his explanation.

Krige handled himself well at the press conference. He didn't get upset, and gave an honest account of what he'd experienced. When the media asked him if an Australian had hit him first, he said it could have been a knee, an elbow, an Australian or one of his own players. He told the media that a lot goes on in ruck situations, and lips get cut. It was all part of the game.

Krige later briefly chatted to Wallabies captain George Gregan to clear the air. Gregan seemed to accept the explanation. But the Wallabies would not be as accommodating about a biting allegation. They were adamant that Brendan Cannon had been bitten and eye-gouged.

The questions from the press put Straeuli on the defensive. They set him up nicely with the old one-two question teaser, and then finished him off by extracting a commitment from him that he would be accountable for the actions of any player found guilty of dirty play. Straeuli was asked whether he promoted thuggery within his team. He said no. Would he take action if, at a later stage, it became known that one of his players had bitten another player or eye-gouged him? Straeuli said yes. What kind of action, he was asked. He said the player would not be selected for South Africa again.

Straeuli responded like a man trapped in a corner, but it was not an honest reply. Straeuli suspected that our player had bitten an Aussie. The player later even admitted it to Straeuli, who continued to select him. You can't clean up the image of your team when you still continue to pick the same offenders. Jones was right when he called the Boks a disgrace, especially because the coach failed to deliver on his promise to expunge thugs and thuggery from Bok rugby. Whatever their pre-match intentions had been of playing within the rules in Brisbane, the Boks had caused irreparable damage.

Straeuli was furious. As his communications manager, I had let him down, as I should have been a step ahead and attended the Wallabies press conference to prepare a defence for him. Straeuli should have been briefed going into the press conference. He would have been more composed, with access to a pre-prepared response that would have appeared forthright but revealed little.

Afterwards, I acknowledged my error to Straeuli, and he agreed that in future I should attend the opposition's press conferences. Jones' media attack had annoyed him. He felt that Jones should have spoken to him privately, and the issue addressed in-house, away from the media eye. When we arrived at the post-match cocktail party, Jones and the Wallaby team manager were having a beer near the entrance. I suggested to Straeuli that he have a chat with Jones to try to save the situation. Jones was having none of it. He blasted Rudolf, saying there was nothing to talk about. What had happened was unacceptable, and he felt that the incidents had been premeditated.

Straeuli denied this, but Jones was defiant. As an international coach, he said he would not tolerate such behaviour. 'It is a fucking disgrace,' Jones said. 'And you know it.'

This exchange upset Straeuli even more. He sought out Rian Oberholzer and asked him to take up the matter with his Australian counterpart, John O'Neill. At that stage Straeuli was still adamant that Bakkies Botha had not bitten an Australian player. He was willing to give Botha the benefit of the doubt, something Jones was not prepared to do. Kempson would also be cited, for a late tackle on Kefu in the last few minutes of the game. I think Kempson had simply had enough of everything – the Wallabies, being on tour with the Boks ... He was very frustrated. Kefu certainly milked the affair, but Kempson is bright enough to know that the incident further engrained the Boks' thuggery tag, which they would take to New Zealand the next week and into the World Cup in October 2003.

Because of their obsession with physical domination and pre-test macho talk, the Boks reinforce the perception that they play with premeditated illegal intention. I spoke about this in private media briefings with the players, urging them to be smarter when they spoke to the press, because they were not bullies. In my three-year association with the Boks, I never heard a team talk or a change-room speech that focused on playing the man and not the ball, or physically beating up another team. I cannot vouch for what was discussed between Straeuli and the players in one-on-one situations. In the team environment, these kinds of things were not talked about.

However, certain individuals tended to explode when calmness should have prevailed. Botha was an example in Brisbane. Krige, much to his and everyone else's disgust, was the aggressor at Twickenham. Straeuli believed in strict team discipline. He enforced a tough team ethic, but when players lost the plot, there were no consequences befitting the crime. Confronting issues, whether disciplinary or any other concerns, is not Springbok or South African rugby's strength.

Krige was rapped on the knuckles for Twickenham and Bakkies Botha escaped a lengthy exile from Bok rugby, despite later admitting his guilt to Straeuli, who in turn sympathised with him. Straeuli, who needed the support of all his players, felt that by backing Botha he would win over the squad. He was a coach who would put himself on the line for his players. Although I understood his motivation, I didn't agree with it.

Straeuli would get involved in a disciplinary hearing and put on a public face of defiance. He would remind the players that in his team no one would be left to fend for himself, and referred to the example of one of his Bok teammates, Johan le Roux, who was suspended from the game for eighteen months for biting the ear of All Blacks captain Sean Fitzpatrick in 1994.

'We left a teammate behind to look after himself in New Zealand,' Straeuli told his Boks whenever they were cited. 'It won't happen in this team.'

Whether motivated by frustration or insecurity, the Boks always talk about their physicality. New Zealand, France and England play the game with as much aggression and passion, but rarely do you hear their players talk up a physical confrontation. Rarely do you see those teams being punished for over-robustness. Smart teams talk about skill and scoring tries. The Boks are more testosterone-driven. Their scope is limited to adjectives that merely reinforce the belief that they are thugs. 'Bold', 'brash' and 'brutal' are words that are too often perceived as complimentary within the Bok squad. France has built its rugby reputation on romance. In close contact, the only romance an opposition player can hope for is to have his testicles grabbed, his eyes gouged and being bitten. The French generally escape the law enforcers because they carry an image of sophistication off the field. The Boks need to talk and play smarter. The only way their reputation will ever improve is if both the coach and manager enforce discipline, mete out punishment and omit those players guilty of thuggery.

The Botha incident should not have been condoned, regardless of how good a player Bakkies is. Straeuli told me in Cape Town in August 2003 that he knew Bakkies was guilty, but had felt obliged to defend him. His argument was that we had to 'protect' our players.

According to Rudolf, Australia would have done the same thing, and he referred to the Ben Tune drug scandal, when the Australian Rugby Union had failed to disclose that Tune had tested positive for banned substances, and continued to select him for the Wallabies. I asked Straeuli whether he would still select Bakkies. He said yes, because Bakkies would be an asset to the Boks at the World Cup. He also guaranteed me that the player had learnt his lesson, and that he would never do such a thing again.

That was hardly the point.

10

Whistling a false tune
The influence of referees

South African players believe that the Australian referees deliberately nail them. I agree with the players. The 50-50 decisions do go against South African teams. Referees will always get away with this, because in areas such as the tackle situation and at the breakdown, so much depends on interpretation.

When Harry Viljoen took over as the Bok coach in 2000, he tried to establish a healthy rapport with referees. Where possible, he wanted to discuss problems with them, and also show them that South Africans were not all big and dumb. Harry wanted to change the perception that anyone wearing a green and gold jersey deserved to be detested. Australian Scott Young refereed Viljoen's debut test against Argentina in Buenos Aires. The Boks won a thriller 37-33, but Young caned them in the second half.

Viljoen was highly critical of Young's performance, but he was not prepared to publicly make an issue of his displeasure. He spoke briefly to Young after the match, saying that he disagreed with some of the decisions. He did not take the conversation further at the cocktail party, and instead asked me to e-mail Young. The tone of the e-mail had to be friendly, and the message should not contain an accusation of deliberate bias by the referee. Viljoen wanted me to point out the inconsistencies in Young's interpretation, and also focus on decisions the Bok coaches felt had incorrectly favoured Argentina.

The Boks' technical team had studied the match tape, and I forwarded Young an e-mail listing twenty-one queries. Our approach was to ask for an explanation so that we could improve our discipline. We considered the correspondence confidential, and we pointed out that we would not be forwarding the questions to SARFU or the Australian Rugby Union (ARU). Young responded in an equally friendly manner, and agreed that he had made mistakes. Of the twenty-one objections we raised, he only disagreed with six. He said it had been a difficult test match to referee, and that he was not privy to a second look on video during the game, but had to rely on what he and his two touch judges saw. His response was enough to convince our players that they were getting a raw deal.

In the next two years there would be other refereeing decisions that angered the Bok players, both at test and at Super 12 level. Australia's Stuart Dickinson featured most prominently as the villain among South African players, but they were also unhappy with Steve Walsh Jr's refereeing in the 14-all draw against Australia in Perth in 2001.

Butch James got yellow-carded for a high tackle on George Smith, when he actually missed him. Smith ducked under the tackle, but the crowd reaction was enough to convince Walsh to sin-bin James.

Bob Skinstad, captaining the side, told Viljoen and me after the game that Walsh had been biased against James, as he had made a remark about the player before kick-off. 'He told me to tell Butch to watch his tackling,' Skinstad said. 'He said it before the game. He was obviously influenced going into the match.'

Skinstad had also been sin-binned for a professional foul. He did not blame Walsh for this, but felt that James had been done a disservice, as the referee had been influenced by pre-match media reports about the perceived illegality of James' tackling. Skinstad wanted to have a go at Walsh at the press conference, but it was decided that he would unnecessarily expose himself to further criticism for being sent off. Harry decided to personally discuss the matter with Walsh. I don't know if he ever did, and I was never asked to correspond with Walsh.

However, our players accused Dickinson in particular of being biased against South Africa. His refereeing of the 2002 Tri-Nations test against the All Blacks in Wellington completely influenced the flow of the match. I won't say it cost the Boks the test, but crucial decisions went against South Africa at vital stages. The Bok coaches were angry. The concerns about Dickinson were raised with Rian Oberholzer, but he said we were being paranoid, and that it was time our players assumed responsibility for their own actions.

Rudolf Straeuli acknowledged that our players' discipline had to improve. He had already started on a public relations drive with the referees, and after the first three tests in 2002, Tony Spreadbury and Wayne Erickson addressed our players in a formal debriefing.

Spreadbury and Erickson had refereed the tests, and they were frank on how they perceived our players and in which areas we needed to improve. Our players asked questions and raised pertinent issues, but they had no place to hide when Spreadbury and Erickson spoke about the weakness in the Boks' technical approach.

It was a worthwhile exercise, although Straeuli felt that Erickson had not been consistent in his application of the law at the tackle in the test against Argentina in Springs in 2002. The Pumas had made the same mistakes, but somehow escaped censure. But the Dickinson complaint paled into insignificance during the Tri-Nations because of the crazy pitch invasion by Bok supporter Piet van Zyl during the home test against the All Blacks in Durban. Van Zyl assaulted Irish referee Dave McHugh, and the public relations exercise Straeuli had established was instantly blown away.

Courtesy of one lout, the Boks were again the brutes of world rugby. No referee was going to do us any favours, despite the Boks trying their utmost to be technically disciplined. The players were angry about the incident, but completely perplexed by the reaction within South African rugby. Everyone apologised to McHugh, but the players felt the incident had nothing to do with them. It had been the action of one idiot.

Van Zyl had damaged the country's image, but the players thought it pathetic that apologies had been made to the Irish community and the referee on behalf of just about everyone in South Africa. The Bok team management and players had shown ample concern, and AJ Venter had even broken Van Zyl's nose with a punch to stop him from further assaulting McHugh. What more could the players have done? The answer is nothing, but not even Venter's defence of McHugh would win the Boks refereeing friends in future tests.

South African referee Tappe Henning had been added to the management team as a referee consultant, and worked with the squad in every session. During the Tri-Nations, the penalty count was reduced from twenty to ten a test. Henning's advice was invaluable, and he also spoke to the players about how referees perceive us. They did not dislike us personally, he said, but the fact that we showed no respect for the laws of the game. Jonathan Kaplan, South Africa's number one referee as far as most of the players were concerned, also offered insights into how referees viewed South African players. Kaplan, André Watson and Henning defended Dickinson's motives, saying he would not deliberately cheat the Boks. This did not reassure Straeuli, who felt that the referees were protecting each other.

Straeuli and I bumped into Dickinson at the team hotel prior to the Scotland test in Edinburgh in November 2002. Dickinson had been assigned to run the touch in the test, and we had chatted briefly to him on a few occasions during the week. His wife and child accompanied him, and the banter was friendly and not rugby-related.

One morning Dickinson was downstairs on his own. A relaxed and mellow Straeuli had a coffee with him. Straeuli suggested to Dickinson that he did not like the Boks or South African players in general. Dickinson denied this, and called the accusation absurd. He loved touring South Africa, got on well with the players and called the game as he saw it. Straeuli replied that this was exactly the attitude that confused the South African players. Many of them had enjoyed a beer with Dickinson after the game, and they felt he was a genuine bloke. But once he ran on the field, it was as if he turned against them.

Dickinson was very taken aback. He assured Rudolf that he never went out of his way to find fault with the Boks. Rudolf mentioned the Wellington test, and did not mince his words. He told Dickinson that he had blown a shocker in Wellington. Straeuli was not interested in debating the issue, and moved on to a discussion on general interpretations at the tackle situation. The chat ended with Dickinson reassuring Straeuli that he had nothing against the Springboks. Straeuli was not convinced, and it would take Dickinson only a few minutes in the test that followed to raise Straeuli's temperature. The Boks won a scrum feed on Scotland's 22-metre line, bang in front of the posts. In rugby you don't get a better attacking set-phase field position. Dickinson intervened, accusing Breyton Paulse of going in recklessly with his boots, and the Boks were penalised. The video evidence afterwards showed that Paulse had not been anywhere near the ball.

Straeuli was adamant that Dickinson was prejudiced against South Africa, despite his protests to the contrary. I shared Straeuli's opinion, as did most of the squad. Once again, our protests evaporated after the Twickenham debacle, when Jannes Labuschagne was sent off for a late challenge on Jonny Wilkinson, and Corné Krige belted a handful of English players. It would have been very inappropriate to question refereeing decisions when we were fortunate that Krige was not red-carded and two more players sin-binned. Oberholzer, fuming at the off-the-ball antics of the Boks, was not interested in hearing complaints about referees. He wanted answers about our players' actions. The performances in a three-test tour had undone every metre of goodwill gained during the Tri-Nations. Dickinson was safe for another few months.

At the annual Super 12 pre-tournament gathering of referees, coaches and administrators, referees' inconsistencies were discussed. No names were mentioned, but it all blew up a few weeks into the 2003 Super 12 tournament anyway. Dickinson was in South Africa again, and doing his utmost to enrage South Africans.

The media attacked his refereeing in two Super 12 matches, and wanted Oberholzer to condemn him. Bound by IRB protocol, Oberholzer said nothing publicly. He took it on the chin, and accepted that the media would reproach him for failing to act against Dickinson. But behind the scenes, Oberholzer asked technical analyst Dale McDermott, SA Rugby's director of referees, Freek Burger, and me to draw up a list of complaints on Dickinson. He wanted each complaint supported with a video clip, and also other referees listed where necessary, so that it would not look like an orchestrated vendetta against Dickinson. We put together a tape, with the majority of the clips featuring Dickinson. This was presented to Oberholzer, who sent it to his Australian equivalent John O'Neill and the IRB.

This is what O'Neill and the IRB received along with the video material.

Referee inconsistency concerns as raised by SA Rugby

Clip No. 1
Highlanders No.14 on Cats No.11: deliberate use of the knee going into the tackle. Referee (Dickinson) reacted immediately and sin-binned the offender. The offence deemed only serious enough for a yellow card, despite the Cats player's

face being cut and requiring stitches. The Highlanders No.14 was subsequently cited and banned for six weeks.

Clip No. 2
Cats No. 2 and No.7 upend Hurricanes No.15 and dump him to the ground in an action commonly referred to as a spear tackle in rugby. Cats No. 2 singled out and sent off (red card offence). Highlanders No.14, the week previously, only received a yellow card for an illegal act that caused facial damage to Cats No.11. We question the consistency in application by the same referee (Dickinson).

Clip No. 3
The match is the Highlanders vs Cats – the same match from which Clip 1 has been cut. The Highlanders No.14 has already received a yellow card for foul play, returns to the field in the 27th minute and is involved in another high tackle on No.11. Tackles him high and then carries through with dragging the player along the ground. Penalty awarded. Referee (Dickinson) calls over the player and again talks to him, but no sending off or second yellow card occurs. Why not?

Clip No. 4
The same No.14 (as referred to in Clip no. 3) has already received a yellow card, has been talked to for a high tackle subsequent to that and now puts in a late shoulder charge on Cats No. 9. This happens in the 48th minute. The referee (Dickinson) does not rule it late or illegal. Why not? No action taken against Highlanders No.14.

Clip No. 5
Hurricanes match vs Cats. Hurricanes' No. 8 is spoken to for off-the-ball action. Referee (Dickinson) deems his action serious enough to call him over and speak to him.

Clip No. 6
The same No. 8 player is spoken to again for off-the-ball play. No action taken by referee (Dickinson).

Clip No.7
The Hurricanes No. 8, having been spoken to by the referee on two occasions, retaliates to the 'spear tackle' on Cullen. His action sparks further player involvement from both sides. Referee (Dickinson) calls No. 8 over but again only talks to him. No caution and no sending off.

Clip No. 8
Now compare the interpretation with the previous week. The Highlanders match. In second half. Kelleher, Highlanders No. 9, puts in a high and late tackle on Cats No. 9. Kelleher drives No. 9 to the ground, nudges him with fist and flicks him with the boot when getting up. Cats No. 7 takes exception to this

off-the-ball act, runs in and pushes Highlanders No. 9 off Cats No. 9, who is lying on ground. Referee (Dickinson) intervenes. He acts more on the retaliation. Reverses the penalty against Highlanders No. 9 and punishes Cats No. 7 for retaliatory shove.

Clip No. 9
All Blacks vs Boks (in Wellington in 2002). Bok centre (13) Joubert puts in a high tackle on All Blacks winger (14, Howlett). Umanga (*sic*) (NZ centre) charges in and punches Joubert. Both players then become locked in a struggle and other players join. Referee (Dickinson) rules a dangerous tackle, penalises South Africa and sends off Joubert (yellow card). NZ centre is not penalised for retaliatory punch or yellow-carded.

Clip No. 10
Hurricanes vs Cats match: Hurricanes No. 8 is penalised and yellow-carded in the 40th minute of first half for a high tackle on Cats centre Jorrie Muller. He is punished with a yellow card but nothing more despite being cautioned on three occasions. During the same movement there is a high tackle on Muller by Hurricanes lock (Paul Tito). No action taken.

Clip No. 11
The previous week in a Super 12 match played in Australia, Stormers No. 12 Werner Greeff is yellow-carded for a dangerous and high tackle. Tito's offence, high and no arms, is of a similar nature. No sending off. What is the Super 12 standard?

Clip No. 12
Hurricanes vs Cats match: Hurricanes No. 9 Spice, in 46th minute, is involved in a head-high tackle on Cats No. 9 Januarie. The action only warrants a penalty, and again referee (Dickinson) calls the player over and the captain. No yellow card. What is the Super 12 standard with high tackles? Is it interpretation or is it applied according to the law?

Clip No. 13
Hurricanes vs Cats match. Cats No. 2 sent off and red-carded for 'spear tackle' on Hurricanes No. 15 in the 39th minute. In the 47th minute, Cats No. 14 (Willemse) is also the victim of a spear tackle by Hurricanes No. 6 and No. 1. The referee (Dickinson) is positioned looking at the tackle. He does not deem it to be illegal. Where is the consistency? Commentators wrongfully identify Hurricanes tackler as Lomu when it is in fact Collins.

Clip No. 14
All Blacks vs Boks test in Wellington. First clip is the set scrum early in the game (7 min 30 seconds). Boks penalised at the scrum set. No caution, no talking to ... an immediate short arm (for a free kick) from referee (Dickinson).

Clip No. 15

All Blacks vs Boks test in Wellington. All Blacks scrum put in forty-three seconds after previous clip infringement. All Blacks too don't engage correctly. This time there is no short arm awarded to Boks. Referee talks to All Blacks front row and calls a reset. We question the consistency in application.

Clip No. 16

All Blacks vs Boks test in Wellington. At the very next scrum, there is still a problem with the engage. Referee breaks up the two packs and calls over both captains and talks to them. No penalties given. Again this happens on All Blacks put-in.

Clip No. 17

All Blacks vs Boks test in Wellington. At a later scrum, 40th minute, there is a problem with the engage. It is a Bok put-in, and immediately there is a short-arm free kick awarded to All Blacks. We question the consistency. Two All Black put-ins and he only deemed it necessary to chat. Two Bok put-ins, and he penalised South Africa on both occasions.

Clip No. 18

All Blacks vs Boks test in Wellington. Obstruction: Skinstad penalised for protecting ball carrier and obstructing NZ defender.

Clip No. 19

In the same match the next two sections of the clip show a New Zealander making contact with SA defender on the decoy run, but it is not deemed obstruction. Immediately thereafter, two NZ players obstruct SA defenders, but no penalty awarded. We question the consistency from referee (Dickinson).

Clip No. 20

All Blacks vs Boks in Wellington: NZ hooker (No. 2) has foot inside field of play and ball does not travel the required five metres from the line-out throw. Referee (Dickinson) rules okay on both counts and NZ score a try.

Clip No. 21

Scotland vs Boks. In 23rd minute. Up-and-under kick and chase. Scotland knock ball on, there is a scramble for ball, the referee calls a halt and gives the scrum feed to Boks on Scotland 22 right in front of posts. Touch judge, Mr Dickinson, intervenes. He points out illegal use of boot by SA No. 14 and recommends penalty to Scotland. The referee complies. Slow-motion replay shows Paulse (SA No.14) on left side of the ruck and the footage clearly indicates there is no boot going in and that SA No.14 does nothing wrong!

Clip No. 22

Blues home match vs Stormers in Auckland 2002. In 68th minute, Blues flanker Parkinson knocks the ball on from a line-out. Referee (Dickinson) rules it is okay and Blues score from the kick-through.

Clip No. 23

Blues vs Stormers. Same match as previous clip and two minutes after previous incident. In 70th minute, Stormers player (Hottie Louw) knocks down the ball, a similar motion, and it is ruled a knock-on. In same match, Blues lock twice plays Stormers centre off the ball after tackle. Referee (Dickinson) does not even penalise player.

Clip No. 24

Hurricanes vs Cats match. At 21-all, in 68th minute, Hurricanes on attack. Penalty and kick to corner. Referee (Dickinson) immediately warns the defending team Cats of the danger of penalties in that zone.

Clip No. 25

Hurricanes vs Cats match. In context of the 68th minute warning received from the referee. This time the Cats are on the attack. It is the 77th minute, the Cats win a line-out and are a few metres from the Hurricanes line. They retain possession and launch a few attacks on the line. They need a converted try to level the game. Hurricanes player deliberately kills the ball on the ground. He is penalised, but no yellow card is awarded for professional foul. Only a caution to the captain with the message: 'I did not get a number but it is one of the two players wearing headgear. The next infringement will be a penalty.'

Clip No. 26

In the context of the tournament and consistency, Bulls flanker is sent off for a late tackle in Brumbies match; Hurricanes No. 9 only penalised for high and dangerous tackle on Cats No. 9.

Clip No. 27

Where is the consistency in application? Bulls flanker sent off for alleged deliberate offside in the red zone. In Hurricanes vs Cats game, only a penalty against Hurricanes player for deliberately committing a professional foul in denying the Cats the ball, also in the red zone.

Clip No. 28

Stormers vs Waratahs. Stormers centre sent off for a high tackle after the touch judge made the referee aware of the tackle, but did not recommend anything other than the player be spoken to. Referee clearly asks if he needs to change the position of the penalty or issue a card. Touch judge says no, and referee in turns does the opposite. Sends the player off.

Clip No. 29

In the same match, five minutes later, Waratahs winger puts in a late and high tackle on Stormers No. 9. Video shows it is late and high. Referee rules it okay and does not even penalise the Waratahs players. He rules a forward pass from the Stormers.

The package was sent by courier, and the relevant people in Dublin and Sydney viewed the tape. No official response was ever received, but Oberholzer seemed content that the message had reached the right people. Dickinson would go on to torment the New Zealanders for the remainder of the Super 12 and in the international season. Meanwhile Straeuli continued to work on gaining favour with referees through a committed technical approach at training. He used Henning to good effect. Our South African referees are among the best in the world. Credit must go to Freek Burger, SA Rugby's director of referees, who has cultivated a culture of excellence among our referees. In 1996, South African referees were despised, and Australian and New Zealand teams felt they were incompetent and biased. Oberholzer had received numerous complaints.

Now André Watson, Jonathan Kaplan, Mark Lawrence, Andy Turner and Tappe Henning were rated in the top ten, with Kaplan and Watson among the world's top three referees.

Our advantage was the skill of our referees, and Straeuli knew they would improve the Boks' discipline. Players were made aware of their weaknesses, and a database was kept of the offenders to measure areas of ill discipline. South African players were vulnerable at the breakdown and ill-disciplined because they did not always back their defensive alignment.

Tournament data revealed that 23 per cent of the penalties conceded by the four South African Super 12 teams was at the breakdown, and 15 per cent at the tackle. Paying attention to detail and working closely with Henning could fix this problem. The players had to take responsibility for an offside penalty count of 18 per cent. It was unacceptable, and exposed the laziness in defence. There is no excuse for going offside. Every player knows where the line is. Henning spent the best part of four months with the Boks prior to the 2003 World Cup and refereed every training session. Players' awareness of the tackle ball situation improved, but huge discipline was still required on match day.

Henning found that the players contested every ball on the ground, regardless of whether it could realistically be won or not. Often they would commit more players to the tackle than was necessary, put their own defence under pressure because of a lack of numbers, and then commit an offence at the tackle situation. This was why they were so heavily penalised. Players were not thinking. They would join from the side, fall over the ball and play the ball when off their feet. Henning focused on making the players use their discretion. The player had to make an immediate decision as to whether it was impossible to win the ball. If so, let the opposition have it, and make sure the defensive alignment is spot-on. He emphasised the importance of knowing which ball to fight for and which to leave.

The results were not immediate, but improvement was seen in every match. The aim in each test was to restrict the penalty count to ten. Ideally, Straeuli wanted to reduce the penalty count to less than ten.

In the last 2003 Tri-Nations test against New Zealand in Dunedin, the Boks conceded only nine penalties in the first seventy-four minutes, and the All Blacks were guilty of conceding seven. In the last five minutes the Boks conceded an additional four in a desperate attempt to stop the All Blacks from scoring. They had almost matched the All Blacks for discipline, and it showed how much South Africa had improved under Henning's tutorship.

Henning was frank with the players, and told them to focus on themselves and forget about the referee. 'At times we can get too caught up with who is refereeing the game,' he said. 'It is one of England's strengths. They take the referee out of the equation. They concentrate on doing the basics well and imposing their style on the game. They are streetwise and a very good side. I refereed them a few seasons ago against France, and they were a pleasure to referee. They were disciplined, played very positively and just got on with the job. If the Bok approach in future can mirror England's, then South Africa will always be in with a chance, and the referee won't be the feared factor our players believe him to be.'

11

The fourth estate

The role of the media

The influence of the South African rugby media on Springbok coaches and local rugby administrators is colossal. But the quality of the rugby media is not of the same standard. Exceptions exist in the print media, where Andy Colquhoun is a class act in his analysis of the game, be it politics, commercial aspects or actual play. Yet even Colquhoun has been hamstrung at times because of a partnership deal between MWP, a sports news agency, in which he is a partner, and SA Rugby. MWP publishes the national team media guides and the impressive rugby annual. His association with MWP has not stopped him from criticising South African rugby when necessary, but this link with the game's governing body means he does not have total independence.

Unfortunately for the rugby supporter in South Africa, there is no such thing as a free or independent media voice. Media constraints, more so in the electronic than print media, hamper freedom of expression, but then television largely determines the perception of the sport. As much as the print media hates to acknowledge the fact, television rules the sport, and in South Africa SuperSport is the media god of rugby. The subscription broadcaster owns rugby as much as rugby owns the broadcaster, and this love affair has confused those players, coaches and administrators who believe the media is there to service the game and the individuals within the game.

This makes it particularly hard for print media writers, who still try to be critics and not fans with free entry to the game. Those select few who still try to do the game a service with their writing are often on the receiving end from players and coaches, who are sensitive to criticism and take it personally. Instead of addressing the criticism, they attack the messenger. In my role as Springbok communications manager, I spent many hours trying to explain the function of the media to players, coaches and, in some instances, administrators. The impact was negligible. Many wanted to use the media as a support base, and were not willing to acknowledge the reporting role of the media during times when critical analysis was required.

Provincialism is exacerbated because of the provincial nature of the print media. The influential daily publications are provincial, and their slant is understandable.

National focus in rugby can be secondary to provincial interest during the course of the season. An example would be the selection of the Bok squad. On many occasions the national team announcement in the media was represented with a different provincial angle in the four regions. The writer was merely playing to his audience, but it added yet another flavour to the boiling pot of provincialism.

Rugby writers on the beat form strong associations with their respective provincial players, and this sometimes emerges when the Boks tour. Journalists feel comfortable with the players they write about on a daily basis at provincial level. When the journalist then covers a tour for an entire national group of publications, he tends to favour those he knows. Players from other regions would comment on the favouritism. The players' deep concern about the media's opinion contradicted their claims that they cared nothing for the press, especially the print media. Our players and coaches are definitely influenced by what is written about them, as well as what is said on television and radio.

The majority of the players take player ratings – a laugh among most of the rugby writers – very seriously. There is always the exception, but I was amazed at how upset some players would be about a rating given to them by a journalist they considered a fool. I would ask them why it bothered them. If they had no respect for the individual's knowledge of the game, why even read the person's daily or weekly contribution?

Players, like anyone else, want to read about themselves. If the report is positive, then they like the writer. If it is unflattering, they dislike him. Their interpretation is that basic. Within the Bok set-up, the rugby media was despised. Players think of the media as vultures, scavengers and a presence that has to be tolerated. Their dislike is exacerbated by the fact that some of the rugby media have never played the game, can't catch a ball and look like they should attend Weight Watchers meetings.

These were issues the players would take up with me. I'd try to explain to them that although Shakespeare never killed anyone, he wrote the most brilliant murder stories. It might help to have played a bit and to have some kind of pedigree, but it was not essential. The right to be a student of the game is not exclusive to those who have played test rugby. I doubt I ever convinced the players, and this ongoing debate about the merits of the South African rugby writer was one of the daily irritations between the players and the media.

The lack of respect is not one-sided. The South African rugby media had a similar disrespect for the lack of intelligence they encountered when interviewing some of the players. It was necessary to try to form a kind of professional relationship between the squad and media, and I was always a believer that the best coverage comes from writers who are reporters – and not supporters – at heart. There is nothing quite as off-putting as a fan with a pen or microphone. And in South African rugby there are way too many fans parading as rugby media.

Attempts to bring the press and the squad closer together never really worked. Individual journalists form alliances with certain players, and, as mentioned, a lot of that stems from associations at provincial level. The players tolerate the media only because they have to. The same applies to a section of the media, who are forced to grin and bear the self-indulgent attitude and aloofness of some players.

SuperSport, the dominant media force in South African rugby, wields the greatest influence on the average punter. Yet they are caught between two worlds: calling the game and selling the game. Their commercial motivation is to sell advertising and satellite decoders. They cannot tell the viewer too often that South African rugby is a circus, as it will have a direct impact on their own product. They have to lure the viewer to the game; rugby is their biggest investment. They spend more than any southern hemisphere broadcaster on buying the rights from Newscorp. The game is as much a SuperSport product as it is a product of South African Rugby (Pty) Ltd and SARFU. More than 60 per cent of SA Rugby's annual income of more than R320 million comes from broadcasting. This gives you an idea of what SuperSport is spending annually on investing in the game. Commercially, it makes no sense to knock the product you have just bought.

This is why criticism of Bok rugby is so mild on SuperSport. They are in partnership with SA Rugby, but the two parties locked horns after Harry Viljoen's resignation as Bok coach. Viljoen had very little time for SuperSport's Naas Botha and Darren Scott, nor were they his greatest admirers. Attempts were made to find common ground between Viljoen, Scott and Botha. In 2001, on the Sunday following the 12-3 defeat against the All Blacks in Cape Town, a meeting was arranged between Viljoen and Scott, who had been critical of Lukas van Biljon's inclusion at the expense of James Dalton.

Scott and Dalton have a good relationship, and Scott believed Harry had deliberately nailed Dalton because of the player's reputation for ill discipline. Viljoen defended the selection by arguing that Van Biljon was the form player, and that Dalton had hardly played in the Super 12. Van Biljon played a blinder against the All Blacks, and Scott admitted the next morning that he could see why Van Biljon was picked and not Dalton.

Viljoen told Scott that if he was better informed he would have known why Van Biljon had been picked. In turn, Scott told Viljoen that if he were more transparent in answering the media, then it would never have been an issue. Both suffered the informal get-together, and in time the relationship broke down completely. Prior to the Boks' departure for the end-of-year tour to Europe, Scott told me that we would never beat England. Not with Harry in charge. I took him a R1 000 bet. A month later I messaged him to find out where he wanted the money paid. England had beaten us 29-9, and Scott had won the wager. He didn't want the money, but he did want a new Bok coach.

Rudolph Lake of *Rapport* also had a few altercations with Viljoen, the most heated of which occurred after Viljoen picked Victor Matfield ahead of Johan Ackermann for the All Blacks test in July 2001. Lake verbally abused Viljoen after the press conference for dropping Ackermann, a Cats player. Lake, who operates out of Johannesburg, seems to be loyal to any team from the Ellis Park headquarters. Viljoen was stunned at the outburst, and was unwilling take part in the discussion, as it was unfolding in front of several South African journalists, among them the Cape Town-based Gavin Rich.

Viljoen told me to take up the matter with SA Rugby and Lake's publication. I contacted Bokkie Gerber, *Rapport*'s sports editor, and he apologised on behalf of Lake. He said he would take care of the matter. Later in the year, Gerber and Lake met with Viljoen for dinner, where Harry played the good guy and acknowledged how much he needed their publication's backing. The meeting was vital, and Lake, who covered the end-of year-tour, was sympathetic to Viljoen despite two defeats against France and England.

Rapport's goodwill towards Harry and the Boks was obvious in their reporting, but in 2001 the relationship between Harry and SuperSport deteriorated. This complicated my professional relationship with Gert Roets, the SuperSport sports editor and producer of *Boots & All*, the weekly rugby progamme. Roets felt that our association could be healthier, and to his credit he requested a meeting with Harry and me to try to establish a suitable working relationship. He explained to Harry where he felt SuperSport could improve, and Harry, in turn, conceded that he could be more accessible in certain areas.

Harry told Gert that the negativity of *Boots & All* annoyed him, and that it caused unhappiness in the squad. Gert drew up a list of questions, and asked me to conduct a survey within the team during the away leg of the 2001 Tri-Nations. Players completed forms anonymously, and I returned the survey to Roets. The only player who was not prepared to take part in the survey was Lions winger Dean Hall, who felt it unfair for him to pass judgement on another person's career. Dean thought it was up to SuperSport to employ who they thought were capable of doing the job. I respected his stance.

This is what I submitted to Gert Roets in answer to their questions:

What do you think is right with *Boots & All*?
A third of the squad does not watch the programme because they have in the past found it negative and boring. Of those who do watch, they enjoyed the concept of a highlights package, the offbeat features on players (although they feel these are done too infrequently) and the personal interviews.

What do they think is wrong with *Boots & All*?
Too many ill-informed people have too much influence. In particular, Dan Retief and Andy Capostagno discredited the show, whereas the hosts should be enhancing the product. Cappy and Dan featured in every one of the squad's

proposals of what needs to change. Their criticism of Cappy is that he lacks understanding of the game and is opinionated about a subject of which he knows little. They also feel he is extremely negative about the Springboks and gets very personal in his attacks on players. They detect a British bias. They reckon Dan is very out of touch with what is going on. He is not actively on the beat, yet presents as someone in the know. They also question his motives in his criticism. There is a feeling among the squad that he is against Harry, and it reflects in everything he says during the show.

What would they like to see more of in *Boots & All*?
Players from the modern era talking about the modern game. The Boks feel too many players, not in the loop, are involved. They want guys involved who have just finished playing the game or are still playing the game. People whose opinions they respect. Again, they would like to see a shorter highlights package and a lot more analysis of the game as opposed to just opinions of a test match or Super 12 and Currie Cup matches.

What would they like to see less of?
Again, they want to see shorter highlights and a lot less of Cappy and Dan.

What are the thoughts on presenters?
On the presenters, the feedback was pretty unanimous. All seem to enjoy Darren and the role he plays. They also don't have a problem with Naas, although the general feeling was that they would like to see him more involved in the field, e.g. attending practices and matches ... so that his opinion can be influenced by what he sees as opposed to what he hears. As was answered earlier, there is very little respect for Cappy and Dan. As with the one criticism of Naas, they also feel that the only time they see Cappy or Dan is at a game, and that they really don't have an idea what is going on behind the scenes.

What are the thoughts on our commentators?
They enjoy Blades [Hugh Bladen] because he has a passion for the game and for the Boks. He calls the game with enthusiasm and gusto and it makes the mistakes bearable. They would like to hear less (as in nothing) from Cappy and Guy Kebble. Too negative and too anti-Springboks and SA teams in the Super 12. In Afrikaans they don't enjoy Uli Schmidt (accusing him of being an ex-player caught up in his own importance and always harking back to his days as a player).

What ideas do the players have that will improve the rugby coverage?
They would like to see a lot more offbeat stuff; behind the scenes and analyses. They want the focus to be on the players. This was highlighted in a previous question, where they answered that they want more player involvement, more fun and a light-hearted side to things where people can see the person behind the player. On a serious note, good and accurate analysis – an idea being

that the Bok technical adviser should play a greater role in this analysis (in conjunction with the *Boots & All* panel). This would help the viewer obtain an accurate assessment of what the team is trying to do, and it can then be discussed whether or not they are succeeding.

I took the comments with a pinch of salt, as I knew how sensitive players are to criticism. I also knew that before I joined the Boks, the majority of the players couldn't stand me. Because I was critical of their performance and willing to raise issues, they regarded me as a troublemaker. It comes with the territory. I knew Cappy had upset them with his off-the-cuff remarks, but I enjoyed his commentary. However, I took him more seriously in his newspaper columns, where there was no restriction on what he wrote. On SuperSport he was bound by the partnership with SA Rugby. He could not be too critical, so he chose to be sarcastic and patronising. I thought the players' criticism of Dan being office-bound and uninformed was valid. I knew that Dan's problem with Harry indirectly stemmed from a problem he had with me. Perhaps Dan felt Harry should have appointed someone more experienced to advise him ... someone like Dan Retief?

I had no problem with Dan's game analyses, and will always respect his achievements as a rugby journalist, but if he was trying to get at me by criticising Harry, he was going too far. When Dan had worked at the *Sunday Times*, he was considered the leading rugby writer in the country. He had an independent voice with which to express his views. When he moved to SuperSport he lost his forum, and very soon his identity.

SA Rugby bosses were angered by Dan's criticism of Viljoen in his SuperSport Internet columns. They argued that Retief had a personal issue with Viljoen. Meetings were called between SA Rugby and SuperSport, and the usual mud was slung across the boardroom table. Dan did not attend the meetings. SuperSport blamed Harry and me for our 'bad attitude' towards them, and for acting unprofessionally. We, in turn, blamed them for being unprofessional, as well as having personal agendas and ill-informed opinions.

Finally, Harry and Dan had it out at SuperSport's offices. The meeting solved nothing. Dan left the room fuming, and Harry wasn't convinced that anything had been achieved. SuperSport backed Dan as a rugby writer, but they also wanted a healthy relationship with the national coach. The situation climaxed at Harry's resignation, when he blamed the media for driving him out of the game. He condemned SuperSport in particular. Harry's words prompted an urgent meeting between SA Rugby and SuperSport. The upshot was a truce when Rudolf Straeuli succeeded Viljoen.

SA Rugby and SuperSport would operate as a partnership and look after each other. Rian Oberholzer hoped to avoid a repeat of the Viljoen situation, wanting to protect Rudolf. He asked for Dan to be muzzled, which he was, much to the journalist's displeasure. Dan had two options: adapt to the partnership, or leave. He chose to stay, and to be fair to him he did not have much of a choice. Media partnerships are stronger than independent voices. There was nowhere for Dan to go.

SA Rugby bosses regarded the silencing of Dan as a small victory in the pursuit of turning the media into a friend and not a foe. SA Rugby wanted the positive accentuated and reinforced at every turn. Criticism had to be constructive, but as we all know, that is a matter of interpretation. Rudolf and I presented a few workshops to the SuperSport commentators, trying to give them insights into his planning, selections and theory about the game. Senior players Joost van der Westhuizen, John Smit, Bob Skinstad and Corné Krige attended one of the workshops in 2003. They raised the problems players had with the subscription channel's paid experts. The players pointed out the perceived negativity of some of the commentators and their lack of information. Skinstad, in particular, did not hold back. He distinguished between objective opinions and those based on hidden agendas. Heinrich Enslin, CEO of SuperSport, wanted to nurture the relationship with Rudolf and the Boks. He understood the value of showcasing the Boks on his channels. He also knew that South African rugby and SuperSport would both be the losers if the Bok coach and his players sidelined them.

Heinrich promised Rudolf, Rian and Songezo Nayo, the deputy-managing director of SA Rugby, that he would deliver a sunshine attitude from his people, but there would be occasions when questions had to be asked and criticism would have to be accepted. Rian and Songezo accepted Heinrich's view, but the message was clear. Rain and thunder would be rare. In 2002 and 2003, it was mostly sunshine from SuperSport. They would give the Boks the benefit of the doubt, and we would give them exclusive access behind the scenes. Their commentators were told to look for the positive in everything, and our players were briefed to always accommodate a SuperSport request.

Viewers were mostly fed what SA Rugby and SuperSport believed would promote the interests of the game. Naming the World Cup squad live on SuperSport in 2003 illustrates the kind of partnership we were nurturing. I prepared a list of questions for Naas Botha to ask Rudolf, who was briefed on the answers in order to ensure that he came across as confident and well informed. Gert Roets invited us to sit with SuperSport's producers, and we selected player footage we wanted the public to see. The footage had to support what Rudolf was saying, and not contradict his words.

The relationship between Rudolf and SuperSport was very strong. Rudolf knew only too well that they, more than any medium, could influence public opinion. If SuperSport backed him, the public would more than likely give him the benefit of the doubt. In interview situations the questions were screened, and Rudolf always knew what was coming. The odd exception was when Joel Stransky would catch him off guard with a bit of wit at a post-match interview. Sensitive as coaches are, even this was brought to the attention of SuperSport's bosses, and Stransky was told to be nice to the coach.

The SABC and e.tv were not seen in the same light as SuperSport because of the minimal coverage dedicated to rugby. This will change as the SABC in particular tries to give the game more exposure. In print, partnerships were forged with the Independent Group and *Rapport*. The Independent Group, made up of more than twelve mainstream publications across the country, was identified as the biggest English-speaking rugby audience. The *Sunday Times* had cut back radically on its coverage of rugby by 2003, and SA Rugby decided that the bigger fish was the Independent Group. SA Rugby's marketing general manager, Gary Grant, was keen on a relationship with the Independent Group. He was successful in bringing them to SA Rugby's media bash. I agreed that the Independent Group's support would be of huge value to us. I also impressed on Gary and Rian that there were editors and sports editors in the group who would not buy into sunshine journalism. A few of them would still stand firm against advertorial content determining editorial content.

It was important for rugby's influential leaders to grow the relationship with editors and regional chief executives. If rugby wanted a better return in the way the product was portrayed, then the likes of Rian had to be on good terms with his newspaper equivalents. Magna Carta, public relations consultants for SA Rugby, spent a lot of energy on information sessions involving newspaper decision-makers and rugby's top structure.

SA Rugby also had to invest money in advertising with the newspaper group. Cash talks, and it certainly eased the pressure on Rudolf Straeuli for much of 2003. SA Rugby knew they could not buy the editorial independence of the English press, but by building a relationship through advertising, the mood certainly swayed towards the positive in most of the Independent publications.

Rapport remained rugby's biggest headache. The paper had been very critical of Nick Mallett in his final six months, and hammered Harry for his love of foreigners' input. The paper knows its market, which is white and conservative. It succeeds because it delivers to its readers what they want to read. What readers desired in 2003 was to know whether the Bok coach – one of their own – would be the one to bring back the World Cup.

SA Rugby built a professional relationship between Rian and *Rapport* editor Tim du Plessis. Oberholzer believed rugby had an ally in both *Rapport* and Du Plessis, from whom he felt that he would get a fair hearing. Oberholzer was as sensitive as the next guy to media criticism, but he was prepared to take any blow as long as the critic gave him an opportunity to have his say. *Rapport* left us in no doubt that if there was an evil that had to be exposed, they would do so, but they also agreed to the concept of working closely with the national squad and South African rugby.

Rudolf and I had to accommodate *Rapport* with exclusive information and allow them access denied to other media. In my capacity as communications manager, I felt that *Rapport* was the only rugby newspaper in the country. Its sports pages were dedicated to rugby, and if we ever needed a newspaper mate, it was *Rapport*. Despite all the marketing efforts to popularise the game in the black market, the white subscribers of *Rapport* were still the main support base of South African rugby at the home test matches.

Rudolf would write a column for *Rapport*, which I would ghostwrite in English and send to their sports editor, who would then have it translated into Afrikaans. Rudolph Lake, who was the paper's senior rugby writer, was given a free ride with Straeuli when it came to access or interviews. Straeuli was very happy with the arrangement. The coverage was very pro-Bok and criticism was minimal, outside of the satirical column 'Boela Vermaak'.

It is the worst kept secret in rugby that the writer of this column is the paper's athletics correspondent, Johan van Wyk. We also knew that if the rugby writers did not want something under their byline, they would pass it on to Van Wyk. He would attack the 'foreign involvement' in our rugby on a weekly basis, have a go at me, and be very sarcastic about Straeuli and the team. His audience was the *volk*, and he delivered a weekly formula that spoke their language. The column would have served a purpose if only South Africans could laugh at themselves. But they can't, and it takes a unique talent to deliver a satirical message. Van Wyk failed 'Boela' in that the satire became very personal and insulting, and was rarely humorous. 'Boela' upset Rudolf, as everyone whose opinions he valued read *Rapport*. We discussed the situation, and he felt that *Rapport* was getting the best of both worlds. They were getting exclusive access, but still putting in the boot whenever it pleased them.

Straeuli wanted to put an end to the column and cut Rudolph Lake out of the loop. He would only continue favouring *Rapport* if they sorted out Van Wyk. I took the matter up with Lake and Rian Oberholzer. The message I received was that the situation had been 'sorted'. For a good two months in the lead-in to the World Cup, Boela Vermaak underwent a change in attitude, and even he found the positive in Straeuli. We were told that Van Wyk was no longer Boela. I never believed this, although I knew that pressure had been applied on the columnist to hold back for a while. In 2002 and 2003, SA Rugby made inroads into controlling and manipulating the rugby media. When a few independent voices accused SA Rugby of doing just that, the standard response was that we 'understood media demands' and were not in a position to influence the opinion of a writer.

Gavin Rich, one of the most experienced South African sports writers, wrote an article for a local rugby magazine addressing the issue. He criticised the way in which SA Rugby bullied the rugby reporters via their commercial arrangements with the writer's publication. The story appeared under the byline of James Stewart, probably only because Rich feared that SuperSport, with whom he has a retainer, would react badly to the article. Oberholzer was angry about the content of the article, but even angrier when he found out Gavin had written it. The two of them enjoyed a decent professional relationship, but Oberholzer's biggest gripe was that Gavin had written the story under a pseudonym. He should have used his own name and been prepared to accept the consequences.

A few phone calls were made to the magazine's managing director, and since then the criticism has never been quite as harsh. Again, rugby's actions had squashed the lone voice of dissent. The magazine had a small readership, but Oberholzer had made his point: SA Rugby controlled the South African rugby media. SuperSport was on board, the Independent Group had a financial interest in rugby because of advertising revenue, Highbury Monarch Publications bought the rights to SA Rugby's *Fifteen* magazine, and SuperSport ran SA Rugby's Internet site. *Rapport* was also nicely tucked away in the stable for most of 2003.

The rugby writers were never paid for their services, although it was discussed as an option. I thought paying a writer was not only unethical, but also a waste of time, as they were not the decision-makers in the workplace. They reported to editors and sports editors. Also, paying a writer was just asking for trouble, because his boss would quickly pick up on an obvious lack of objectivity. On the issue of money, the media had accused me of allowing myself to be bought when Harry Viljoen hired me. For all I know, that might well have been his motivation, so there was no point in arguing. I had made a decision to work with the Boks and had committed myself to their cause. I was batting for the Boks against my old team. In the time that I was with the Boks, I was not a journalist. I thought like one, but I acted like a spin doctor. That was my role for three years, and I knew the jungle I was about to enter. Everything I did during my time with the Boks was to benefit the team or South African rugby. In 2000, a week into the tour of Argentina, Gavin Rich wrote an article about the barbaric nature of the team's initiation, and how unhappy the players were with the caning part of the ritual. The article was accurate, and I knew that Rich had obtained his information from sources inside the squad.

Joost van der Westhuizen was livid. He approached Gavin during a reception at the house of the South African ambassador in Buenos Aires. Joost attacked and Gavin defended. I backed Joost, as he was the Bok; I now worked for the Boks. A month earlier Gavin had been my colleague, and he is still a friend. But he understood the game. The media's issues would always be important to me, but my loyalty lay with the Boks. I did whatever I could to ensure they were given good press.

If I could present a glossy image of the Springboks, then I was doing my job as the team spin doctor. To be honest, it wasn't particularly difficult, as so many of the beat writers were lazy in their work. A lot of rugby writers in this country operate on press releases and a phone call to the coach. They don't know the game, and do very little to improve their knowledge. I would send out a press release and see it repeated verbatim in certain publications. The only change was the writer's byline above the story.

Magna Carta, SA Rugby's PR consultants, kept files on the articles by the beat writers. It was a taxing exercise, but it allowed me to inform the squad accurately about items that appeared in the media, and about who had written what about whom. In the first year, Straeuli used to encourage me to share the daily headlines and the significance of the coverage with the squad. The purpose was to keep the squad informed, but also to make each player responsible for what he had said to the media. However, in the last few months of his tenure, Straeuli did not want the players exposed to what was being written. Paranoia had taken charge of all decision-making. Newspapers were also banned from the team room.

Robert Denton, who had been a media officer with the Boks in the early 1990s, was famous for the only answer he ever gave to a journalist's request: 'Let's have a drink.' As a journalist, it used to appal me that Bok management thought that by buying you a drink they had won you over to their side. In my first year with Harry, I tried to limit entertaining the media socially by introducing professional structures that would provide sufficient access to players and coaches. In 2001, Oberholzer would regularly call me to his office. Journalists had complained that I never bought them a drink or took them for dinner on tour. They would tell Oberholzer that I did not return calls, had made mistakes in press releases and had an agenda against the media. Oberholzer told them to put their complaints in writing, and they would be investigated.

No one ever did. I knew who the journalists were, because Oberholzer would tell me. I asked him to judge my effectiveness according to the amount of access the media had to the squad, and the professional nature of the relationship the players and I had with the press. As an example, in 2001 more than 1 500 interviews were conducted with our players. That certainly constituted access, but it always occurred in a structured environment. Oberholzer approved of this, but advised me to be more street smart with the media. Be friendly. Be their mate. Buy them a few drinks. Don't be aloof; play their game. In 2002 and 2003 I changed my approach and bought lots of drinks. Oberholzer told me that the boys spoke a lot more highly of me. They felt I was doing a better job!

Too many rugby writers let themselves down when they cover tours because of their lack of professionalism. I am not talking about having a pint or a good time. I had lots of pints and plenty of good times when I covered the Boks as a beat writer, and while I was a part of the Bok squad. My criticism relates to the manner in which journalists cover their beat. I am judging their work ethic and not their personalities. The beat writers' laziness used to endlessly frustrate players and coaches, making it all the more bizarre how much attention their articles received from the team.

The level of analysis by South African writers is generally poor. Of the mainstream newspaper rugby writers, Colquhoun is the best, and he deserves respect. *Sunday Times* sports editor Clinton van der Berg is perceptive, fair and forthright. He calls it straight, without avoiding the issues. However, his promotion in 2002 to sports editor means he spends less and less time on the rugby beat. The *Sunday Times'* reduced rugby coverage has also impacted on his influence.

Rapport's Louis de Villiers writes beautifully, but he is not confrontational enough in his articles. His private opinions are much stronger than those you see in print. Occasionally he produces a great line at a press conference, but his public utterances are all too rare. In terms of entertainment value, De Villiers was the most popular read among the Afrikaans players. Even some of the English squad members would take the time to read his match report, as it was so entertaining.

JJ Harmse, another of *Rapport's* writers, has a good knowledge of the game, but his provincial bias is blatantly obvious. The Afrikaans dailies are very quote-driven, resulting in very little analysis of the game. The bulk of their copy consists of quotes from a player, coach, former player or recognised authority on the game. These so-called experts' subjectivity emerged all too often, with the same experts venturing an opinion on the same players. This was typical of the 'dial-a-quote' mentality that drives the dailies. Although the Afrikaans daily newspapers do a thorough job, they don't promote their rugby writers. They want reporters and not writers. It is a pity, because youngsters such as Herbert Pretorius and De Jong Borchardt have heaps of potential, but both are forced to operate within the parameters of their newspaper group's editorial policy, which is to find more value in the comment of a former player than what their own beat writers have to say.

Rapport's strength is that their rugby writers are dedicated to the beat. Their coverage of the game in this country is the most extensive, and their writers are considered authorities on the game in South Africa. It was therefore important that we used these writers to our advantage to get our message across.

We were starting to influence the flow of information from within the team through Rudolf's columns and the weekly player ratings. The manipulation of the player ratings caused a lot of unhappiness among the *Rapport* rugby writers, who quite rightly argued that they should independently allot the players the rating they felt was merited, be it 2 out of 10 or 9 out of 10.

Straeuli told Lake that his job, and the atmosphere within the team, were complicated by the ratings, and that *Rapport* had to educate the public about a player's worth. Straeuli might want to drop a player, but then the paper rated him a 7 out of 10. Straeuli wanted the paper to follow his lead in assessing the players. Lake, having raised Rudolf's objections with his boss, agreed to consult with us after every game. He would be the only journalist allowed in the change-room area. I would tell him what rating Rudolf thought each player should be given and why, and the next day the ratings would conveniently reflect Rudolf's sentiments. As mentioned earlier, the players took those ratings very seriously.

Very few of the Springbok players knew how to manipulate the media to their advantage. Bob Skinstad had his own marketing plan and knew what he wanted from the media. He had suffered so much abuse from the press that he had become immune to their criticism. When he captained the Boks, it was a chore for him to speak to the media, although he had an ability to turn on his smile like one would turn on a light.

More than any player I worked with, Corné Krige understood the value of being portrayed as the good guy in the press. He played the game to perfection, and was charming and intelligent enough to convince the media that he actually cared about them. He was a pleasure to deal with from a media perspective. Among the senior players, Joost had no respect for the media, but he played them to his advantage. And they obtained their quotes from him – one hand washing the other.

Generally players were naive, and having been a journalist on the beat for ten years, I knew how easy it was to prise information from a player. You only need one player in the squad as your informant in order to know the ins and outs of every important team discussion.

Viljoen and Straeuli both wanted tighter control over the media. They did not want our players commenting on every pertinent issue. I established a media system that guaranteed access to all the players, but on our terms. Players had to be interviewed during specific times at the team hotel and in a structured environment. It was a way of controlling the flow of information, and it also meant the player could be properly briefed before facing the press. For a lot of players the media experience is overwhelming, and they say the silliest things. It was important that the squad spoke in one voice, and that no mixed messages surfaced from within the squad. Journalists feast on inconsistencies; I had to sever their supply. I tried hard to educate the players about the role of the media, in order for them to accept that the media could never be their friend. There was no such thing as 'off the record'. If it had been said, it would appear in one form or another at some time. I would brief the players as a squad, but a lot of the education took place in one-on-one discussions.

I referred to the media as the 'beast', and promoted an understanding of the 'beast'. To conquer the animal, I told the players, you have to know it. I believed that those players who had a disregard for the press would be eaten alive by the media. They would be unprepared for the interview, give the questions no thought, and then get the fright of their lives when they read their quotes the next day. I don't accept that a player is ever misquoted. It is a lame excuse. If players prepared for their weekly press session with the same application they exhibited in training, then the media could be a wonderful medium for self-promotion and promoting the team.

There have always been a handful of rugby writers who know exactly what information they want to obtain from the player in an interview. I asked the players whether they ever attended an interview knowing what they wanted to achieve. Very few did. The players needed to learn how to play the media game so that it would benefit them as well as the journalist. This is an example of a typical media briefing made to the Boks:

What do we need to know about the beast?
- He/she is loyal to the story
- He/she is not your mate
- He/she has no loyalty to you
- You are not an individual, but a SOUNDBITE
- You cannot control the beast. You can control yourself

How do you beat the beast?
- You prepare for the contest, as you would when playing a test match
- You know the opposition's game plan
- You counter this with your own game plan
- 'Knowledge is power'
- If you know, you can manipulate
- You control the flow of information

Accountability and consequence
- This management does not accept the excuse of a 'misquote'
- Think before you talk … you will be judged on what you say …
- You are accountable for your pearls of wisdom

Non-negotiable team media ethics
- You do not operate outside of the team media structure
- You do not comment on your teammate
- You do not talk game-plan specifics
- You do not comment on SA Rugby policy
- You stab your 'mate' in the heart and not in the back

Springbok media structure
- Maximum of two sessions a week, including post-test match Saturday
- All interview requests forwarded to team communications manager
- Interviews at team hotel in set out times
- No interviews at field, unless with communications manager's approval

- No private telephonic interviews, to avoid excuses of being misquoted
- No player columns, be it print, magazine or Internet, unless approved and ghosted by the communications manager
- Dress code for interviews: full tracksuit, T-shirt of the day and *takkies*
- Punctuality is non-negotiable

Areas of potential trouble
- Watch what you say at after-match functions
- Pubs, nightclubs
- Supermarkets
- Hotel foyers
- Gyms
- Just about everywhere

IN THE MEDIA JUNGLE, 'OFF THE RECORD' DOES NOT EXIST

I explained that once the player has said something, it would never be forgotten. Journalists also need to confirm things that have happened; it was not always about a quote. Many a times as a journalist I did not want to quote the player, but I wanted him to confirm the specifics of an incident that had occurred.

In camp dealings with the media
- There would always be an advance briefing
- Who is interviewing you, for whom and potential agenda
- Team message
- Television training
- Ongoing individual education

Springbok media philosophy
- Control our own soundbites
- Look after each other
- Educate each other
- Back each other
- Put the team first
- Look at ourselves
- Take accountability
- Respect each other

In 2002, Clinton van der Berg wrote a column in which he referred to the Boks as robots. He said they revealed nothing in interviews, were dull and said absolutely nothing of any relevance. I took that as a compliment. It meant I was doing my job. The next step was to teach the players how to say absolutely nothing but to do so with style and personality. They could still be characters, even if they were not giving away soundbites. They could offer interesting quotes, if not anything of relevance about the team or the test match.

The players called me 'Soundbite', because that is what I would reiterate in every discussion. They were not individuals but soundbites. In a thirty-minute interview, just one throwaway line could make a dramatic headline.

In the build-up to the test against England in 2002, Robbie Fleck had been asked how physical the match would be. He said it would be like a war. This is how the players speak. But it was reported a bit more dramatically: "'It is war,' warns Fleck.'

That is the nature of the industry, and the players had to appreciate that the media were the scriptwriters of their weekly plays. I spent a lot of time trying to teach them to think like journalists in an interview situation. I knew which players were linked to which journalists, as rugby writers talk among themselves, especially in the early hours of the morning after a few drinks. To obtain information from a writer was not difficult, especially if the trade-off was the promise of exclusive access to a player, to a training session or to the coach. I knew with whom the players were in cahoots, and the players knew it as well.

Media is big business in rugby, and Straeuli, for one, was surprised at how big a player the press had become since the 1995 World Cup and the advent of professionalism. It was essential to maintain databases on who was being interviewed and who was writing what. Many of the writers don't keep track of their own work. To brief the coach and players properly, I had to maintain an accurate and extensive database. I had to arm the squad member with the necessary information, as the player had to have his own aces in the interview. He had to know whom he was dealing with, and what the potential pitfalls were. He also had to know the interviewer's provincial affiliation. There is no unity among the writers, which makes it easier to manipulate them. Each one is searching for his little bit of exclusivity, and it isn't difficult to play one off against the other.

In 2000 Harry called a meeting with the South African press on tour in England. Clinton van der Berg had written a story about a Bok player who had slept with a woman in the team room. The player was single, and Viljoen argued that the incident was not in the public interest. He asked Clinton whether he thought the story was in the public interest, or would the public merely find the story interesting? There was a difference. The journalists argued the issue among themselves, and took Harry's side and not Van der Berg's. To me it was not so much a case of who was right or wrong, but that the media ought to band together and back their own guy. Bok management would then have seen that the press hunted as a pack. Instead, we knew that they could be divided, and that one could be played off against another.

It reminded me of an incident that occurred when I was a journalist. Balie Swart had insulted Gavin Rich in front of several media guys. Instead of telling Balie where to get off, most of them laughed at the put-down. Journalists are seldom united in their cause, but, despite this, there are a few strong voices on the game in South Africa.

John Robbie, on 702, calls it as he sees it. He has also added another dimension to SuperSport's coverage, but the television version of Robbie is a lot milder than the rampant radioman. Don't ever forget that SuperSport is in partnership with SA Rugby. Too many of the other 'expert' commentators wear too many hats to be straight talkers. Stransky, for example, is a director of Megapro, SA Rugby's commercial agents. Naas has interests in rugby academies linked to SA Rugby, and was the manager of the national under-21s in 2002 ...

The joint ventures that I helped promote as Bok communications manager have bitten me on my return to journalism. There are publishers and broadcasters who won't look at my work because it is deemed too controversial and too critical of the manner in which the game is being run. My opinions might be harmful to the partnership. That was always the risk I had to take when nurturing these sunshine collaborations as an employee of SA Rugby. It would be hypocritical of me to cry injustice now.

However, it doesn't mean that I will stop asking questions. I'll applaud when SA Rugby gets it right, but I won't shut up when they get it wrong. The public in this country deserve a rugby media that is strong enough to operate with an independent voice. As readers, listeners and viewers, they have a right to be informed. This kind of rugby media does not exist in South Africa.

Unfortunately, partnerships between the media and rugby are in vogue, and will stay fashionable for as long as the one is prepared to financially invest in the other in a mutually beneficial relationship.

12

Descent into darkness
Rudolf Straeuli's self-destruction

In 2002, Rudolf Straeuli would often make me laugh with his dry sense of humour, brilliant one-liners and honesty, which went AWOL in 2003. On match days he would talk about 'smelling the fear' of the player as opposed to seeing it.

'I'll know if they are nervous and aren't sure if they can win,' he told me on more than one occasion. 'I only have to smell the change room. If it smells like shit, then I know we are in shit. When players can't get off the toilet before a game, then I know it is going to be a shitty eighty minutes.' I never hung around the change room for long enough before a match, so I could never test the theory. But there was always enough information in the mannerisms of the players to set my own heart racing or my stomach churning.

Calmness was usually a good sign. In test matches where the players were calm in the build-up, bantered a bit and looked half disinterested, you knew they were sure they'd done everything possible in the preceding week. A better team would have to beat them. On Saturdays when the vocals were at high decibels and each player was psyching the other up in the countdown, when the opposition's qualities were insulted or their nationality attacked, then I knew we were in for one of Rudolf's 'shitty' afternoons.

Straeuli encouraged a calm approach. He experimented with music in the change room to create a certain atmosphere. One Saturday it could be something that soothed the soul. On other match days, if he felt the energy level was low, he would lift the spirits with some pretty decent high-energy music. He also asked the players what made them feel comfortable. But in 2003 he was not so accommodating, and certainly not as experimental. With the exception of the Newlands test against Australia and the Dunedin clash with the All Blacks, the mood in the change room was usually tense that year.

I can say for certain that the Rudolf Straeuli I worked for in 2002 was not the man who defied all logic in his decision-making in 2003. Power can change an individual's personality. Paranoia and power make a self-destructive combination. In 2003, Straeuli embarked on a power trip, taking Mr Paranoia along as his travelling companion.

Straeuli and I had first met in 1994. It was a Friday evening before the

Springboks' third and final test match against the All Blacks in Auckland. The Boks had already lost the series 2-0. At the time, I was working as a journalist in New Zealand. Straeuli entered the Loaded Hog, a popular bar at Auckland's Waterfront, after eight in the evening. He was with several of the non-test-playing squad members. He confronted me about a piece I'd written on Bok fullback Gavin Johnson. I defended the article, and the discussion turned into an argument. Straeuli, seven foot tall, told me what he thought of me. In turn, all five foot seven of me let him know what I thought of him. He called me an embarrassment to South Africans, and I told him that he was an embarrassment to the Boks. He had captained the midweek side against Taranaki, which the Boks won 16-10. At the time, Taranaki were one of the weaker first division teams. On television Straeuli had described the win as a 'big one' for the Boks. I said it was a disgrace that the Boks had struggled to beat Taranaki. The argument became heated, and it must have taken a lot of restraint from Straeuli not to knock the living daylights out of me. He eventually left, saying I was not worth talking to, and his teammate Chris Badenhorst called me a c**t in Afrikaans.

A year later I was back in South Africa, and *SA Sports Illustrated* asked me to interview Straeuli. I wasn't sure if he would speak to me, but gave it a bash anyway. He agreed to see me, and I assumed he had not made the connection that I was the little guy with the big opinions from New Zealand. But he had. We ate lunch, and I apologised profusely for my behaviour, which I blamed on a combination of Jack Daniel's and Mark Keohane. He said he was as much to blame, adding that he had matured, and after five minutes we moved on to more pertinent issues.

Now, eight years later, we were in New Zealand again, and working side by side for the Springboks. Straeuli mentioned the bar incident to the team prior to the 2002 Tri-Nations test against the All Blacks in Wellington. He used it to illustrate why South Africa was so important to so many people, and why the Boks are held in such high esteem. He said that I could have settled in New Zealand, but that I had wanted to return to South Africa to write about the Boks. Now I was working with them. He told the players how tempted he had been to beat the crap out of me in 1994, but that he hadn't because it was clear I had passion for the Boks. The anecdote raised a laugh among the squad. I considered my relationship with Straeuli to be healthy.

On the Friday evening we went for a captain's run at Wellington's WestPac stadium, and the groundsman had pulled the covers over the cricket pitch. It meant that we could not use the full length of the field to practise our drills. It was a deliberate ploy that every home team uses, and it only adds irritation to the build-up twenty-four hours before a test. We knew that the All Blacks had been allowed to use the entire field, so Straeuli and I proceeded to pull the pegs out and remove the covers. We were psyched up for the match, and were not going to be sidetracked by Kiwi distractions. The groundsman was furious, but we didn't care. Nothing was going to disrupt our match preparation. It was the most confident I'd felt about the Boks beating the All Blacks in five years. There was an incredible buzz in the Bok squad: Straeuli and Tim Lane were connecting as a coaching team, and the squad felt a sense of urgency. In his first few months as coach, Straeuli had given the players a voice. He promoted open communication, as well as a spirit of confrontation when required. He wanted each guy to speak his mind. Straeuli wanted to avoid secrets, or 'bullshit', as he called it. He also wanted the guys to have fun. When I reflect on the first months in 2002, I still struggle to understand the dramatic reversal in attitude in 2003.

In 2002, the players laughed. Straeuli laughed, and he would make the squad laugh with his understated but hilarious sense of humour. In one amusing incident in 2002, Straeuli was woken up at four on a Sunday morning after the Boks had beaten Argentina. A man, his face bleeding, accused Bob Skinstad of having beaten him up an hour earlier in a Johannesburg nightclub. On telling the squad and the media the story, Straeuli was asked what he had said to the man. 'It was four in the morning. I said: "Good morning."' This was Straeuli humour at its best.

The squad became accustomed to being relaxed around Straeuli. He was hard on the players at training, but not destructive in his criticism. At times I thought he could have been harsher, but he wanted to win the players' trust through his actions, and not through fear. The Boks had won four in a row in 2002, which helps the mood in any squad, and even though we were beaten 41-20 by New Zealand, everyone believed we had little to be afraid of in the return test against the All Blacks in Durban. However, before the Durban test, the Boks still had to play Australia in Brisbane, and Straeuli knew he had a difficult week ahead because of the disappointment of the defeat against New Zealand.

The youngsters in the squad were deflated. So much effort and energy had gone into the New Zealand match, and in the end it had turned on a shocking refereeing decision by Stuart Dickinson. Straeuli, captain Corné Krige and manager Gideon Sam had stayed behind in New Zealand on the Sunday because of a disciplinary hearing, in which Krige was cited for biting Scott Robertson. He was never found guilty. The squad had left the hotel at 4.30 on the Sunday morning, but two flight delays meant we arrived in Brisbane at three in the afternoon, when we should have been there at nine in the morning. Everyone felt sorry for themselves and for each other. We were tired, and convinced ourselves that we were the victims of a scheme to derail our preparations. It was a very depressing Sunday afternoon in Brisbane.

Straeuli, Krige and Sam linked up with the squad on Sunday evening, and Straeuli immediately detected the lack of enthusiasm for the Wallabies match. On the Monday morning, he addressed the squad. He told them that it was great to be in Australia, and that we should consider ourselves fortunate that we had come by aeroplane, and had enjoyed a meal and a drink on the aircraft. He whipped out the local paper, and showed the team the lead article on the front page. Some guy had made it to Australia after being at sea in a wrecked dingy for sixteen days. He had survived on seawater and his own urine. Straeuli told the squad: 'Now *he* has reason to be pissed off, but he's just happy to be here in Australia.'

It was more of Straeuli's subtle charisma. The mood changed almost immediately, and to put the finishing touches to an impressive team talk, Straeuli told the squad that any player who was too sore to train on Monday afternoon should book a flight home through the logistics manager Mac Hendricks. Players who had been in doubt for the test on Sunday evening ran in front at training on Monday. No one wanted to go home. Players and management wanted to be a part of the Bok set-up in 2002.

We lost against the Wallabies, but with two minutes to play trailed them 33-27, after being 24-3 down after twenty-five minutes. The fightback was remarkable, and indicative of the spirit in the squad. We had a fresh approach, and the Kiwi and Aussie press wrote of a Bok team that was unlike the traditional white South Africa in the way they spoke, acted and played. We were likened to the French, and afforded the same escape clauses the French receive from foreign media. Sure, we should have won and it wasn't appropriate to clobber a few of their blokes off the ball, but in losing we had played some great rugby. The press started to write about the skills of the Boks, the game breakers and the pocket rockets, as Brent Russell, André Pretorius, Breyton Paulse and Bolla Conradie were affectionately nicknamed. No mention was made of 'Boers' or 'Boerish Boks'.

Straeuli, a walking caricature of the stereotypical Afrikaner in the eyes of the world, was doing a lot right. He was changing global rugby perceptions, and seemed genuine about an all-out attacking philosophy, which embraced what Tim Lane had introduced with the backs. The 2002 Boks did not talk about the history of the jersey or the tradition of Bok rugby. They focused on beating everyone and playing brilliant rugby. Straeuli told them to show the world they could play rugby. Self-expression in 2002 would be replaced by paranoia in 2003.

Tiaan Strauss, former Bok test captain and Wallabies No. 8, was asked to present the team jerseys on the eve of the Wallabies test in 2002. Strauss, a good mate of Straeuli's, had been living in Australia since 1996. Before he spoke to the team, Brent Russell asked who Strauss was. Russell had never heard of him. Bob Skinstad thought it very funny. 'He only played about 150 games for Province,' Skinstad said. Earlier in the week, former Australian master flyhalf Mark Ella had praised André Pretorius in a newspaper column. Tim Lane and I mentioned the compliment to Pretorius, who did not know who Ella was. Straeuli loved this kind of anecdote.

'We have some great youngsters,' he said. 'They don't know who did what for the Boks or anyone else, and they don't care. There is no baggage with these youngsters. That's a good thing. No one has poisoned them, and they also don't carry the baggage of apartheid South Africa.'

I liked Straeuli more and more. I defended him to the media in 2002, not because I had to, but because I believed in him. We had started the year not trusting each other, and I had heard he was going to fire me because he considered me a 'Harry Viljoen man'.

I'd confront him when the time was right, but when I was first told that Straeuli had said I was the first guy he was going to boot from the management team, he was not even guaranteed the Bok job. Straeuli's appointment was in doubt because, according to Rian Oberholzer, his interview had not gone particularly well. The board was disappointed in Straeuli's interview, but very impressed with Rudy Joubert's presentation. Joubert, then coaching Cardiff in Wales, had flown to South Africa confident that he was the best candidate for the job. Stormers coach Gert Smal had declined to apply for the position. The press had quoted him as saying that he was concerned the appointment had already been made, and therefore felt it would be a waste of time applying for it. He wasn't far wrong, although for a while Joubert cast doubt in the minds of the board members. Keith Parkinson was Straeuli's biggest supporter, and most of the board agreed that Straeuli's success with the Sharks – two Currie Cup finals and a Super 12 final – was a good enough recommendation. Straeuli rushed his interview, as he wanted to get back to Durban that afternoon to take charge of the Sharks training session. Oberholzer told me that Straeuli had not applied himself enough, because he was trying to fulfil his Sharks coaching duties on the same day as his interview. Joubert, by all accounts, was outstanding, and afterwards he hung around SA Rugby's offices catching up with several former colleagues and friends.

Having finished at 5.30 in the afternoon, Oberholzer invited a few of us, including Joubert, for a drink at Billy the Bums, a local bar near rugby's head office. By ten in the evening just Joubert, Oberholzer and I were left of the original group. Joubert was in fine form, telling Oberholzer what team he would pick in the first test, who he would drop from the national squad and just how the Boks would play in 2002. Joubert was great entertainment value, but he did himself no favours in boasting about how he was going to 'fix' Bok rugby. Joubert's indiscretion cost him dearly. When he eventually left, Oberholzer told me that there are always two interviews a candidate had to pass in applying for a big job: one in the boardroom, and one in the pub.

'Rudy passed the one in the boardroom,' Oberholzer said. 'But I think he's just failed the one in the pub.' The next day I was told to book two flights, one to London and one to Sydney. If Joubert was given the job, I would spend a week with him in Cardiff; if Straeuli was appointed, I would fly to Australia. During the week I had contact with both Joubert and Straeuli about the arrangements. Joubert seemed more confident than Straeuli that he had the job. What Joubert didn't know was that he'd done himself considerable damage in the post-interview drinks session.

Straeuli was given the job, and I spent the week with him in Sydney. He returned to South Africa a fortnight later, was replaced as the Sharks coach, and flew to Cape Town, where we worked non-stop on various matters in the next week. I confronted Straeuli about the rumours of my early demise. He denied them, and said he could not confirm my position with the Boks because we had never worked together. He needed a few weeks to see how I worked and to give me a chance to get to know him. We spoke openly, and I said I was committed to being involved and that my loyalty was to the Bok coach, regardless of who he was. Straeuli quizzed me about my relationship with Harry. I pulled no punches, saying I was upset with Harry for doing a runner, and that I thought he had let a lot of people down. Straeuli asked whether I still spoke to Harry, and I said we spoke occasionally, but that I hardly ever saw him. I wasn't going to rubbish Harry – he is a decent guy, but I thought he had acted selfishly by resigning, as he had persuaded so many people to join the Boks.

My impression was that a thirty-year-old Viljoen had accepted the position of Bok coach, but the celebrated forty-year-old businessman was the one who actually had to do the job. Viljoen didn't need the politics and the nonsense, and he certainly did not need the media and rugby administration to police him. Financially, he is worth a bundle, and when you break everything down, Harry never recovered from the Ellis Park test defeat against the French in 2001. That night his spirit was crushed, like a heavyweight knocked out with the first punch in a title bout he had waited a decade to fight.

Straeuli mentioned that he had heard of some 'trouble' I had been involved in during the last week of the Bok tour in 2001, when we were in the United States. He wanted to know why the team doctor had to stitch up my butt and finger in the early hours of the morning. If only I had a war story to tell, but the reality of how I was injured was far less dramatic than the injury itself. The team had enjoyed an end-of-season dinner on the Wednesday evening prior to playing the United States. It was a fantastic night and everyone had a good time. Copious amounts of alcohol were consumed, as everyone felt relief that the season had come to an end. Most of the guys had flown their partners to Houston, but I was among a handful whose partner had remained in Europe or South Africa.

Joe van Niekerk, Nike's Mark Pollard and I ended up having a few drinks in a late-night bar. A few locals invited us back to their place for a drink, but once there, the drink turned out to be a few joints. We had the common sense to leave, as the last thing we could afford was being caught in that kind of company. We had to climb a security fence to leave the building, and I went first. My jeans caught on the spike of the fence just as I was about to jump. As I tried to stop the jump and unhook my jeans from the spike, I put my right hand's middle finger through another spike. I lost my balance, fell, heard a rip in my jeans and experienced a strange sensation as I hit the ground. I felt nauseous. The spike had lodged about half a centimetre from my anus, and had torn a chunk of flesh out of my rear.

Pollard and Van Niekerk, initially guffawing with laughter at the hilarity of the fall, then realised I had done some serious damage. We walked across to the same pub we had left a few minutes earlier, called a cab and made it back to the hotel, where I went knocking on team doctor Craig Roberts' door. In my mind, he was about to perform a minor miracle. When Roberts saw my finger, he said it looked quite bad. I replied: 'That's not the problem Doc,' and dropped my rods. The doc earned his annual salary in the next thirty minutes, putting twenty-five stitches into a jagged chunk of flesh.

The team members thought the entire episode hilarious. I was the 'butt' of every joke that week. But they also felt for me, as it would take a month before I could sit down. On the aeroplane journey home the stitches burst, and I spent most of December on my stomach trying to recover. Joe, who had enjoyed a great laugh at my expense, would break his ankle within ten minutes of the test match against the US. We were seated behind each other on the aircraft, and we found that quite amusing. Neither of us could sit properly. The flight from Houston to London was painful; both of us felt like damaged goods going home.

Straeuli told me that the executive members had said that I had been involved in a pub fight. I asked him how it would have been possible for me to get twenty-five stitches up my arse in the shape of a fence spike during a pub brawl. I could only give him the facts, but said if he wanted to call Van Niekerk and Pollard then and there and ask them what had happened, he should do so. Straeuli never did. He told me that all sorts of stories were doing the rounds about me within the executive. I couldn't change what people were saying, and I wasn't going to try. I assured Straeuli of my full support for him as Bok coach, and that I would do whatever I could to make his job easier. But I wasn't going to be fucked around. I was either in or out, and he accepted that he had to make a call one way or the other.

We spent five weeks travelling the country together, and got to know each other socially. I had given Straeuli my commitment, and after the five weeks he said that he backed me. We would form a close bond, built on trust during our professional relationship, and in 2002 I believed in Rudolf Straeuli and what he wanted to do with the Boks. He spoke the right language, rated the right players and respected Tim Lane's philosophy. Those were happy times, and the 2002 Tri-Nations campaign ranks as my most enjoyable experience with the Boks. Corné Krige and Bob Skinstad were the perfect combination to lead the team, James Dalton's charisma in the team set-up added an interesting dimension, and the pocket rockets ensured an adoring audience. Black player representation was not an issue. Five black players had game time in the 60-18 win against Samoa, the most representation ever in the history of a Bok test match, and three black players starred in the 33-31 win against the Wallabies at Ellis Park.

The team was confident, perhaps even arrogant. In the build-up to the 2002 test at Ellis Park, both the Springboks and Wallabies did their preparations in Durban. One day the practice fields were double-booked, and the Wallabies had to wait for us to finish. The rain was pouring down, and they started practising on an adjacent field, with only a shed separating them from us. The Boks finished their training and got back on the bus. As they drove past the Australians, Straeuli instructed the driver to hoot. Once he had their attention, Straeuli waved at them. They looked really pissed off!

In 2002, after the Tri-Nations, we knew that we could win the World Cup. At worst, the team would make the semi-finals. The pack would have to improve, which it would, but the backs were nothing short of sensational. Their defensive frailty could be corrected, but you cannot teach Louis Koen to be André Pretorius, Joost to read a game like Bolla or ask Stefan Terblanche to step like Brent Russell. Straeuli had impressed me with his work ethic and his willingness to back Tim Lane all the way. I knew that in 2002 he had picked players Lane rated more than he did. When we talked about selections, he said that while he did not always agree with Tim's preferences, he had to give him the players he wanted in order to get the best out of the backs. Straeuli could see the benefit in this, because of the way we played in the Tri-Nations and in the two tests before that against Argentina and Samoa, in which the Boks scored fourteen tries.

In 2002, I spent many evenings with Straeuli, talking about life as much as rugby. On the away leg of the Tri-Nations he did not police the players. If they wanted to go out for a few drinks, he was cool about it. He gave them freedom of choice, and they showed him the respect expected from a professional athlete. In Brisbane, where we based ourselves for the away leg of the 2002 Tri-Nations, Straeuli would invite the South African media into the team dining room area to interview him during lunch. He encouraged interaction between the media and the players, and arranged a half-an-hour drinks session every evening, where the players chatted informally about the day.

If the player wanted a beer, he had one. Most drank soft drinks or mineral water, but for those who enjoyed a cold frostie, it was not frowned upon. Straeuli played pool and darts with the players, and even challenged a few of them to a game of table tennis. But he was the man in charge. Straeuli conducted a video session with the South African media to explain his thoughts on the game in Brisbane. This occurred in his hotel room while we all sipped a few beers. The South African journalists on tour were given access ordinarily reserved for squad members, as Straeuli wanted them to experience first hand that something special was brewing in Bok rugby in 2002.

I felt privileged to be in the Bok change room between June and August 2002. In 2003 I would be made to feel like the enemy, and I know I was not the only one who felt that way. The turnaround in attitude, approach and playing style was beyond comprehension. In only a few months, the Straeuli who I had come to respect and believe in went walkabout. The person who pitched up for work at the start of the 2003 international season resembled a politician in the old South Africa. Everyone and everything was mistrusted from the outset, a lack of frankness in dealings with the players and management was evident, and paranoia was rife.

Tim Lane had been given the boot a week before the start of the international season, the pocket rockets were consigned to memory, and bumper-car rugby was reintroduced as the means of transport to the World Cup. Having added security consultant Adriaan Heijns to the team's list of consultants, Straeuli found himself glorified as one of the most important figures in South Africa. He believed and overestimated his own importance. Paranoia replaced personality. Players who smiled at their freedom in 2002 now grimaced with fear in 2003. Brisbane 2003 was a lifetime away from Brisbane 2002.

After the Pretoria shambles in 2003, when the Boks were humiliated 16-52 by the All Blacks, I spoke to Corné Krige about arranging a meeting in Brisbane, where we were to play Australia, to clear the air. He said he had given it a lot of thought after the Pretoria defeat, and wanted to call a meeting attended only by the players. I felt it was important that the entire squad be there. Corné called one meeting for the players, and another with the squad and management.

At the Brisbane meeting in August, Corné, Joost and Robbie Kempson were the main speakers. When Joost blamed the press for a number of problems, I also had my say. I said that it was time the squad looked at one other and practised a bit of introspection. There was no trust among the squad members, and provincial and race issues had to be addressed. Joost agreed that an element of trust was missing.

Kempson focused on the practical inadequacies of training. He challenged forwards coach Gert Smal on his training methods. It did not go down well. Gert defended himself, and, despite agreeing with Kempson, the players did not back him. Typical of the South African 'yes-sir' mentality, they said they would do whatever the coach wanted. Kempson looked at me, bowed his head and hardly said a word again.

The players' failure to speak up did not surprise me, because Bok players don't express their views in a team situation. Within the squad, players believe whatever is said will be held against them, and South African players, generally, don't challenge the system. In private they are very opinionated, but put them in a meeting and they say nothing – the financial implications are too costly. If a player gets dropped because he has spoken out, it could cost him anything between R500 000 and R1 million.

However, the players did complain about the poor communication from management, the many pointless mind games, and the lack of clarity and honesty. (Not unlike the concerns raised in the meeting in Cape Town earlier in 2003.) But few were prepared to pursue the concerns. The one-sided nature of the discussion persuaded Gideon Sam to intervene, and he told the players that it was a disgrace that they were not using the forum to speak out, clear their hearts and find solutions to obvious problems within the squad. The players now had to take their destiny into their own hands and speak up for what they felt was right. He said that he did not want to read about him being a '*kak* manager' ten years from now, and one who did not give them a forum or opportunity to speak.

It was a very impressive speech, but the players hardly responded, opting rather to say nothing. I found the meeting disturbing, as it highlighted just how much fear the players had for their position in the team, and how wary they were of airing an opinion that could be held against them. They felt that they were being spied on by their own security, and that the coach allowed them no space or privacy.

Rudolf thought the session had been positive, but nothing was resolved. Issues had been aired and debated, but there was no conclusion. The week in Brisbane, prior to the Tri-Nations test against Australia, was crazy. The security situation had become ludicrous. CNN had asked to do a behind-the-scenes documentary on the Boks. It was a very good public relations opportunity for us, and I took the decision to go ahead. I told them that Monday, the Boks' quietest day, would be best for filming.

Straeuli reacted badly. He said that the players had just suffered a 50-point defeat, and he did not want CNN following them around making them believe they were superstars. He wanted no intrusion. It made for an embarrassing situation. A compromise was reached when Straeuli agreed to let our own video analyst, Dale McDermott, film the players in off-the-field situations. These included physiotherapy consultations, time in the pool and hanging out in the team room.

I needed to send the tape to CNN in London by courier, and asked Dale if he had completed filming. He said that he had, but the camcorder was missing. He thought a player might have borrowed it to do some filming, and said he would get back to me. I walked into the team room in the afternoon, and asked him if he had found the camera. Straeuli was present, and he said that the camera was not gone – I needn't worry. I said that was good, as I could now send the footage to CNN.

But McDermott did not have the footage – the camera had been stolen. Hotel security video footage showed Victor Matfield leaving the team-room door open. The door led out onto the hotel arcade, and some street kids had slipped in a few minutes later and stolen the camcorder.

Instead of addressing the player's negligence, Straeuli bizarrely ordered McDermott to tell each player he had simply misplaced the camera. Dale had to re-shoot all the footage with a new camcorder. The players mocked him about the camera, which naturally looked different. Of course they realised that the other one had been stolen, but Straeuli reasoned that if the players knew there had been a theft, they might think it was Australian management looking for game plans and the like. It was absurd. I could not believe the mentality.

I phoned Songezo Nayo to fill him in on the levels of paranoia within the team, the intensity of the security and my general concerns about the team meeting that took place earlier in the week. He told me to be positive and keep the spirits up, and said that everything would be discussed when the squad returned.

There were other problems in Brisbane. Gcobani Bobo missed a team meeting, and Corné Krige reprimanded him. Bobo went to see Krige and told him he did not feel like attending any meetings, or even training. He was only on the tour to make up numbers anyway, and the coaches had no faith in him. I sat with the reserves during the match against Australia, and Straeuli used everyone except Bobo. The midfield pairing of De Wet Barry and Jorrie Muller had been ineffectual on attack, and with the Boks fifteen points down with fifteen minutes to go, Bobo knew he was not going to play. He pulled his jersey over his head and started to weep. He had lost all faith in the coaching staff. It was a very poignant moment.

That night on the reserves bench was both testing and amusing. An Australian yob took up position right behind the bench. The crowd at the Suncorp Stadium is very close to the pitch. The players could hear every bit of abuse this guy was screaming. He singled out Bok hooker Danie Coetzee as his target, and he let rip. I have never seen a player so rattled by spectator abuse.

At the line-out in front of us, the yob would scream: 'Come on No. 2. Fuck it up for your team again. Miss your jumpers you c**t …'

And so it went.

Inevitably Coetzee got yellow-carded for a professional foul, and had to sit right in front of this bloke. The abuse continued. Coetzee was fuming. He turned to the bench, and said in Afrikaans that if only he could, he would shut this guy up. The squad members were also getting fed up with him as he continued to bark out the insults, telling the Boks how useless they were. Defensive coach Ray Mordt, a good man with a wonderful sense of humour, broke the tension. For about twenty seconds he eyeballed the bloke into silence, then turned to us and said: 'I would like to fuck him up, but you can't argue with him. He is right. We are playing like c**ts.'

Everyone started laughing. It was a rare moment of light relief.

Once back at the hotel the paranoia continued, especially after Robbie Kempson and Bakkies Botha were cited. The world was out to get us once again! Security was stepped up, if that were possible, and team doctor Uli Schmidt sarcastically let the management know what he thought of the 'clandestine' daily Bok operation.

Schmidt had blown his top in Port Elizabeth a few months earlier about the ridiculous security measures. He had attacked the over-the-top methods in a team meeting, jumping up and pulling Prestik from a keyhole in the team-room door. 'Look at this!' bellowed Schmidt. 'What is this? … What is going on here? Come on, we are not the President of America. We are a sports team.'

At a management meeting, Schmidt told Gideon Sam that he felt like an outsider in the squad. He did not know when he could enter a room or even if he was allowed to enter the room. Everything was secretive. He did not know what he was allowed to say and to whom he was allowed to speak. Sam defended the security situation, and said Adriaan Heijns was simply doing his job.

Schmidt was not convinced. He lost it further, and in a moment that was both serious and incredibly funny, he grabbed at his chest like a madman and mimicked testing for a heartbeat with a stethoscope. 'Imagine me doing this to every player every morning … "Sorry, just checking to see if you're still breathing. I just want to make sure you're still alive. I am the team doctor. I am only doing my job …" Come on!'

Schmidt sat down, exhausted at the absurdity of it all. There was silence. Straeuli then only added to the skit-like nature of the outburst by telling Schmidt, in a serious tone, that he had made a good point. Schmidt, who would often joke that the Bok set-up was one big movie and we were merely props in it, just shook his head. It was not the only time he would despair at being part of Bok management. In Brisbane, Schmidt and Ray Mordt attended a Brisbane Broncos training session. When Straeuli asked him how it had gone, Schmidt said it had been brilliant. 'I felt more welcome at their training session than I ever do in this team.' He was no longer prepared to hide his feelings.

But there was still more to come from the script of Walter Mitty. Straeuli had wanted to bamboozle the Aussies. He was convinced they would spy on our training sessions, and announced that the team would be training at Ballymore on the Wednesday night. He invited the South African media along.

At around 5.30 p.m. a South African journalist phoned, asking why training had been cancelled. I said I was not aware it had, but would find out. I got hold of Mac Hendricks, who had told the journalist that training had been cancelled. Mac said that the security consultant had told him, in effect, to mislead the media, as Straeuli did not want them there. I was furious. Straeuli had invited the press, and now he was lying to them. We would look like clowns if they found out the team had trained. I asked him why I was not consulted on the issue. He replied that he was only carrying out Straeuli's instructions.

I went downstairs and explained to Straeuli that it would be a major story if we had lied to the media and they then found out the truth. I phoned the media and told them that training was not cancelled, but that the video session would take place first, and the training session would be a lot later than scheduled. It would impact on their deadlines. If anything happened, I would let them know. I told them that Mac Hendricks had misunderstood what the coach had meant.

To allay any suspicions, I added that it was just a standard last run of the week, and that not even I was going. It would only be Straeuli, the assistant coaches and twenty-three players, as Gus Theron's fitness was to be determined. This, too, was nonsense, because Theron had already been ruled out. But Straeuli did not want me to inform the media, and they did not question my explanation. The team trained, at normal time, at an alternative venue. Instead of going to Ballymore, they went to the grounds of the University of Queensland. This is how comical it gets. They moved venues for privacy, but a student party was under way at the varsity. Squad members later told me that the Boks had trained with drunk students screaming 'Aussie, Aussie, Aussie!' all the time.

Brisbane's end could not come quickly enough. And when it ended, it was with the drama of Bakkies Botha taking a piece out of Brendan Cannon's shoulder. New Zealand would be better. I was always convinced of this, and so was the entire squad. The Boks believed that the winter conditions in Dunedin would favour them more than the All Blacks. They would play a simple, forwards-oriented game, and just keep the ball with the forwards.

We prayed for rain, and although it did not come, the late-evening kick-off in Dunedin was never going to bring out the best in an All Blacks line-up missing four of its regular pack.

The New Zealand media were very kind to the Boks in the week preceding the game, backing them and hammering the Aussies for being whingers. Corné was outstanding that week. He took on all the media responsibility, and spoke with charm and sincerity about being in New Zealand and wanting to redeem himself after the fifty-point loss in Pretoria. Straeuli was also good value, boosting the All Blacks at every opportunity. New Zealanders love it when opposing teams talk up the All Blacks and the New Zealand rugby culture.

Straeuli had settled on his team early, and picked Selborne Boome at No. 8, without discussing the selection with the player first. Boome did not believe it was the right match in which to experiment. He was suspicious of the selection, and said as much. Straeuli tried to convince him that he could add value to the line-out options. It would mean having Geo Cronjé, Victor Matfield and Boome, all tall men, starting. The line-out was an area in which the Bok coaches felt they could dominate the All Blacks.

Boome trained the first session at No. 8, and when the media questioned this, I told them that Juan Smith was not feeling well. Straeuli was thinking of using Boome as a replacement loose forward during the match, and just wanted to give him time in the position. But Boome was reluctant to play at No. 8, and after having a chat with him, Straeuli told me that the player thought he was being set up to fail. It was not the case. Straeuli really believed that Boome could add dimension to the line-out and back-row play. But Boome opted out of the starting line-up, and Straeuli had to announce a revised team.

The players were very calm in Dunedin, perhaps feeling that the situation could only improve after the Pretoria and Brisbane defeats. On the Wednesday evening, we had a great team dinner. As previously in Cape Town, the players had determined the kind of week they wanted. The preparation was more technical than physical. After dinner I went to a local student club with Gcobani Bobo, Ashwin Willemse and Lawrence Sephaka. Bobo and Willemse were our tickets in.

There were probably a thousand people in the club, and as we walked in, local students started chanting: 'Bobo … Bobo …' People wanted their pictures taken with Bobo and Willemse, and many wanted to chat to them. They told Willemse that he was the best No. 11 in the world. He was the man. You could see the shoulders of Bobo and Willemse lift. They were being treated like rugby players by the New Zealanders – and seen as darn good ones.

We had been at the club for about thirty minutes when All Blacks Jerry Collins and Kevin Mealamu appeared. They came over to Bobo, Willemse and Sephaka, and greeted them with a handshake and a hug. They told them to have a good one, and that they'd see them on the park on Saturday. There was respect among 'the brothers', as Willemse called them.

Bobo was psyched up for the game. He knew that Rudy Joubert did not rate him, and he also felt he was being set up to fail. If he crashed against the All Blacks, it would give them the excuse to tell the world that he was not good enough. He kept on telling me he was going to have a 'big one' in Dunedin. 'Playing the All Blacks in New Zealand,' Bobo said. 'It does not get better. If I cook here, they can never question my ability to go against the best again.' Bobo went on to play the game of his life in the green and gold jersey.

The day after our nightclub excursion I told Rudolf about the exchange between the 'brothers'. Straeuli had selected three black players in the starting XV, and while he publicly expressed enthusiasm, privately he was concerned. I said he had nothing to worry about – the All Blacks didn't think the guys inferior or see them as quota players. They were rugby players. I also told him that Bobo and Willemse were pumped for the game. I got on really well with Willemse and Bobo, and admire them for who they are, both as people and as rugby players. They are good guys.

Saturday is the worst day of the week when there is a night match. The day is long and monotonous. The players drift in and out of the team room, sleep, eat, sleep and try to keep themselves busy.

Ashwin and I were chatting outside the team room when Louis Koen told him there were people from Caledon, Willemse's home town, who had asked to speak to him. They wanted to wish him well for the match, and were waiting in the foyer. Ashwin was intrigued.

'Where would the brothers get cash from to come to New Zealand to watch me play?' he laughed.

We went into the foyer, Ashwin looking for some young coloured guys; instead, three white Afrikaans-speaking men jumped from their seats and charged towards him.

'Ash,' they said in Afrikaans. 'We are from Caledon. You have done us proud.'

Willemse sat with them for a while and chatted. On returning to the team room he was very taken aback.

'Wow, ' he said. 'I did not expect that.'

The match was a disappointment, because the Boks could have won it with a more adventurous last twenty minutes. Straeuli refused to introduce either Neil de Kock or André Pretorius in the last quarter, with the Boks trailing 19-11. Louis Koen had a shocker with his kicking, both out of hand and at posts. As the clock ticked down, one felt that the coaches were actually happy to finish with an eight-point defeat. Either that, or they had never believed we could win.

The press spoke to me in the tunnel after the game, and they hammered Straeuli for not making the substitutions. I went into the dressing room to prepare Straeuli for the press conference. 'Make sure they are positive about the result,' he said. 'Your job starts now.' I said they were not positive. They were pissed off that he did not substitute the players, and we had better have answers for them. To this day, Straeuli believes I set the media up to ask him about the substitutions.

After the press conference, the South African reporters were invited to the change room, as they would not see the players again until we were back in South Africa. I knew they needed to obtain reaction quotes from the players for the Monday publications. Straeuli agreed to let them in. Many players were not happy about it, but it was explained to them why the journalists were entering a place players considered off-limits to any pressmen. Some of the journalists asked me whether it had been Rudolf's decision not to make substitutions, or if all the coaches had agreed, because they could not believe Gert Smal and Rudy Joubert would have left Neil de Kock and Pretorius on the bench. I said that Rudolf makes the call, but with 'buy-in' from his coaches. I was concerned that Joubert may have told the journalists that it had not been his call, as he had a habit of chatting to the rugby writers and letting a few pertinent things slip, just to cover himself.

I asked Rudy and Gert whether they were happy with the calls, as journalists were suggesting they weren't, after which Rudy approached Rudolf and told him I was undermining him. Rudolf then confronted me. It was one of those nights, and it seemed as if it would never end. Close to midnight, Gideon Sam launched a vitriolic attack on me in front of half the team because I had dared ask Straeuli to change the Sunday management meeting in Dunedin to an afternoon meeting in Sydney. Several management members had asked me to inquire about changing the time.

Sam, using very abusive language, accused me of undermining his position as team manager. The altercation took place in the presence of several players and management members. When I responded by saying I would not be spoken to in that manner in front of the squad, asking that we take the matter outside, he used the following phrases repeatedly: 'Fuck you' and '*Fok jou*'. I further objected to a finger being waved in my face, and said as much. I was told that: '*Ek sal jou steek ... ek sal jou hard steek mannetjie*' ['I will screw you ... I will screw you hard, little man'].

Subsequent to the argument, I requested a private meeting with the coach, during which Straeuli said that the matter would be dealt with in the morning. I was incredibly upset at what had transpired in the team room, and my attitude while speaking to the coach was aggressive. He told me to calm down, and that we would speak in the morning. On the way to my room, I called Gideon Sam and asked to see him.

In his room I expressed my disgust at the language he'd used, his behaviour, and the fact that it had taken place in front of players and management members. He reiterated that I had undermined his position as team manager, saying that I had shown him no respect in approaching the coach when he had made the call on the management meeting. Sam suggested that I'd done so because he was black. I told him that was rubbish. Our voices were loud, and neither of us wanted to back down. Straeuli entered the room, and our discussion continued in his presence.

In the end I apologised for approaching the coach to request the change, which was viewed as undermining the role of the manager. I accepted responsibility for that. But I made it very clear that I refused to be spoken to in such a manner by anyone, more so by the manager of the team and a member of the SA Rugby (Pty) Ltd board. I was stunned at his outburst, as I had the highest regard for his leadership and for him as a person.

The background to the incident was less dramatic, which made Sam's extreme reaction even more perplexing. Gideon had informed the management en route to the post-test function that there would be a meeting at 8 a.m. the next morning. The function started just after eleven in the evening, we would only get back to the hotel by midnight, and the players wanted all of management to have a beer with them. Realistically, no one would get to bed before 2.30 or 3 a.m., and we had to be at the airport by ten in the morning to fly to Australia. During the course of the function, management members asked whether I could request that the meeting be changed to later in the afternoon.

We had an entire late afternoon and evening in Sydney, and it made more sense to hold the meeting then, as everyone wanted a sleep-in. I asked Rudolf to discuss the change with the manager, as I felt it would carry more weight coming from him rather than me. I assumed that Straeuli would mention that he also thought it a more convenient arrangement. Instead, he told Sam that *I* thought it would be better. Sam exploded, and afterwards the mood was very strained.

Being given the aeroplane ticket home was like winning the Lotto. Brisbane and Dunedin felt like twenty-odd days of being in a psycho thriller with such a bad plot that it could easily have been a black comedy. I needed to laugh, and I don't think I was the only one. A few days at home would provide some sanity and relief. I had to return to the real world and be with real people. I did not know it, but the week in Dunedin would be my last test experience with the Boks. Six weeks later I would walk away from it all, disillusioned with Bok management, the lies and the insistence on keeping the sport white.

The significant security presence in 2003 only added to the paranoia that pervaded the atmosphere. All telephone calls were blocked to rooms, no one was given a team rooming list, you could not contact a teammate by telephone unless you knew his room number, and every movement was policed. Players objected to the intensity of the security, as did some of the management. Heijns defended himself by saying that he was merely doing his job and complying with the job description the coach and manager had agreed on. These measures might have been acceptable if we were carrying around state secrets and going to war on behalf of our country. But for God's sake, we were a sports team, even if Straeuli did not see it that way. Heijns had convinced him we were 'targets', of whom or what I never quite figured out. However, Straeuli believed Heijns, and now answered only to himself. Anyone who questioned Straeuli, he believed was against him. He started making mistakes in his team selection, game strategy and the composition of his squad. He refused to acknowledge that he had done anything wrong. Straeuli still sees nothing wrong with the infamous *Kamp Staaldraad*, and has yet to apologise to the nation.

Straeuli lived as if he was the president of the country, always in the presence of Heijns, who had now become his personal minder. Heijns would warn him that he was a 'target', and Straeuli believed it. Bok players had never thought of themselves as a security risk in the new South Africa. Heijns, a former South African Police Special Task Force commander, convinced them that they were under threat every time they went out. There were some outrageous stories, like the alleged bomb threat during the charity Bok dinner in aid of the Chris Burger and Petro Jackson fund. When the squad left the Cape Town Convention Centre, Straeuli told me it was a blessing we had Heijns and team security, as there had been a bomb threat, but it had all been sorted out.

Heijns was very good at his job and was an outstanding operator, but he'd found a real-life Walter Mitty in Straeuli, who believed everything he told him. I don't believe for one minute there was a bomb threat at the convention centre. I don't believe the Boks' lives were ever at risk, or that Straeuli needed a 24/7 surveillance team headed by Heijns. Straeuli was starting to live in another world where everyone was the enemy, be it wives, brothers or family friends. Criticism was interpreted as conspiracy, and in every statement he would find some ambiguity to confirm a suspicion he may have had. It was exhausting to be a prop in this rugby tragedy. In 2002, Straeuli had been a rugby coach who was living a dream. In 2003, he was an ordinary man made to believe that he owned the planet. He did as he pleased, and showed those he dealt with very little respect. He told players they were in the World Cup squad and then didn't pick them. He shafted Tim Lane, and never admitted that he wanted to get rid of Butch Watson Smith. Instead of telling Watson Smith he wanted him out, Rudolf convinced Rian Oberholzer why he could not work with him. Oberholzer then dealt with Watson Smith, who agreed he could not work with the Bok coach.

Straeuli had stopped fighting his own fight. Others were doing his fighting for him, and he created a security buffer between himself and the rest of the world. One night in 2003, Straeuli, Heijns, Dale McDermott and I were having a nightcap in the hotel bar in Durban. Straeuli finished his drink at around ten, and said goodnight. Heijns jumped up, and I asked him where he was going.

'Walking the coach to his room.'

I laughed.

'He is seven foot tall. If anyone needs to be walked to his room, it is me – all five foot, seven inches of me.'

Heijns disappeared and returned a few minutes later, comfortable that the coach had been safely tucked into bed. In 2002, Straeuli had walked tall. In 2003, he ducked and dived around every corner. Mike Greenaway, a journalist covering the 2003 World Cup in Australia, relates a hilarious story that occurred at one in the morning at fast-food joint Fast Eddy's in Fremantle.

'I was getting a burger after being out for a few drinks, and I looked up and saw Heijns scouting the place,' Greenaway said. 'I then saw him motion with his head, and Straeuli walked in. When Straeuli saw me, he seemed visibly embarrassed at what I had just witnessed.' Straeuli and his security man had become one.

When Straeuli left SA Rugby's offices for the final time in December 2003, he sent his faithful personal assistant, the charming Merril Cleal, through the front entrance. Merril, an elegant and dignified woman, passed the media with her head held high, carrying Straeuli's personal belongings. Straeuli slipped out the back emergency exit with Heijns.

13

A house divided
Racism in the Springbok team

Rudolf Straeuli was very unsure about the composition of the provisional 2003 World Cup squad. Injuries were adding to his confusion, with conflicting opinions on the fitness of several World Cup candidates. He selected thirty-six players for the one-week training camp, to be held at the Pretoria High Performance Centre, and the final thirty would eventually only be finalised on the Saturday morning of the squad announcement. He did not want to make an early call on Bob Skinstad and André Pretorius. Rian Oberholzer had cautioned him against making a decision he would regret.

Oberholzer, a World Cup director, knew the ins and outs of the competition's regulations better than anyone at SA Rugby. He advised Straeuli that it was easier to lose a player following a failed fitness test than to include a star player once the squad had been finalised. What he was trying to say was, if Skinstad or Pretorius are in your plans and you are worried about their fitness, pick them subject to a fitness test. Don't ignore them and select two other players who are inferior in quality.

Straeuli was torn between trusting his gut instinct, which was to take Skinstad and Pretorius along as game breakers, or being accused of giving the duo preferential treatment. It was a difficult situation, and what made it worse was that Straeuli had about twenty different opinions pounding his ears on the subject. I agreed with Oberholzer, believing it to be common sense to keep the options open for as long as possible. From the outset, Straeuli had maintained that he needed Skinstad's game-breaking skills. He had taken a lot of flak for picking Skinstad in 2002, but the player had rewarded him with a very good Tri-Nations performance.

Skinstad, focused and fully fit, is of enormous value to any side. He has to be managed carefully, and Straeuli backed himself to get the best out of the player in 2002. Tim Lane was also a believer in Skinstad's class, and Lane's positive reinforcement about the player swayed Straeuli. The original plan in 2002 had been for Skinstad to captain the Boks on the end-of-year tour, leaving Corné Krige at home to have whatever operations he needed and to rest. Straeuli wanted a refreshed Krige to be in peak condition for the 2003 World Cup.

In the 2002 Tri-Nations tournament, Krige had led the Boks, but in two of the tests Skinstad had taken over the captaincy when Krige was forced out of the match due to injury. Straeuli was very worried that Krige would not physically last the 2003 season. But then Skinstad injured his shoulder in the last fortnight of the Currie Cup, and missed the 2002 tests against France, England and Scotland.

Incidentally, Skinstad was also going to captain the side against Samoa in 2002, but his involvement in a nightclub fight meant that Straeuli overlooked him as part of the player's internal disciplinary punishment. Skinstad was fined R10 000, and Straeuli felt it was inappropriate for him to lead the Boks – even more so because the test was at Loftus in Pretoria.

In his first year as coach, Straeuli had huge plans for Skinstad. He took the player's personality out of the equation and looked at his attributes as a rugby player. He was in no doubt that a more skilled No. 8 in South Africa did not exist. No other No. 8 had the hands of Skinstad at the base of the scrum, and none could take the opposition Nos. 8 and 9 out of the game with a pass from the base of the scrum like Skinstad.

In 2003 this viewpoint would change through a combination of bad luck for Skinstad and the addition of new coaching staff, some of whom were not convinced that he was an asset. The Bulls factor played heavily on Straeuli's mind. In 2002 Victor Matfield was the only Bok player from the Bulls. In 2003 the tight five, the halfbacks and one of the loose forwards were from the Bulls. Straeuli started to wonder whether Skinstad would be an asset or a hindrance for the pack.

Unfortunately the player, in the last few months leading up to the World Cup, did not help the situation, due to a combination of illness and injury. In the final analysis, had Straeuli's coaching support staff pushed for Skinstad, he would have been included in the World Cup squad. They didn't, and therefore the player's World Cup participation was always doubtful. Skinstad was savvy enough to have been aware of the situation. He had his sources within the team and squad set-up. He was also not fooled by Straeuli's promises.

André Pretorius was another matter. Again, had Lane been there, Pretorius would have made the squad. But the Boks' backline coach was now Bulls coach Rudy Joubert, who favoured Louis Koen as the number one flyhalf. Also, he quickly fell in love with Derick Hougaard during the five-day camp, especially after Koen announced that he had signed for the French club Narbonne.

For six months Joubert had talked down the claims of Hougaard and given him only two starts in eleven Super 12 matches. Now the young kid was being fast-tracked for World Cup glory, but only as a back-up to Koen. Straeuli was not sure about Hougaard, although the media pressure was getting to him. The press, especially up north, felt that Hougaard should have been in the side for most of the international season.

The squad arrived at the camp at the Pretoria High Performance Centre on the afternoon of Friday 22 August, where Robbie Kempson requested a meeting with Straeuli. I asked him if it was urgent, as Straeuli was in a coaches' meeting. Kempson said he was pulling out of the World Cup. He needed an operation on an injury that could be career threatening if he did not undergo surgery immediately. He wanted to inform the coach.

Kempson had been brilliant within the squad context since being drafted in from overseas. The players responded to his attitude, professionalism and knowledge of northern hemisphere rugby after playing there for two years. Kempson kept to himself, but the players respected him for his work in the gym and on the field. He was the kind of tight-five forward Straeuli felt we had lacked in 2002. Kempson had 'mongrel'.

Kempson, though, had become disillusioned with the Bok set-up. I enjoyed a very good relationship with him. In a team environment that was becoming more conservative and Afrikaans-dominated by the week, we had our Englishness in common. I know Kempson had been very put out by management's attitude after he was cited in the Brisbane test. We heard that Kempson was to be cited while at the post-match cocktail party, and team manager Gideon Sam confirmed this as we were leaving the event.

He told Kempson that he had been cited, and that it was up to him to acquire his own legal representative if he wanted one. Sam told him that the hearing would start at 9 a.m. He was very abrupt and unsympathetic towards Kempson, who said his lawyer was in New Zealand, and it was now 1 a.m. there. Kempson would be unable to get in touch with his lawyer in order for him to board a flight from New Zealand to be in Brisbane by 9 a.m.

The matter was handled very poorly. Kempson ultimately retained a Brisbane lawyer, and his disciplinary hearing started late on the Sunday afternoon. In a team 'clear-the-air' meeting in Brisbane before the test match, Kempson had criticised the coaching methods, which he felt were outdated, and suggested a change in attitude. I fully agreed with him.

The coaches were working really hard, but quality sessions are not always measured in time, but in value. Unfortunately, although many in the squad agreed with Kempson, he did not receive any backing at the meeting.

At the training camp in Pretoria, I sensed that Kempson wanted out, and asked him whether he was bailing because of the set-up. He denied this, reiterating that he had to undergo the injury.

Straeuli was also suspicious, and I told him that I knew Kempson was having trouble operating in such a conservative system. In my view the player could have the operation later, and we needed to convince him to stay. In order for that to happen, a few things would have to change.

Straeuli spoke to the player, and Kempson said he would be guided by medical opinion. What followed was a mess. The specialist's report was sent to the Boks' medical staff, but his secretary had sent the wrong report, including the rough draft containing the specialist's consultation notes. The specialist was of the opinion that Kempson could have the operation after the World Cup.

Kempson was being paid by SA Rugby, but was still on Ulster's books. Before any decision on the operation could be made, it had to be established who would pay for it, and if he did have the operation, if Ulster would resume paying him. Ulster agreed to take over the paying of Kempson's salary, as the player would be fit for the European Cup in December. Kempson was gone, but had the situation within the squad been different, I believe he would have stayed and had the operation after the World Cup.

On day one of the camp, the Boks' World Cup campaign had suffered its first casualty, although Straeuli would not announce Kempson's departure to the squad until it was made official a week later, the day before the World Cup squad announcement and nearly a week after Kempson had already left Pretoria. On the Friday evening when the squad assembled for the first time at the Pretoria High Performance Centre, Straeuli addressed the players about the seriousness of the camp and the responsibility attached to a World Cup campaign. The daily schedule was discussed, and each member of the management team was given the chance to speak to the squad about his particular portfolio.

The evening's most important talk was by logistics manager Mac Hendricks, who gave the players the relevant times of the first day's activities, and explained how the communication about each day would work. Hendricks also read out the rooming lists, emphasising that there would be no room swapping, and that no player from Johannesburg or Pretoria could stay at home in the evenings. The coach wanted all the players to sleep at the High Performance Centre.

Straeuli had drawn up the rooming list himself, and had done so for specific reasons. He did not want familiarity. He wanted players out of their comfort zones, and he especially did not want provincial cliques further entrenched. The forwards were told that they had to be at the gym promptly at 6.45 a.m. on the Saturday morning. The backs had to be there at 8 a.m. The sessions were split to accommodate the entire squad.

Clint Readhead, one of the team physiotherapists, and I accompanied Straeuli to the first session on the Saturday morning. I knew it was going to be very demanding physically, because Straeuli had told me he wanted to ascertain the squad's fitness.

Stormers and Western Province lock Quinton Davids did not arrive for the morning session, and Straeuli established that Geo Cronjé had swapped rooms.

When Rudolf told me about this, my initial response was that both players should be sent home – one for tardiness, the other for making a mockery of team protocol. But Rudolf said that he would sort it out. Quinton eventually arrived with the backs for the later morning session, and in the early part of the training Joost, in his capacity as a senior player, told Quinton in Afrikaans that if he were ever late for another session again, he personally would chase him away. Clint Readhead and I witnessed the exchange between the two players. I agreed with Joost's attitude and his no-nonsense approach to the situation.

The mood at the session, which entailed boxing and running, was very tense. Physically, it proved a demanding session for Quinton, and he was worked over. His fitness levels were not good, and his body took a pounding. After the session Rudolf told me that he would address the issue at the afternoon practice. He was going to make both Quinton and Geo realise that they should have respect for each other and team protocol by making them run the grass embankment around the rugby field. They would do it together and learn what it meant to be teammates.

During the afternoon session, both Quinton and Geo were singled out by the coach and told that they would be taught a lesson. The players who, according to the coach, had 'agreed' to the swap – Gcobani Bobo and Fourie du Preez – were also punished, while Corné Krige and Robbie Kempson were also part of the *koppie* [hill] session. Corné could not take part in the contact session because of a sternum injury, and led from the front in the *koppie* punishment, while Kempson, who also could not train contact, voluntarily joined the *koppie* run for the last forty-odd minutes. Davids, especially, was shattered. On a few occasions he wanted to quit, but Krige and Kempson kept him going. When it was over he slumped to the grass, exhausted. Kempson helped carry him to his room.

During the session, which had started at 11 a.m. and finished just after 12.30 p.m., Rudolph Lake of *Rapport* dropped in to watch the training. He asked me why six players were running hills while the others were training contact. My excuse was that none of them could take part in the contact session for various reasons. When Rudolf saw me chatting to Lake he walked over, and told Lake that he was teaching a few guys a lesson, but that he was not to write about it. I told the coach later that I had already told Lake that there was nothing untoward about the training, as the players were carrying various niggles and could not take part in the contact session.

After the *koppie* session, Rudolf felt that he had sorted out the situation and that the players had now bonded. The Afrikaans phrase he used often in the next two days was: '*As ek met hulle klaar is sal hulle mekaar oopmond soen*' ['When I have finished with them they will be kissing one another open mouth']. However, that evening Kempson went home because of injury and Geo, in the interim, had asked Mac Hendricks if he could move into Kempson's room. Mac agreed, but this apparently upset the black players, who wanted him to go back and room with Quinton. Schalk Burger, who would soon be flown in to join the squad, was to room with Quinton, but the black players felt that this was a management cop-out, and that they were not confronting the issue.

Corné had been alerted to the fact that the situation had caused dissatisfaction among the black players, and he called a meeting with them. On Sunday he told me that the black players were very upset by the incident and that Geo, in not sharing a room with Quinton, had 'taken a stand'. Now they were also taking a stand by insisting that Geo move back in with Quinton. According to the black players, Cronjé had insulted all of them by refusing to room with Davids, and by not wanting to use the shower and toilet after Davids had used these facilities. Ashwin Willemse said that Geo had shown the black players no respect as people with his actions. The only way they were prepared to look past the incident was if Cronjé and Davids moved back in together.

According to Corné, Quinton was very upset and angry about the situation. He wanted Corné to arrange for the next practice session to involve contact, when he wanted to physically 'fuck Geo up'. Corné told me that he would not accept a white player who would not share with a black player. Not in this team. Corné wanted to see the coach, because as the captain of the team he would not condone any form of prejudice or racism.

I spoke to Rudolf after Corné had seen him, and he said that he would be calling both players in to sort out the matter privately. Rudolf wanted the situation resolved before team manager Gideon Sam arrived, to prevent it from becoming a political issue. Gideon had been in Canada on Commonwealth business, and was only due in after the weekend. I advised Straeuli to send both players home and make an emphatic stand to the squad that he would not tolerate this kind of behaviour. Later, Rudolf told me that the matter had been sorted out, and that there was no longer a problem.

Straeuli had earlier asked me to phone Rudolph Lake to make sure that nothing was going to be written about the incident in the Sunday paper. I didn't phone Lake, but instead spoke to him at the Saturday evening Springbok Nike World Cup kit launch in Sandton. On the way to the launch, Rudolf informed me of his concern that Quinton was not up to standard. He was not good enough to go to the World Cup. Rudolf admitted that he had a problem with his 'players of colour' (his term), and that he was going to struggle to find six to take in the squad of thirty. Quinton was to make up one of the six, but Rudolf felt he was not good enough. Neither was Dale Santon.

Straeuli asked me whether I thought there was a chance of getting away with only four 'players of colour' in his World Cup squad. I said no, but perhaps he could get away with five if he was direct with Rian Oberholzer and Songezo Nayo about Quinton, and told them that the player was not up to World Cup standard. In my opinion, if they were convinced that Quinton was wasting everyone's time, they would approve five black players in the squad 30.

At the launch I sought out Songezo, and explained that Quinton had missed the first session because he had overslept. Any player who wanted to go to the

World Cup should have a bigger hunger than that, I thought. Quinton's attitude, I said, was not good, he was struggling to keep up with the other players, and it would be window dressing picking a player who clearly was not good enough to make the squad on merit. That is how I felt. Songezo agreed that no allowance should be made for any player, regardless of colour. I told Rudolf that I had spoken to Songezo and that he was aware of his feelings on Quinton.

On Monday 25 August, Dale Granger, a rugby reporter at the *Cape Argus*, called me to say that he had heard of an incident involving Geo and Quinton at the weekend, based on the one not wanting to room with the other, and that both had been physically taken to task by means of a *koppie opfok*. He could not believe this was happening in Bok rugby in 2003, and asked why the hell we, as management, had put the two together.

Granger also wanted to know how archaic our set-up was if the coach reverted to a military-style punishment in a professional national rugby squad. We discussed whether in this day and age players should be 'fucked up' by means of military-style *koppie* runs. Afterwards, I informed Rudolf that the papers had got hold of the story, and of my concern about the ramifications. Rudolf thought I was making an issue out of nothing. The incident would simply go away, as everything had been 'sorted out'. However, he was very upset that the media knew about the episode, and wanted me to try to find out who the source of the story was. I disagreed with Rudolf's assertion that the matter had been dealt with; it was not as simple as that. Because of the political ramifications and the history associated with the South African game, the incident had the potential to turn into a big story. It was not something I believed could be sorted out with a *koppie opfok*.

On several occasions during the course of Monday and Tuesday I spoke to Dale Granger, and asked him where he had obtained his information. He told me that Quinton, very upset by what had happened, had called his girlfriend, and had also spoken to his teammate and good friend Bolla Conradie. The incident had been discussed among the players at Western Province as well. Granger also informed me that Thelo Wakefield, the WP manager, had confirmed both the incident and its racial nature. I took this information to Rudolf, who said that he had spoken to Quinton, who had denied ever calling anyone, and said that the journalist was lying. My response was that the journalist had called me to tell me what had happened; all I was doing was conveying the message. I did not know whether his source identification was accurate or not. All I knew was that the journalist's story was pretty precise. Rudolf would inform Gideon Sam about the incident, but first he wanted me to find out more, as he couldn't believe Granger's information had come just from Quinton. Both Straeuli and Corné had asked Quinton whom he had spoken to, and he denied telling anyone about the incident.

On top of everything, Rudolf was very concerned about the black representation in the squad. He needed finality on whether he could get away with only four black players, or whether he was going to have to take six. He called Rian Oberholzer and asked if Rian could fly to Pretoria, as he wanted to finalise the squad that day. When Rian arrived for the meeting with Rudolf on the Tuesday to discuss the squad, I joined them just after 2 p.m. Rudolf had asked me to give them a few minutes on their own before joining them. They were discussing the squad composition, focusing on black player representation. Rob Benadie, a consultant for SA Rugby, and Adriaan Heijns, the team security consultant who had also assumed the role of assistant logistics manager, were also present.

Rian was emphatic that no fewer than six black players would be agreed on. He reminded Rudolf that he, as the Bok coach, had promised six, and he, as managing director, would accept no fewer. Rudolf initially said that there were only four, five at a push, but not six black players good enough to make the squad, but Rian did not buy this. They discussed all the candidates, and Rian wanted to know why black players whom Rudolf did not believe in were brought to the camp, among them Dale Santon and Quinton Davids.

Rudolf's response was that none of the other black players outside of the squad were good enough to play test rugby. Rian disagreed, saying that he would not even try to convince people that there weren't six qualified black players in South Africa capable of making a national squad of thirty. He mentioned a player such as Breyton Paulse, who along with Ricardo Loubscher and Bolla Conradie was classified as a black player who had played test rugby and was, in his opinion, good enough to make the squad.

Rudolf said he could draft Bolla in and pick him if he dropped Quinton and Dale, but he could not make up six if it was strictly a merit selection. I reminded them that it would be impossible to bring Bolla in, as the press release I had sent out the day before quoted Rudolf as saying Robbie Kempson's likely unavailability had meant a reshuffle in the combination permutations. One back had to drop out, and that was at scrumhalf. This was why Fourie du Preez, one of the original three scrumhalves at the camp, was sent home. At least that was the story spun to the media. We could not announce just a day later that Bolla had been invited – that would smack of window dressing. Rian agreed, and told Rudolf he would have to work with the seven black players at the training camp. Rian refused to accept that fewer than six would make the squad, stressing that this was non-negotiable, and that there would be no further discussion on the issue.

Rudolf showed Rian his intended match 22 to play England. Just as Rian was about to leave, I inquired whether the issue of Geo and Quinton had been sorted out. 'What issue?' Rian asked. Rudolf said there had been an incident, but that he had dealt with it. 'What incident?' Rian asked.

Rudolf told Rian about the room-sharing episode, and how it had upset

Quinton and the other black players, but that both players involved had been punished – one for being late for training, the other for not being prepared to share the room. Rian was not to worry, as the matter had been dealt with. I spoke up and said that it was not that simple; the press were aware of the story. I gave Rian a breakdown of the information the media was privy to, and who in the media had contacted me.

At this point Rian became angry, and wanted to know from Rudolf what had happened. Rudolf told him that Geo had moved out because he did not want to share with a black player, and after the *koppie* session he was ordered to go back in with Quinton. Instead, Geo opted to take the room vacated by Kempson. This really upset Rian, who raised the point that even after the *koppie opfok* the player had still not returned to his allotted room. Rudolf, at this stage gesturing for Rian to give him a chance to speak and explain, said he had called the player in again, along with Corné Krige, and it was made very clear to him that he had to share the room with Quinton, and that we as a squad did not promote any form of prejudice in the team. His only option was to do as instructed or leave the squad.

Corné later confirmed that both he and the coach had told Geo emphatically that if he wanted to have a future in this country, not just as a rugby player, but as a South African, then he needed to learn to get to know and accept the black players in the side. He had to show them respect, as they felt his refusal to use the shower after Quinton had used it made them feel dirty, and was a sign of disrespect.

Rian said that he would not tolerate any form of racism in the Springbok squad, and then told Rudolf to remove Cronjé. But according to Rudolf the player had shown remorse, and was now amenable to the idea of sharing. He defended the player's behaviour on the basis of his cultural upbringing, and said that Cronjé was not being a racist. Rian pointed out that Cronjé's actions certainly implied that he was a racist. One could hardly believe that the player was a racist one minute, but ten minutes later, after being ordered to room with a black player or miss out on the World Cup, he was no longer a racist!

However, Rudolf insisted that the player was not a racist, mentioning that Geo had even called home to his father for advice and to explain what had happened. Geo's father allegedly told him that it was okay to share with 'them' [*hulle*], as he had been in similar circumstances at the mines where he also had to share with *hulle*. Geo, said Rudolf, had had tears in his eyes, and knew that he had made a mistake. But that was not good enough for Rian, who realised that there obviously was a problem in the team, and wanted it dealt with via an investigation. Rudolf thought Rian was blowing the matter out of proportion.

'Listen to yourself,' Rian said to Straeuli. 'I am starting to get worried when you justify or attempt to justify this kind of thing. You are the coach.'

Rudolf tried to further explain the situation, saying that the player was uneducated about the way things worked in the team. He cited the example of the players no longer praying before a game. 'He [Geo] thinks the black man [Gideon Sam] has taken that away,' Straeuli said. 'I had to explain to him that this is not the case. It was a team decision that each player does his own spiritual thing.'

Rian reiterated that he would not tolerate such a player in the squad, but Rudolf continued to defend Cronjé by saying that he was not the only one who had a problem sharing, and that he should not be singled out. Rudolf claimed that the problem was not just white on black, but also black on white, and not just at the World Cup camp ... Then he mentioned Joe van Niekerk moving rooms with Gcobani Bobo in Dunedin in the week before the 2003 Tri-Nations test against the All Blacks.

I interrupted Rudolf to explain that the only reason the two had moved rooms was because Bobo snored and Joe couldn't get any sleep. Bobo and Joe were also good friends, and thus the matter was irrelevant. In my opinion, if a situation existed where whites and blacks had a problem sharing, then we had an even bigger problem on our hands than just one isolated case. Rian told us that he was taking the matter out of Rudolf's hands, and that Cronjé would not be going to the World Cup. He could not afford to have the team tainted by an incident of this nature.

Rudolf was still against dropping Cronjé from the squad. The player, he argued, added value to the team, and he warned of the backlash from the conservative white element.

'I have seen your match 22 against England,' Rian said, 'and he is not in it, so I do not consider his absence weakening your team for that match. Secondly, I don't care about what a white minority is going to think. The player did not want to share a room with a black player, and I want him out of the team.'

When Rudolf again introduced the white versus black debate and the ramifications of isolating white support, Rian said it was not a very hard choice to make: there were 40 million blacks and 2 million whites in South Africa, and he would rather live with 2 million being upset because a white player was sent home for not sharing with a black player, than 40 million black people with no confidence in SA Rugby because we tolerated this kind of prejudice.

SA Rugby, Rian said, and he as MD, had a commitment to transformation, and he was not prepared to compromise. But Rudolf said he was looking at the matter from a 'rugby perspective': 'I have to make a rugby decision,' he said.

'Don't come with that fucking [Nick] Mallett bullshit to me,' Rian said angrily. 'We don't make "just" rugby decisions in this country. There is a bigger picture and you knew the deal when you took the job.'

He said Rudolf had two choices: either don't pick Cronjé and explain it as a selection decision, and SA Rugby would then take up the racism issue, or pick

Cronjé and have him removed. Rian suggested the first scenario in order not to destroy the player's life. SA Rugby would be in a position to help the player with his 'problem'. The second option would be a disaster for the player, said Oberholzer.

During the discussion, Adriaan Heijns suggested that both players be dropped from the squad and that we move on. Rob Benadie questioned just how much the media knew, before asking whether it was possible to squash the incident. I said the media knew everything, and even if we tried to squash the story, we were losing sight of the bigger picture in South African rugby. Benadie then tried to offer Rian advice, who reacted by telling him to 'fuck off'.

'I will not squash anything, and I make the decisions here, not you,' Rian said. 'You are a consultant here. I remain the boss.'

The mood was very strained. The meeting ended shortly after 3.30 p.m., and Rian left for the airport.

14

The show must go on

Controversies and cover-ups

Rian was on his way to the airport when I contacted him on my cellphone. He was very disappointed in Rudolf's attitude and outlook, and was adamant that Geo Cronjé would not go to the World Cup. On the Tuesday evening, 26 August, Gideon Sam arrived. Rudolf informed him about the incident between Geo and Quinton Davids, and I also spoke to him, expressing my concern that the media was aware of it and that journalists could look to run the story close to the team announcement. Sam said he would deal with it. Rian had already spoken to him – he knew what was going on.

I spoke to Dale Granger again on both the Tuesday and Wednesday. After I promised not to reveal his source, he told me that Martin van Schalkwyk, a Western Province player, had given him the information. Granger asked me not to reveal the player's name to management as Gert Smal, Van Schalkwyk's provincial coach, was also assistant coach of the Springboks. According to Granger, the incident was common knowledge among the Province players. He also knew about the shower and toilet episode.

In strict confidence, I informed Rudolf of Granger's source on the Wednesday evening after training, and much to my disgust I would find out later that he had asked Rudy Joubert to call Martin van Schalkwyk to confirm that he had spoken to the press. Because Joubert had coached Van Schalkwyk at Boland, Straeuli assumed that the player would confide in Rudy. According to Straeuli, Van Schalkwyk had denied being Granger's informant. Martin had then called Dale, who in turn phoned me, wanting to know why I had spoken to Rudy Joubert about the matter. Dale was understandably upset that I had betrayed his confidence, and I assured him I had never spoken to Rudy Joubert about it. I only established that Straeuli had asked Rudy to make the call to Van Schalkwyk on the Friday before the World Cup squad announcement.

On Wednesday 27 August, at the open media day, Archie Henderson, sports editor of the *Argus*, said he wanted to speak to me. It was about an issue of which he knew I was aware. I agreed to call him from training that evening, when things were less hectic. When I got hold of him later, he wanted to know why Mac Hendricks had called his journalist, Dale Granger, to find out why he was writing the story about Cronjé and Davids. Mac had asked who Granger's source was, and if the information had come from within the squad. Mac even confirmed that 'an incident' had occurred, but that it had been dealt with and had only been a misunderstanding. On the basis of Mac's confirmation, coupled with their sources, Henderson said they would be running the story. He did not say when.

The Boks were training at Loftus while I was having this conversation on an adjacent field. The backs were on the main field, and the forwards were doing scrumming drills on the outer fields. Adriaan Heijns stood near Straeuli. I phoned Heijns and told him there was trouble coming. I only wanted to mention it to Rudolf, as I did not want to pull him away from the session. I would speak with him in detail after training. When I saw Rudolf later, I asked him why Mac had made the call. He could not answer me. I had had the situation under some sort of control, but now the papers were going to run with the story because Mac had confirmed that the incident had taken place. I had been confident of keeping the media at bay until the team announcement, as I knew Cronjé would not be included in the squad and that SA Rugby was going to investigate the incident afterwards. This would also cause minimal disruption to the team preparations.

That evening I entertained the press at a media dinner with the squad, and returned to my room at around 11.30 p.m. A message awaited me from Dale Granger, asking me to call him. I SMS-ed him back to say that I would call him in the morning, but in a return message he said it would be too late. I phoned him. Granger said that they would run the story in the morning to make the afternoon papers, as they had enough information and other publications also had the story.

Granger told me the gist of his article, which was factual and accurate. He also knew about the incident between Quinton and Joost. Quinton felt that Joost had taken Geo's side, and was aggrieved when Joost threatened to chase him away from the camp. Granger said that Joost had also asked Davids what he thought of Bolla Conradie, a question Quinton felt was unfair, given that Joost was a senior Bok and Conradie was Quinton's friend. Granger had it on good authority that Joost had also told Davids: 'Don't bring your Western Province manners here.'

Granger would be writing that Davids had requested a meeting with Mac Hendricks after the *koppie opfok* (Granger's words), and that a meeting between Corné and the black players had also taken place. Granger wanted a response from team management, and would be calling Rian Oberholzer later in the morning. I said I would get back to him.

I woke up Straeuli just after midnight to explain the situation, after which we also woke up Gideon Sam. We called Rian at about 1 a.m. Rian's advice was to have the player removed from the camp immediately, but both the coach and manager thought this unreasonable, preferring to discuss the matter when everyone was a bit calmer.

Adriaan Heijns called both Corné and Joost to the room to discuss Granger's allegations of their involvement in the incident. Corné confirmed that the black players were upset by Cronjé's actions, but Joost denied he knew anything at all. Rudolf reminded Joost that he did know about the incident, as he had personally spoken to Quinton at the gym. Joost suddenly remembered, but said that he had not spoken to Quinton after telling him off.

I asked Joost if he had ever used the words 'Western Province' when speaking to Davids, and he repeated that he hadn't spoken to the player. We discussed how best to resolve the matter. I explained the possible media implications to Rudolf and Gideon, and mentioned that there was a coloured faction in Cape Town who knew about the incident, and who were opposed to the Boks because of the lack of black representation. I had been informed that Thelo Wakefield, the WP manager, and Peter Jooste, a WP administrator, knew of the incident, as did the coloured journalist Andrew Koopman, but I could not confirm this because of the hour.

Gideon retorted that these guys were not anti-Boks; they were anti-black. According to him, the Africans in SA Rugby were going to show the coloureds that they could administrate the game. Gideon was very vociferous, and used colourful language.

I was asked how I knew for sure that Granger was going to write the story, and I said he was not bluffing. Granger had too much information, and it was too accurate. Heijns said that no proof of the story existed, and Rudolf added that we could not respond to something when there was nothing on paper. I explained that the story had not been written yet, as the newspaper would only appear on Thursday, mid-morning, in Cape Town. For all I knew, the story was still in the journalist's head, or on his laptop, or in the work queue on the newspaper's computer system. Granger had told me what he was going to write; I had not seen the copy. Straeuli and Heijns asked whether I could obtain a copy of the story once it was written, and I promised to try, but I knew that Granger was not supposed to send out a copy. Everyone was exhausted. Gideon suggested we try to get some sleep; we would reconvene at 6 a.m.

Straeuli and Sam went to bed, and Heijns, Van der Westhuizen, Krige and I left at around 3 a.m. I went back to my room, called Granger, and asked if it would be possible to see a copy of his piece before management would comment. But he was only planning to write the story at 4 a.m. for his 7 a.m. deadline. Also, he would only be able to get hold of Rian, for his comments, at 6.30 a.m. I conveyed to him that the coach and manager felt he was bluffing, as they had seen nothing in print. Granger agreed to write the article before 5 a.m. and send me a copy, which I could show the coach and manager as proof that the story was going to be published. It would not contain Oberholzer's quotes, as Granger would only speak to him later.

Granger e-mailed me a copy of the first-edition story, which I printed out, and then I called Rian. I read the article to him to prepare him for his 6.30 a.m. call. Rian would tell Granger that an investigation was to be conducted into the matter, and that the player had been removed from the camp that morning.

After our conversation, I showed the coach and manager the printout. Joost and Corné joined us. Initially, Rudolf and Gideon discussed the possibility of Geo making a statement, apologising to the nation for what he had done. He would admit that he had made a mistake, and was prepared to receive counselling. They felt the reconciliation theme was the best way forward for the team, and had also touched on the subject earlier in the morning. But Rudolf would need to spend time with Geo to establish if the player would be willing to do this. I mentioned that we had about thirty minutes before the newspaper's deadline, and the idea was shelved. Everyone agreed that it was more important to save both players' careers, and that the team's World Cup preparations should not be damaged because of the matter.

All four men studied the printout, which mentioned Joost's alleged provincial remarks, as well as Uli Schmidt's comment, made a few years back, that black players could not play rugby. While reading the statement to Rian earlier, he had said that the paragraph referring to Uli was unfair, as he had apologised for the remark. Rian asked me to speak to Dale about removing the paragraph, as it had nothing to do with the current incident. I mentioned it to Dale, who agreed that it was irrelevant, and omitted the reference from the final story.

Rudolf wanted other details either removed or amended. I told him that I did not have the power to remove things. The Uli paragraph had only been deleted because Dale had acknowledged that it was not relevant to the current situation. This was not a press release we were sending out, but a copy of a news story. We were not even supposed to have a copy, and the only way I had managed to prise it out of Granger was to tell him that before we commented, we wanted proof that he had written the story. Rudolf and Gideon wanted a copy of the amended version, with Rian's comments. I said I would call both Archie Henderson and Dale Granger, but I doubted they would consent to this. It was not allowed. I made the calls, but naturally neither would send me a copy.

Dale not only deleted the Uli Schmidt paragraph, but also softened the allegations of provincial bias initially directed at Joost. I eventually obtained a printout of the story off the Internet just after 8.30 a.m., and took it to Gideon and Rudolf. Gideon informed me that we were waiting for an SA Rugby statement to arrive, after which he would address the team. The statement arrived at 9.45 a.m., and Gideon addressed the team shortly afterwards.

At the meeting I was stunned at how the focal point was being shifted towards SA Rugby (Pty) Ltd. Gideon read out the statement, emphasising that it was SA Rugby that wanted the investigation, and that management and the team had to abide by their decision. Both Geo and Quinton were seated with the squad during all of this. Rudolf then addressed the team, and said that they should not believe what they read in the papers and that the truth will out. He offered his support to both players during this 'difficult period'. Corné then told the players that the squad stood behind them, but that everyone had to accept the outcome of SA Rugby's investigation, and 'move on'.

Not one of the three speakers mentioned racism, prejudice or the abuse of team protocol. I was amazed that this incident was not used to reinforce to the squad that nothing of this sort would be tolerated. In my opinion, both players' departure was glorified. Geo would go home and be back once everything had been cleared up; Quinton would spend a few days at a hotel to avoid media pressure. Ironically, he would have been more protected in the squad set-up, because the squad was off-limits to the media.

Rudolf's concern was that the Bulls players would react negatively to Quinton remaining and Geo going.

Rian informed me telephonically that SARFU's legal consultant, Adri Brandt, and SARFU's head of disciplinary matters, Christo Ferreira, would be arriving in Pretoria at around 2 p.m. to conduct interviews and complete an investigation into the incident. Early on the Thursday evening I needed to talk to Rudolf, but could not reach him. I tried Adriaan Heijns, who told me that they were at the hearings. Team management had not informed me about the hearings, and I did not even know where they were being held. When I asked Heijns, he mentioned a hotel without divulging its name.

I asked if Mac Hendricks was there, and Heijns confirmed that he was, as well as a few of the players. I later established that other than Quinton and Geo, Lawrence Sephaka, Dale Santon, Gcobani Bobo, Joost van der Westhuizen and Corné Krige were interviewed. Later that evening I asked to see Rudolf, as I was disturbed that I had not been informed about the proceedings. I was not being trusted with the information in my capacity as communications manager. Rudolf said he would see me in the morning.

I confronted Mac Hendricks and asked him why he had called Dale Granger when he, as logistics manager, had nothing to do with the media. I wanted to know whether he had been instructed to do so by Gideon or Rudolf, which Mac denied, saying he'd thought that he could save the situation. He had taken action on his own initiative, thinking he could help resolve the matter. I reminded him that the media was my field of expertise – why had I not been consulted? He could not give me an answer.

Rudolf called me just after 6 a.m. on the Friday morning, 29 August, and we met on the balcony next to his room. He informed me that he was going to put some tough questions to me, and he wanted some honest answers. I agreed, but said that I, too, would be putting some tough questions to him, and I also wanted honest answers. He asked me if I thought Geo was a racist. I certainly thought he was, given the Quinton incident, the conversation I had been privy to between Rian and Rudolf, and information received from within the team. I had also been in the physio room when Geo inquired '*of die apie nog kolf* ['is the monkey still batting'], referring to Monde Zondeki in the cricket test match between South Africa and England. I had mentioned this remark to Rudolf at the time, and had expressed my concern at its racial nature. Back then, Rudolf had told me not to blow it out of proportion; he would 'sort it out'. I had also mentioned it to Corné when he gave me feedback on his meeting with the black players.

When Rudolf asked me whether I felt there was racism in our team, I replied that there definitely was, citing examples. It was my job to canvass opinion all the time, to be the eyes and ears of management, and to pre-empt potential conflicts. The aim was not to squeal on any individual, and this was what upset me when Rudolf said that Quinton was not a team player because he spoke out about the Geo incident. He added that we should not rule out that Quinton could be playing the race card trick for fear of losing out on squad selection. I took exception to this, and said that I, too, would have spoken out if it had happened to me. We had to look at the incident in the context of our country's history and our rugby history. The black player felt he had been prejudiced because of a white player's actions.

Black players felt subtle forms of prejudice and racism we were unaware of. They felt that white players received ample playing opportunities, but opportunities were limited for them. They were still making up a quota, be it four, five or six. The coaches did not instil confidence in the black players, but they could not complain for fear of being prejudiced further. I explained this to Rudolf, who became defensive, asking if they had ever accused him of being a racist. They hadn't, but they did feel uncomfortable with certain statements that had been made, which I expanded on the next day when we spoke about the race issue prior to the World Cup squad announcement.

Rudolf wanted to know whether I thought he was a racist. I said no. However, he was culturally too close to the Cronjé issue and too concerned about how his stance would be interpreted by the whites, especially up north. Because he had previously worried about the impact Cronjé's axing could have on him in the community, I suggested that he was more concerned about the consequences of acting against Cronjé than about the incident itself. His judgement was being clouded by these considerations. I also mentioned the conservative attitudes that were being promoted in the composition of the team. Rudolf maintained that he would root out racism at the boot camp, which was to start the day after the squad announcement. I said he could not. It would take time, and for us to fix it we first had to acknowledge that a problem existed. There is more to racism than one player verbally abusing another. It comes in various shapes and forms.

Then Rudolf told me that he, Gideon, Corné and Joost had come to the conclusion that I had leaked the story to the media. I was, to say the least, shocked. I wanted to know what this allegation was based on, but he could not give me a straight answer. The way the story had developed made them suspect me, and they did not trust me. I made it clear that if I had wanted to leak the story, I would have done a better job, and I would have caused myself less stress. I certainly would not have woken everyone up at midnight and worked through until 2 p.m. later in the day to try to ensure that the situation was handled properly.

I took great exception to the accusation, and told Straeuli I would meet individually with the other guys who supported the charge. Straeuli also wanted to know whether I had ever manipulated his decisions through the media, which I never did. After all, I only needed to speak to him and convince him of my point of view if I wanted to manipulate a decision; I certainly did not need to complicate matters by working through the media. All I had to do was knock on his door and talk to him.

Straeuli asked what my greatest criticism of him was, and I mentioned his paranoia: the clandestine manner in which the team was being run, lending his ear to people who further fuelled his paranoia, the lack of communication, the mind games played with individuals, the constant changing of arrangements, the inconsistency of his decision-making, and trying too hard to please every provincial and racial faction before making a decision. He had to make the calls, good or bad, and live or die by those decisions.

While contradictions abounded in his selections, he wanted total control, and felt he could fix every situation. I added that we also had to seriously address the racial issues in our team, specifically referring to the Cronjé incident as an example of a problem he felt he could fix internally, but which was bigger than that. We discussed other rugby matters as well, and at the end he asked where we stood. I replied that I wanted to go to the World Cup, but that things would have to change. I could not operate without trust.

Rudolf wanted to speak to Rian, and I recommended he fly to Cape Town to see him for a private meeting, as their relationship would have taken a severe pounding after Tuesday's discussion. Rudolf flew to Cape Town later that Friday morning.

Afterwards, I informed Gideon of the details of my discussion with Rudolf. I reiterated that I would not be party to any racial cover-up in the Bok squad. It might be my job to spin stories around selection and match results, but I refused to lie when it came to prejudice or racism.

I mentioned my concerns about his management style, which lacked consistency and sensitivity to the mood in the squad. Gideon said the inconsistencies had come about because of the ongoing changes in the daily schedules, which he blamed on Rudolf. I alluded to the build-up to the All Blacks test in Pretoria, which had been a shambles, especially the fact that no one was prepared to tell anyone where the squad was staying on the Friday night. It created uncertainty and anxiety.

Gideon told me that not even he, as manager, had known where we would be staying, and agreed the week had been a 'disaster' (my word, not his). I also expressed my disappointment at the lack of trust in me, and referred him to several incidents where I felt I, in my capacity as communications manager, had not been trusted with information necessary to do my job.

Rian called me after my meeting with Gideon to tell me he had seen the investigators' findings, and that it smacked of a team cover-up. Nothing appeared to have happened, and he refused to believe this, given the conversation he had had with Rudolf a few days earlier. I was appalled, and asked why I was never questioned. He could not give me an explanation.

I made it clear to Rian as well that I would not be implicated in covering up a racial incident. It went against everything I stood for, and there was no way I would accept the investigation's findings, knowing what had gone on. I could also not work with people who had lied about an issue such as this. He said he would call me once he had met with Rudolf.

When I spoke to Corné on the Friday afternoon, I expressed my disgust at having been falsely accused of leaking the story, and he apologised for doubting me. I argued that I had had three years of opportunities to 'sink' the team – why would I leak stories now, five weeks before the World Cup? I added that the issue was not about who spoke out, but about the incident itself. Corné could not explain why he had suspected me, but admitted that when someone plants enough seeds of doubt, you start doubting. Naturally, I asked him who had planted the 'seeds of doubt', and he named Adriaan Heijns.

I told Corné that I would speak to Adriaan about this, and continued talking about the Cronjé incident, reminding him that he had informed me of the serious-ness of the situation after his meeting with the black players. Why had he felt the need to see the coach after the black players' meeting if the matter had not been serious? He agreed that it was serious. I also reminded him of his statement that he would not tolerate any racism in the team, and that any player who would not share with a black player did not belong there.

I wanted to know why he had not told the real story at the hearing. Rian had informed me that Corné's evidence to the investigating team had been vague. I asked Corné why this was so. He replied that he did not want to be the person responsible for ending another player's career in this country, or destroying a player's life. He felt he had given the investigators enough information for them to dig deeper, without him being responsible for sinking Cronjé.

I told him we could not wish away the situation, and that it had to be dealt with. Corné grasped the seriousness of the matter, and agreed that Cronjé could not go to the World Cup. He also agreed with me that no fewer than six black players should be included in the squad. I told him that I knew Gcobani Bobo had met with him in Brisbane and explained his unhappiness about simply making up black numbers on the tour. Bobo had been late for a meeting and was fined. He told me in private that he had felt like not pitching up at all, and that he had expressed his feelings to Corné. The Bok captain had said that he was aware of the issues, and that they would be addressed.

The final person I confronted about the allegation made against me was Adriaan Heijns, who admitted that he had assumed I was responsible for the leak, but that he was wrong. He apologised. I was extremely pissed off, and told him as much.

Later in the afternoon Rian called me, and in a conference call we discussed the press release that would go out following the investigation into the Cronjé incident. Apparently, evidence of racism was inconclusive. When I suggested that such a finding would evoke angry reaction and allegations of a cover-up, which I also felt it to be, and suggested that they at least admit that an incident had occurred and that team protocol had been compromised, Rian interrupted me and said that his investigators had found no evidence of an incident.

'That's great,' I said, 'because the coach has fucked them both up physically for an incident, and the logistics manager has admitted there was an incident to the media. Now your investigating team cannot even find evidence of an incident.'

Based on the findings, the team protocol contravention was worked into the press release, and it was agreed that it would go out on Saturday afternoon so as to minimise reaction. Cronje's omission and let-off would be secondary news to the announcement of the World Cup squad.

I spoke to Rian privately a while later, and again expressed my concern. I asked him if the squad had been finalised, and he said that it had. I asked him who the two flyhalves were. He said Koen and Pretorius. On the Friday evening I was having dinner with Bok public relations manager Anne Lee Murray, when at around 9.45 p.m. she received an SMS from Zelda le Grange, PA to former president Nelson Mandela. Mr Mandela was looking for Rudolf urgently. The SMS inquired whether Cronjé was in or out. I could not get hold of Rudolf on his phone, and contacted Adriaan Heijns, who said that Rudolf was with him and that they were talking to Geo Cronjé near the player's house in Pretoria.

Rudolf was trying to convince Geo to go for counselling, which Rudolf confirmed to me on the Saturday morning. It was a remedy discussed in Cape Town between Songezo Nayo and Rian Oberholzer. I told Rudolf that Mandela was looking for him. He said he had already spoken to him, but did not expand on the details of the conversation. I called Rian Oberholzer and informed him that Mandela was getting involved, should he not be aware of it. It was the first he had heard of Mandela's phone call to Straeuli.

On Saturday 30 August, Rudolf met with his assistant coaches to finalise the squad. I spoke to Rian shortly after this meeting, and he informed me that there had been one change to the squad: Pretorius was out and Hougaard was in. Straeuli did not want to take a chance on an injured player. I met with Rudolf later in the morning, and he showed me the squad, repeating what Oberholzer had told me: he was not going to risk a player struggling with fitness.

SA Rugby would be releasing the statement on Geo at around 12 p.m. When Straeuli saw the release, he lost it. The release stated that if any new evidence came to the fore, SA Rugby would revisit the situation. Straeuli felt SA Rugby was leaving the incident hanging in the air. He wanted the release changed, threatening that if it were not he would not announce the squad.

The situation became very tense. To Straeuli it was a clear indication that SA Rugby wanted to 'sink' him and hang him out to dry. In the current situation, the squad would go to the World Cup under suspicion of racism. Straeuli did not want that. He also maintained that if reporters attacked Geo in the media, he would never go for counselling. He did not want Geo to be branded a racist or his career destroyed. Straeuli contacted Songezo Nayo, wanting to call off the team announcement. He also left a message for Rian, who was flying to Johannesburg from Cape Town, saying he was not going to announce the squad.

In the meantime, Gideon, Rudolf, Corné and I held lengthy discussions about the implications of the Cronjé incident. I again raised the issue of racism in the squad. Adriaan Heijns said it was not for us to fix the problems of South Africa, but of the team. That was my point exactly: before we could fix it, we had to acknowledge that it existed. We had a race problem in the squad and it was causing serious problems. Rudolf asked why everything had run smoothly in 2002, and I told him to look at the squad composition, both players and management. Corné agreed, saying that the Bulls players were a problem. I added that the black players felt isolated by the Bulls players.

Corné mentioned an incident that had occurred when a few Bulls players were leaving the gym, and a group of black supporters wearing Bulls jerseys approached them for autographs. The Bulls players walked off in another direction, and Corné spoke to the supporters and signed their jerseys. Afterwards, he took up the issue with the Bulls players, explaining how the Boks and every province needed black support. He was upset by their attitude towards their black supporters. I said that racism came in various forms, and the worst was when black players were alienated in subtle ways. I mentioned examples of black players telling me that a white player's attitude was different when he was around other white players, as opposed to when he was on his own in the company of black players. Rudolf wanted to know whether black players had ever had an issue with him. I said no, but that Bobo had mentioned a conversation between the two of them in the week after his initiation. The tradition is for the new caps to sit with the coach. Bobo was chatting to Rudolf, and the coach told him how well he had done to make the team, and that he was there on merit (something Bobo took exception to, as it implied that not everyone was there on merit). He says the coach, in praising him, said that he owed it to 'his people' not to mess up the opportunity, as players such as Owen Nkumane and Kaya Malotana had done before him.

I also recounted another incident involving Bobo. Following his initiation, Bobo had complimented Joost on playing eighty-plus tests, and called him a Bok icon. This occurred in Port Elizabeth after the test against Argentina. Joost told Bobo that he had the chance to be an icon for 'his people'. Bobo's feelings were that he wanted to be an icon for all South Africans, not just for black people.

Bobo told me on the night before the World Cup squad announcement, in the presence of physio Clint Readhead, that he had a 'history' with Bok assistant coach Rudy Joubert, which dated back to when he was nineteen. Bobo had given up playing rugby. Rudy, then SARFU's director of coaching, was furious that they later wanted to invest more time and money in him, a sentiment he bluntly shared with Bobo. Now Joubert was coaching Bobo at national level, and the player felt the prejudice during the training runs. He might be given an opportunity, but the white player would be given more than one opportunity.

I asked Bobo about the investigation, having been told that he had revealed nothing when questioned. His response was that black players were in the minority, and that the subtle prejudices would always exist. The best approach was to say nothing and get on with making the World Cup squad. Bobo wanted to be selected for the World Cup, and speaking out would count against him.

When I approached Ashwin Willemse, he asked me if I had been sent to canvass opinion and find out what the black guys were thinking. I had, but my intention was not to burn the black players. I wanted to try to find a solution, because we had problems in our team set-up and no one was prepared to tackle the issues. Willemse and I had spoken at length overseas about the subtle forms of prejudice within the squad. He seemed unconvinced that there was a solution, saying an open forum or one-off meeting solved nothing when you look at the colour representation in the squad. The black players were in the minority. He also said that when Quinton Davids initially spoke to him about the Cronjé incident, he told Davids to ignore it and accept that this was the way things were. When Davids could not handle the situation, the black players advised him to see Mac Hendricks.

Willemse said he did not care for colour, but that he wanted respect for his ability as a rugby player and as a human being. He was willing to offer that to every player and management member in the squad. At the time, he was thinking of going overseas in 2004 to play club rugby, as black players were constantly up against it in South African rugby. He mentioned that he had been made to feel like an outsider from day one, and that a player such as Derick Hougaard, who had not played in one test, was treated with more respect and made to feel more welcome in the national set-up. Naturally, it upset him.

When I mentioned these examples to Rudolf, he said that players could sometimes be 'over-sensitive'. I pointed out that it was not just the black players. Some guys complained that the Bulls players did not show Corné the necessary respect by insisting on calling Joost 'cappie'. This irritated those players from outside the Bulls region. Rudolf merely reiterated that players were being too sensitive, and that he would get rid of any racism and provincial differences at boot camp, where the squad would learn to become a unit.

Other race issues existed that disturbed me, which had been reported to the coach, including the situation with the physiotherapists. Apparently certain white players did not want to be treated by the black physio Matime Diali. I gave Rudolf the figures submitted to me by Clint Readhead. In the week of the Dunedin test against the All Blacks, thirty-eight consultations and/or treatments occurred. Diali was responsible for eight, and Readhead for thirty. Readhead was concerned about the situation, which had become uncomfortable. The two physios had tried to find a solution in Brisbane by making players book appointments under physio one and physio two. This did not work, as the players would stand at the physio room door and ask Readhead which physio he was.

Moreover, Readhead had told me that Geo Cronjé had refused to be strapped by Diali in Cape Town in the build-up to the Australian test in July, when the player was part of an extended national squad.

Also, every team selection announcement was preceded with a discussion about the number of black players in the squad, and I asked Rudolf how I was supposed to explain this to the media. In 2002 Rudolf had selected as many as five black players in his match 22, and on occasion started with four. Black player representation was seldom an issue.

However, in 2003 the starting number never exceeded three, and on two occasions only one black player started, which was an issue to the media and to me. Rudolf justified this by saying that he had to pick the strongest team, and that we could have no 'passengers' in the big games. If he selected more than three or four black players for the lesser internationals, then people would expect the same in tests against Australia and New Zealand.

Ironically, when we beat Australia in Cape Town, three black players were on the field; when we competed well against New Zealand, three black players started the match. I was still upset about a confrontation between Gideon Sam and myself, which had occurred in Dunedin. White players and management felt, as I did, that it had been a racist attack. Management members were also unhappy that Gideon was quick to discipline white management, but excused kit master Philip Malakoane's mistakes because he was 'under pressure'. We felt that everyone should be treated equally, both in good and bad times.

The situation in the Bok squad was not healthy, and the World Cup squad announcement was only a few hours away. Rudolf still had to inform the players who had not been selected for the World Cup. The most emotional response was Jaco van der Westhuyzen's. He was in tears, and Straeuli told me that the player's first question had been whether Ricardo Loubscher had made the team. Many of the white players felt that this was a race selection. André Pretorius had driven from Johannesburg to see Straeuli. The talk lasted about a minute. Pretorius was angry when he left, just shaking his head on the way out.

Pedrie Wannenburg, a member of the squad all year, could not believe he had been given the axe. Straeuli questioned Wannenburg's attitude and commitment rather than his play. Straeuli felt that the player lacked maturity and did not appreciate the importance of the World Cup.

Oberholzer arrived at around 3 p.m., spoke briefly to Straeuli and calmed him down. The show, he said, must go on. The squad would be announced according to schedule, despite Straeuli's protests. SuperSport had paid a lot of money for the exclusive rights to broadcast the announcement, and Oberholzer was not going to consider delaying it. The press release on Geo Cronjé would not be altered. Oberholzer would not budge on that either. Straeuli had no choice. The World Cup announcement would be made on time. Everyone was to put on their best smiles. After all, it was supposed to be a wonderful occasion.

15

The end of the road
Resignations and early exits

On the day after the World Cup squad announcement, the Sunday newspapers criticised Geo Cronjé's omission from the team, and *Rapport* hammered Rian and me, implying that we had conjured up the whole racial incident. No mention was made of Rudolf Straeuli's involvement. Cronjé was portrayed as a martyr and Quinton Davids as the villain.

On 30 August, the squad left Pretoria late on the Saturday evening for what would become the infamous *Kamp Staaldraad*. I flew to Cape Town on the Sunday morning, and went to the office on Monday 1 September. Straeuli and I had spoken on the telephone on the Saturday evening at about 9.30 p.m., and his last words to me were to 'put out all the fires' in Cape Town. We have not spoken since.

I felt very disillusioned on the Sunday evening, and for the first time felt that I could not go back. All my belongings had remained behind in Pretoria, as I was due back on the Tuesday. But I had had enough. I made up my mind that evening, but spoke to no one about my decision.

On the Monday I saw Oberholzer at SA Rugby's offices in Cape Town. I told him I could not believe how the story had been misrepresented in the Sunday press, and how the board and executive members had publicly gone after him. The Monday papers had quoted executive members as saying they were going to discipline Oberholzer. Rian was preparing for a board meeting to explain the situation. I told him I could not work in an organisation where the managing director was made to look like an idiot, and those in the wrong were glorified. He shrugged, saying that he had got used to it – that was SA Rugby. I said I would never get used to it, and wanted to hand in my resignation. Rian asked me to think carefully about my decision. In the meantime he wanted a report detailing the events in Pretoria to present to the board, including the reasons why I could no longer work with Straeuli. I would mention the spying incident involving Australia in Cape Town and the biting incident in Brisbane as contributing factors to the breakdown in trust between the two of us. I also told him that Straeuli had asked me to control the situation in Cape Town, but that I had refused to do so.

Oberholzer needed the report in two hours, so I typed up an abbreviated version and told him I would give him a more detailed account on the Tuesday morning when I handed him my resignation letter. Oberholzer asked me if I could not wait until after the World Cup to resign, but the World Cup was not even a consideration. Going to the World Cup was to have been a career high. For three years I had battled through the highs and lows of Springbok rugby, but what had happened in Pretoria had huge ramifications on what we were trying to achieve in South African rugby. It was a separate issue to the World Cup. Suddenly, the World Cup seemed all but irrelevant. Rian understood my standpoint, but said that he had a business to run and a team to send to the World Cup. He had to try to salvage the situation.

I gave him the report in confidence, and said it was important to inform the press why I was leaving, because over the weekend the media had speculated that I had leaked the story. If I walked out without explanation, the assumption would be that I had, in fact, been guilty, and had been dismissed. I did not want to confuse the issue.

Oberholzer accepted my reason for wanting to release a press statement, but made it clear that I would not qualify for a package if I resigned. I did not want SA Rugby's money. I quit and was paid until the end of September, in accordance with the Labour Law Act, and also paid out for twenty-two leave days owed to me. Songezo Nayo also asked me to wait until after the World Cup to resign. I was disappointed that he, as a black person, thought the World Cup more important than rooting out racism and prejudice. There was no right time to resign. The incident had happened and the matter had to be addressed. Nayo said he understood, and apologised for even asking me to reconsider. I announced my resignation in a press statement. The media frenzy started immediately, but I refused every interview request on both the Tuesday and Wednesday because Oberholzer had given me a commitment that my concerns would be investigated.

On the day I resigned, I watched for three hours as the 'missed calls' ticked over on my cellphone. They totalled 141. My voice mailbox was full. I would clear it, and by the time I finished, it would be full again. Magazines offered money for the report. I refused. How could I make a moral decision to walk away and then sell a report given to the MD in confidence? Overseas cash offers were made in voicemail messages, but I never responded to any of them.

The Boks were due back in camp on the Wednesday evening, 3 September. An open media day was to be held the next day. Up until this point I had said nothing to the press. The board had indicated that there would be a full-scale investigation after studying my report, and had informed the media of this.

On the Thursday afternoon I received a call from a Johannesburg-based journalist, who said the Boks had 'gone for me' at the press day. I expected nothing less. Apparently, the Boks had denied that there was any racism in the team, and Corné Krige even said that I had 'jumped' before I was 'pushed'. He told the media that I was about to be fired. Krige looked very foolish the next day when Oberholzer informed the media that my job had never been on the line. There had never been any suggestion of me losing my job. Krige made some bizarre statements at the press day. When asked whether there was racism in the team, his reply was that it depended on the 'interpretation' of the term racism. Then he assured the media that there had never been a problem in the squad. Every other player said something similar. Breyton Paulse was paraded in front of the press, and he said that things were great. Paulse had not even been at the camp when the Cronjé–Davids incident occurred. Joost van der Westhuizen denied that racism and provincialism existed in the team.

The squad had attacked first, and I retaliated. John Maytham interviewed me on Cape Talk, and the interview was also aired on 702 Talk Radio on Friday 5 September. I gave a full account of what had happened, and also wrote a piece for the Independent Group's Saturday publications, which appeared on 6 September.

In between resigning and doing the interview, the Minister of Sport and Recreation, Ngconde Balfour, asked to see me. I visited his office in Cape Town and handed him a copy of the report. He said he had already read it. The report was doing the rounds within SA Rugby and would later be leaked, from within the organisation, to *The Citizen*.

Balfour called it 'explosive stuff', and promised swift action. He was outraged, and said racism would not be tolerated. He asked me if I thought the Boks should be withdrawn from the World Cup. I said absolutely not. The World Cup had nothing to do with this – deal with the issue and identify those who were involved. Get rid of them, and allow the squad to get on with their preparation. I said Straeuli and Gideon Sam should not go to the World Cup for the manner in which they had dealt with the issue. Balfour was close to Sam, who had taught him at school. He seemed confused by Sam's apparent acceptance of the situation, and asked me why the manager had not taken a stronger stand. I could not answer him.

The SABC, in the meantime, wanted the investigation opened to the public. This unnerved SA Rugby, as there could then be no cover-up. For two days the issue was debated. The discussion would continue the following Monday, 8 September. That afternoon I received a call from someone at SA Rugby's offices. The person told me that Songezo Nayo, SARFU president Silas Nkanunu, Gideon Sam and Minister Balfour had all been in a meeting, and they were on their way to Durban, where the squad was staying. A press conference would be called, and the word at SA Rugby was that the investigation was going to be postponed until 2004. I felt deflated. Balfour had promised not to take any more nonsense from SA Rugby, yet here he was, backing a postponement. It made me question how serious he was about transformation and expunging racism from South African rugby. One moment he was criticising the Boks to me, the next he was having drinks with management and telling the media that the Boks would be going to the World Cup with the country's backing. He would deal with the racism, but only after the World Cup.

I had never heard such a pathetic denial. The half-cocked apology offered by Sam and Straeuli, who acknowledged that they could have handled the incident better, only confirmed how rotten things had become in the Bok set-up. Balfour and Sam have a long history. Sam used to be his teacher; it was obvious who was still the pupil. Once at the World Cup in Australia, players would continue to deny any ill feeling between one another. I knew this was nonsense, but the contradictions would gradually emerge as time passed. I know players don't keep a record of what they say from one week to the next; I was the guy who used to do that for them to ensure that they avoided contradicting themselves when speaking to the press.

Joost van der Westhuizen, who had sworn to God that he never mentioned the words 'Western Province' to Quinton Davids when the Bok management questioned him in Pretoria, told the Afrikaans daily newspaper *Die Burger* just the opposite. One of the issues that had emerged from the Quinton–Geo incident was provincialism. Davids had told people in Cape Town that at the training camp, Joost had said to him that he was 'not at Western Province', which Davids had interpreted as provincial bias.

Joost had denied it emphatically, saying he did not use those words. He told management that he would swear on the Bible. Now, five weeks later, he told the journalist a different story: when he told Quinton that he was 'not at Western Province', he had simply meant to emphasise that this was a national camp. A harmless enough statement had one not known the background. It was the start of the unravelling within the squad. As the World Cup effort weakened, the players became disillusioned. Word started to filter back of unhappiness among the black players. Again, rumours of provincialism circulated.

Over the course of three weeks I had been told, by various sources, of *Kamp Staaldraad* and what had happened there. Initially I could not believe it, but with each different source confirming the same story, I started to investigate exactly what had taken place during the four days when Straeuli took the World Cup squad into the bush. Images of *Staaldraad*, printed in newspapers after the World Cup and shown on television, would shock the world. Players were forced to strip naked, deprived of food and water, and put in a pit for four hours while the anthems of New Zealand and England were played over and over. These were just a few of the images shown. It was like something out of Auschwitz.

Argus sports editor Archie Henderson and I wrote about the camp for the Independent Group. Upon the Boks' return to South Africa, I contacted Dale McDermott, who had filmed everything, and asked him whether he had any footage. He said everything had been confiscated, and he had nothing. But I'd heard that he had still images, and I cautioned him against the ramifications of defending the camp. The story was going to be written, and with or without pictures, enough squad members had spoken to me to confirm what had taken place.

Many stories were written on the camp revelations, but Bok management denied the allegations. In their wisdom, they decided to release footage to *Carte Blanche*, a current affairs programme on M-Net, to defend the camp. They were going to show the world that *Kamp Staaldraad* was media sensation more than anything else. The arrangement with *Carte Blanche* was that they would present their side of the story; *Carte Blanche* was not to probe too deeply. McDermott was upset that the footage he had filmed had been given to *Carte Blanche* without him being told about it. He only heard about the plan through a source at M-Net. He contacted Adriaan Heijns, who confirmed that the footage would be shown on television on the Sunday.

McDermott then phoned to tell me that they were going to show the footage on *Carte Blanche*, and that he did have still images. He was prepared to make them available to the media, as he suspected that the team were going to distort the truth about the camp on television. Heijns had called Bok centre Gcobani Bobo and asked him to appear on the programme in defence of the camp. Bobo told me about it, and added that he had declined. He then gave me an on-the-record statement in which he said that the camp had done nothing for him, it had been a joke, and certainly had not made him a better rugby player.

Bobo was the first player to speak out publicly against the camp. Privately, many players spoke about what had happened, and expressed their outrage and humiliation. The television footage left the public dumbfounded.

Yet Joost van der Westhuizen defended the camp, saying that it had helped break down provincial and racial barriers. I ask the question: If no provincialism or racism existed, as the Boks had told the media at the Thursday press day, why was it necessary for the camp to 'break down' these non-existent 'barriers'?

Corné Krige mentioned how 'emotional' the experience had been in the pit, and how the squad 'had sorted out huge problems … Ashwin Willemse telling the players how it felt to be black in the squad'. Again, the same Krige who, on press day, was recorded as saying that there was nothing wrong, now admitting that 'big problems' had been resolved? As the pressure intensified, more players came forward. Willemse confirmed that certain racial incidents had taken place in an article in *SA Sports Illustrated*; Dale Santon, Ricardo Loubscher and Breyton Paulse would all comment on racial prejudice and the unhappiness of the black players at the World Cup. *Rapport* also revealed that Davids had told his mother, 'the Boer did not want to share a room with [me]'.

Krige disappointed me the most. I had enormous respect for him as a person, but he had not been completely honest about me and about what had happened in Pretoria. A Cape Town journalist telephoned me after the World Cup, alleging that Corné had told him that I was being paid by SA Rugby, and urging him to investigate this. The journalist did, and found the information to be misleading and false.

To this day I have never trashed Krige – the inspirational captain of the Boks and a religious family man. I guess I don't have to. His actions speak for themselves.

* * * * *

Brian van Rooyen stepped in as the new SARFU president on 5 December 2003, and promised to expunge racism and racists from the game. Two weeks before his election as rugby's new chief, I met with him in Johannesburg for an *SA Sports Illustrated* interview. He thanked me for having had the courage to speak out, and said that if he was appointed he would ensure that the game would not tolerate the kind of attitudes I'd highlighted in my report.

But in the first week of March 2004, Van Rooyen told the media that there was nothing racist about what had gone on in the Bok squad, that both Geo Cronjé and Quinton Davids had been done an injustice, and that the sport needed to 'move on'. There would be no investigation and no independent hearing into the events. SARFU wanted to forget that anything had ever happened. SARFU's new boss based his decision on the original statements taken from the players on Thursday evening, 28 August 2003, two days before the World Cup squad announcement. According to Van Rooyen, these statements made it clear that no racism existed, only 'cultural differences'. He dismissed my objections as the findings of an individual with an axe to grind with the sport.

However, the evidence was damning, because all the players had told different stories in different interviews. Even SARFU's internal investigating team had acknowledged in their report that the evidence was littered with contradictions. In his first interview, Davids told investigators that he had never had a problem with Geo Cronjé. In his second interview, he admitted that he had 'felt hurt' by what had occurred between them. What follows are the contradictions and lies told in the original investigation, which was terminated because the investigators had an aeroplane to catch!

Quinton Davids' first interview
1. Joost never reprimanded me at the gym.
2. I was never unhappy about anything.
3. There was never a problem between Geo and myself.
4. He never refused to share the bathroom facilities with me.
5. Joost never spoke to me because I was late.
6. I have no knowledge of Joost saying 'don't bring your WP manners here'.
7. I have never spoken to anyone about anything, not my family, the WP players or the players in this squad.
8. I was not emotional about anything as reported in the newspaper.
9. I have nothing else to say. This is the truth.

Quinton Davids recalled for a second interview

1. I felt hurt that he would not talk to me.
2. After the first punishment he moved out again.
3. He refused to shower in the same room.
4. Joost confronted me at the gym on the Saturday morning and told me not to bring my WP manners here. This upset me because he said it in front of other players.
5. When Corné called the black players together, Dale Santon mentioned that Geo wouldn't share a room with him earlier in the year in Durban.
6. I asked Corné if he could arrange a contact session so that I could beat [Cronjé] up.
7. The coach spoke to both of us about the situation.

Corné Krige's first interview

1. I was aware that Joost had reprimanded Quinton and I agree with it because he was late for gym.
2. During my meeting with the black players Quinton told me he was unhappy about what had happened.
3. Davids told me that Cronjé had made him feel dirty because he refused to use the same bathroom facilities.
4. Having spoken with the black players I knew the situation was serious and I took it up with the coach.
5. Quinton initially told me that he had spoken to his girlfriend.
6. Quinton asked me for a contact session so that he could sort the other guy out.
7. The coach and I met with Geo, and the coach gave him an ultimatum to move back. Told him that no player was bigger than the team. I am aware that the coach had spoken with Geo and the player had problems because of his background, religion and the way he was brought up.

Corné Krige recalled for a second interview

1. Quinton told me he was scared he would be punished again and he felt he had done nothing wrong, either the first time or the second time.
2. He said Geo had shown him no respect.
3. Dale [Santon] mentioned Geo would not share a room with him in Durban.
4. Dale said Cronjé had taken a stand against the black players.
5. The black players said he had made them feel dirty by not using the same bathroom.

Rudolf Straeuli's first interview

1. Joost took Quinton on because he was late for gym and I supported him, as it was his right as a senior player.
2. Geo asked me if he could move in with Jaco van der Westhuyzen after the punishment. I knew there was a problem but did not know what it was.
3. Myself and Corné spoke to Geo and I gave him an ultimatum that he move back in with Quinton or leave the camp.

4. During our conversation he called his father, who told him it was okay to move back in with Quinton.
5. I never noticed that Quinton was 'emotionally battered'.

Rudolf Straeuli recalled for a second interview

1. Mac Hendricks told me Quinton was unhappy.
2. When I spoke to Quinton he told me he was unhappy and very upset about what had happened.
3. Geo told me he had a problem regarding his religion and wanted to know why we did not pray as a team before the test. He wanted to know whose decision it was. I told him the four captains and Gideon Sam had decided that.

Geo Cronjé's first interview

1. I was not aware that Quinton was upset about anything.

Geo Cronjé recalled for a second interview

1. I didn't share with Dale in Durban because he snores.
2. I did phone my Dad and told him what was happening at the camp and he mentioned to me that in 1968 he had to share with people of colour.
3. If selected to go to the World Cup I have no problem with any black or brown players in the squad.

Joost van der Westhuizen

1. As a senior player I took him [Davids] on and I told him that if he was ever late again I would chase him away.

Dale Santon

1. Quinton told me he was unhappy about what had happened. I told him to see Mac Hendricks.
2. I can't remember Geo not sharing with me in Durban.

Gcobani Bobo

1. I didn't know what was going on. No one spoke to me.

Subsequent to the camp and the World Cup, black players went on record to say that racism was still a problem in Bok rugby. Among these players were Gcobani Bobo, Breyton Paulse and Dale Santon. Bobo said he had lied in the original interview when he'd said that he knew nothing, because he feared victimisation and omission from the World Cup squad. The players, in one form or another, confirmed the accuracy of my report in their original statements, but all of them refused to mention the word race in the only statements they provided on 28 August 2003, which was contrary to what they had told me and what Straeuli had told Rian Oberholzer.

After the World Cup, black players told a different story. They also mentioned that they feared they might suffer further prejudice if they spoke out, and Bobo, in particular, said he was insulted by SARFU's findings that racism had played no part in the incident. In media interviews in March 2004, Oberholzer confirmed the accuracy of my report involving dialogue between himself and Straeuli, and he also reiterated that Straeuli had told him that Cronjé had not wanted to share a room with a black player.

Van Rooyen defended Cronjé and Davids, and refused to revisit the original investigation, despite what the black players now said in the media. Certain questions remain unanswered. For example, why did Cronjé feel it necessary to phone his father to find out if it was all right to share with a black player? Cronjé's father's response, as recorded in Cronjé's statement and relayed to Oberholzer through Straeuli at the Pretoria High Performance Centre in 2003, was that it was 'okay' to share with black people. Cronjé senior had done this in 1968. Cronjé senior did not say that it was all right to share with rivals or teammates who were not considered one's friends, but specifically with black people. This bit of dialogue was conveniently ignored by SARFU's new regime. They rubber-stamped their approval of the flawed internal investigation, and ascribed the incident to a cultural misunderstanding between two players. No hint of racism was found. And on the day SARFU's new regime announced that racism did not exist in the game, Blue Bulls chief executive Gary Boshoff spoke publicly about the prevalence of racism in South African rugby. The conflicting views encapsulate the magnitude of the problem, and emphasise rugby's continued reluctance to deal with the issue.

16

In the corridors of power
From Oberholzer to Van Rooyen

The mood of South African rugby's elected officials changes with the direction of the wind. SARFU president Brian van Rooyen called his own organisation 'rotten to the core', but failed to mention that nine of the fourteen provincial presidents who make up the game's hierarchy from the previous regime are still sitting pretty in their plush seats.

But Van Rooyen is wrong. I don't agree that his provincial presidents are rotten. They are simply inept at running a professional game. They remain in the corridors of power today, flying first class, taking the wife along to test matches and on business trips, always arranging executive meetings on the eve of test matches, and constantly mumbling about the salaries paid to the players and the evil of professionalism. Provincial presidents supposedly represent the best interests of the Boks. Instead they ride on Bok successes and deride Bok failures. In the three years that I observed these hangers-on after test matches, they seemed to derive as much pleasure from Bok defeats as you'd hope to see when the team won.

But there were some exceptions. The late Jomo King was a class individual, and on an administrative level his death was a blow to both the Lions Rugby Union and South African rugby professionalism in general. The KwaZulu-Natal Rugby Union's Kevin Dunkley was another who bravely swam upstream for a few years, but he left before his sanity deserted him. Ronnie Masson, once he gave up his provincial hat and concentrated only on South African rugby as the senior vice-president of SARFU, always put the needs of South African rugby first. Sadly, this is where the collective goodwill of provincial administrators towards South African rugby ended.

A new regime hardly seems to have improved the situation. When I attended the announcement of Jake White as Springbok coach in February 2004, the South African rugby administrators made me cringe. They looked as if they had stepped out of the 1970s. It certainly felt as if some of them had been around since then. These executive members rule by division and conflict, and the national interest is secondary to provincial priorities. Isolation made strongholds out of our provincial unions, and in the professional era it has become a financial drain to keep fourteen unions operative.

This is not merely my opinion, but a fact that was highlighted by an independent investigation into South African rugby. In 2002, Accenture, an independent consulting company, was paid R2 million to assess the administrative and structural strengths and weaknesses of the South African game. During three months of intensive probing and questioning, more than 100 stakeholders representing every aspect of professional and amateur rugby were interviewed. The results were revealing and the proposed changes enlightening, as they were built around a philosophy that prioritised national interests over provincial concerns.

Accenture offered solutions to the rugby administration, but their practical implementation would be a problem. The suits in South African rugby aren't professional businessmen tasked with enforcing the changes; they are provincial presidents who sip cocktails and travel in style. Their own comfort and the interests of the provincial unions take precedence over everything else.

Uli Schmidt, the Springbok team doctor in 2003, was horrified at the insular attitudes of the administrators on the eve of the test against the Pumas in Port Elizabeth. The executive was in town for a meeting, which predictably coincided with a home test match, and Schmidt met some of them for a drink on the Friday evening. He would later tell Rudolf Straeuli and me that he couldn't believe how negative these provincial presidents were towards the team, due to the financial implications of a possible World Cup success. Schmidt told us they'd argued that the financial incentives on offer to the players would mean less money for the provinces. The best result for them would be a competitive World Cup for the Boks, but no glory. Schmidt, who was passionate about the Boks, was both shocked and disgusted at the lack of unconditional support for the national team. I told him he should work at SA Rugby's headquarters – then their attitude would not come as such a shock to him. In my time with the Springboks, I experienced first hand Rian Oberholzer's frustrations when he had dealings with the presidents.

The person I've been asked about the most since my resignation is Rian Oberholzer. The public perception of Oberholzer is very negative. The man in the street thinks he ruined South African rugby and was a law unto himself. This is nonsense. Oberholzer made mistakes, as any individual in his position might have done. He had enemies – again nothing new – and his petulance with the media and disregard for them in his last year did him no favours. But he was very good at his job and he was an asset to South African rugby. The public persona of Oberholzer is far removed from the private individual. His bark was so impressive that he never had to bite. This is the way he wanted it, as it is not in his nature to be aggressive.

Ask his staff about him. He might have been difficult, moody and, often, a pain in the butt because he was a stickler for punctuality and office etiquette, but he was very loyal to his employees and the Bok players. Oberholzer was the frontman for South African rugby and enjoyed the status, but he hated the malicious nature of the media. He was particularly irritated by constantly being referred to as Louis Luyt's son-in-law. When I first met Oberholzer in Sydney in 1996, he said he did not have a problem with criticism, as long as it was aimed at him and not the fact that he married Luyt's daughter. It is something that bugged him to the end. Contrary to media belief, Oberholzer was not South African rugby. He certainly did not make every decision on his own, and had a healthy regard for the input of Ronnie Masson, who served as senior vice-president to SARFU president Silas Nkanunu.

Oberholzer also spoke very highly of Derick Minnie, an independent board member, who enjoyed success in the business world and served as an independent on several prominent corporate boards. Oberholzer nurtured the relationships he felt worthy of the effort, and regarded the rest as acquaintances he either tolerated or suffered. He was politically astute. His biggest victory had been when he managed to get the government on rugby's side after Luyt took former President Nelson Mandela to court in 1997. Oberholzer chose rugby over blood and terminated the family relationship. It saved South African rugby, and no one should be allowed to forget the choice he made then. Luyt, for one, has never let him forget.

Luyt and Oberholzer had been close in the past, and the former had once been Oberholzer's mentor. Luyt taught Oberholzer how to play the power game within the corridors of South African rugby. This is why Oberholzer never complained publicly when he was shafted at the end. He was not in virgin territory. He had done his fair share of political manoeuvring and manipulation during his time at SA Rugby, or he would have been gone long before he actually walked away. Oberholzer knew six months before his resignation that a revolution was under way. He had mentioned it to me while I was still with the Boks. All that could save him and Silas Nkanunu was a successful World Cup campaign. Matters had reached a stage where the Boks' series of poor performances would have a domino effect on the majority of the game's decision-makers. This is one of the reasons why Oberholzer backed coach Rudolf Straeuli to the end, as he needed to give the national team every possible chance to succeed.

Oberholzer was loyal to his coaches. Whatever the Bok coaches wanted, they were given. Oberholzer never refused Harry Viljoen or Rudolf Straeuli anything. He would cut back on other budgets to accommodate the Springboks, and he would fight the provincial presidents and his board members to justify player salaries and annual budgets for the best training camps and practice facilities. But he also isolated himself from players, as he refused to hide his disappointment in their poor performances. On several occasions he lost it in the change room. In Paris in 2001 he gave the senior players a blasting. It upset Viljoen, the coach at the time. When I expressed my disappointment in the performance to Oberholzer, Harry accused me of adding to the negative atmosphere. We were talking in the change room and Viljoen, quite rightly, felt the conversation should have taken place outside.

But when we were hammered 53-3 by England at Twickenham, Oberholzer was more tactful. The players were physically drained and in tears when he walked into the change room. Some were vomiting, and Corné Krige was nearly unconscious due to exhaustion. Oberholzer spoke to the team about their courage, and praised their commitment in putting their bodies on the line after being reduced to fourteen men for the last hour of the game.

Afterwards, Krige's moments of madness in the match would be shown to the world, and Oberholzer spent forty-eight hours trying to convince the IRB not to take any further action, which could have resulted in a lengthy ban for Krige. Privately, Oberholzer expressed his disgust to me, Krige and Straeuli. He demanded that the coach discipline Krige, but he wanted the matter dealt with internally. Publicly he defended the captain and the team. Because of this, he copped a lot of abuse in the media.

When Straeuli coached the Springboks, Oberholzer was equally brutal in his assessment of the team, especially after the defeat against France in Marseille in 2002. The players were embarrassed after that performance, and many refused to look the coach or the managing director in the eye. This did not stop Oberholzer from making unflattering comments to the players. The only bit of humour that night occurred when Rian asked Bakkies Botha what the hell had happened for him to be sent off. Botha looked at Rian and said he had kneed the French player off the ball.

'It was stupid of me,' Botha admitted.

'At least you're big enough to admit you made a mistake,' Oberholzer said, and they shared a laugh about the stupidity of the act.

In 2002, Straeuli was very wary of Oberholzer. He respected Oberholzer's role as the managing director and answered to him as the boss. In turn, Oberholzer backed Straeuli unreservedly. In February 2004 I had dinner with Oberholzer, the first time we'd seen each other since his resignation. I told him that I wanted it placed on record that I thought he had 'fucked up' by backing Straeuli after the World Cup exit. Oberholzer replied that he 'owed' it to the national coach to give him his support.

'I had a responsibility as the managing director,' he said. I argued that as the MD his responsibility had been to get rid of the coach, particularly when one took into account the events that had transpired prior to and during the tournament, both on and off the field. We agreed to disagree. This issue was one of the few things we disagreed on in a period of three years. The other was *Kamp Staaldraad*. Oberholzer maintained that he agreed with the boot camp in principle and had signed it off, unaware of exactly what it would entail. However, Adriaan Heijns says Oberholzer had known exactly what the players were to be put through.

Whatever Oberholzer may or may not have known, I believe he was wrong for agreeing to the camp. He was clutching at straws. I have a lot of time for Oberholzer and huge respect for his ability as a rugby administrator. I also admire his resilience. To survive for as long as he did in South African rugby takes some doing.

Rian spent a lot of his time pulling daggers from his back, and towards the end he also took a few in the chest. In an ironic twist, the man he introduced to SA Rugby as an independent board member, current chairman Theunie Lategan, would be among his biggest detractors at the end. Lategan aligned himself with André Markgraaff, Brian van Rooyen and the northern conservatives, who conspired to remove Oberholzer from his post. By the time the Boks were eliminated from the World Cup, Oberholzer knew that he was history. Word had filtered through to Sydney, and the message was clear: Take the package deal, or leave with nothing. He took the package deal, negotiated one for Straeuli, and the two men left with a failed World Cup as their legacy and a combined R5-million payout.

Oberholzer will be forever linked to Straeuli's World Cup disaster, when his legacy should be the filling of the commercial coffers and his fight for transformation, which was more vigorous than that of any black administrator in South African rugby. He was successful commercially, and he engineered the split from SARFU so that businessmen could run South African rugby like a business. He wanted to take the professional game away from elected officials, but too many compromises were made along the way for these dinosaurs to have disappeared completely.

Oberholzer proposed a board that would include four elected provincial presidents and three independent members, but SARFU's executive would only agree to the change if the number of provincial presidents on the board doubled, with the majority of the provincial presidents represented on the board. Oberholzer compromised in an effort to make the company operational. In theory, SA Rugby had a board, but in practice the elected officials were still the decision-makers. They, and not Oberholzer, appointed the national coach. This decision, as with all the big decisions concerning company policy, tournament structure and the national team, would come down to a vote. And this vote could change from morning to afternoon.

One example occurred in June 2002. The provincial presidents had agreed to a strength-versus-strength Currie Cup. They had also accepted the majority of Accenture's proposed changes to streamline the game in order to make it more cost-effective, productive and professional. The decisions were made at a Friday think tank, and would be ratified at an official meeting on the Saturday afternoon. However, a Bok function took place on the Friday evening, where provincial presidents started questioning their earlier decisions. As each whisky hit the palate, someone else changed his mind.

Certain press people were informed of the situation, among them *Rapport*'s Rudolph Lake. Some of the provincial presidents even approached Lake to tell him that it was unconstitutional for the board to make decisions. At this stage the Sharks Rugby Union and Western Province did not have representation on the board, and they influenced fellow provincial presidents to drop the idea of a Currie Cup restructuring. Rumours were flying about a possible court case between the provinces and SA Rugby, and that the media was going to be used to publicise the fight. Oberholzer had well-placed sources in every province, and was aware of the various opinions bandied about that night. There was a lot of backstabbing going on.

Oberholzer informed me of the situation, and said that he would talk to me the next morning. I was staying with the Boks at the Pretoria Police College.

Oberholzer called me on the Saturday morning and told me to meet him at the Palazzo Hotel in Fourways, where the board was meeting. Once I arrived, he informed me that the provincial presidents were trying to derail the strength-versus-strength proposal, and that all sorts of bartering had gone on the previous night. The only way to rein them in would be to use the media first. We called Rudolph Lake at *Rapport* and gave him the exclusive lead about the agreed changes and their consequences for professional rugby in South Africa. In turn, we needed him to nail the provincial presidents for trying to resist change. I briefed Lake, and then Oberholzer spoke to him about the narrow-minded attitudes of the presidents. Lake agreed that they were holding South African rugby back, and indicated that he would push Oberholzer's view in the paper's lead story the next morning.

But later that morning news broke that disgraced South African cricket captain Hansie Cronjé had died in an aeroplane crash. Cronjé's death dominated the news and sports pages, and while Lake wrote the rugby story, it was not displayed as a prominent piece. Nevertheless, he had a go at those resisting change, and praised the Accenture report and the decisions taken on the evidence of the report. The rugby crisis had been averted.

Accenture concluded that unhealthy provincialism was an evil in South African rugby. As a result, there was limited faith in decision-making at executive and board level, and as the mindset of provincialism outweighed regionalism and nationalism, there wasn't enough accountability across the board. South African rugby had clearly not made the transition from an amateur organisation to a professional board. The fourteen-team Currie Cup was not beneficial to the strength of the Springboks, and financially the handouts to fourteen provinces were a drain on SA Rugby as the game's custodian.

Accenture analytically dissected each union and found that half of them were in trouble financially, and at least two were a financial liability. They recommended a reduction in the number of professional provinces from fourteen to twelve, and splitting the domestic competition into two sections of six each, playing strength against strength. The executive and board agreed in principle that it was the only practical way forward, and consented to all the proposed changes. Less than two years later, the same presidents who voted for these changes would agree to scrap every decision, as Van Rooyen disagreed with the system. The provincial presidents had never bought into it.

Oberholzer would not have been surprised, given the dithering nature of these provincial presidents. Now, in 2004, they have assumed total control of a game played by professionals, involving professional partners. The corporate identity, established to govern the commercial aspects of the game, has been knocked down by the same group of elected officials who in 2001 agreed that in order for rugby to prosper, a company had to be be established. The motivation to form a company was based on the need for financial saving and quicker and more decisive decision-making.

However, SA Rugby could not escape criticism that it was keeping the elite in charge while reducing SARFU to an amateur organisation run by blacks. It was as if the whites had retained the money while the blacks had the grind of amateur rugby: the whites had the glitz and the blacks the gravel. Tension existed between SARFU and SA Rugby employees. The perception was that those in SARFU were not as important as those at SA Rugby. The money was upstairs, and the influential people were those operating under the Pty Ltd banner. Provincial presidents saw their control of the game slipping away, which is why they resisted a company board of directors with only minimal representation.

It was naive to assume that with a company controlling professional rugby, provincialism would be killed off and decisions would be made quickly and without the hassle of committee meetings. However, the tax benefit of having both a company and a non-profit national governing body was substantial. SARFU's annual turnover is an estimated R320 million. When the company was formed, it was taxed on only R200 million. R60 million was given to SARFU to administer amateur rugby, and a non-taxable R60-million grant was allocated to the fourteen provinces.

The company, SA Rugby (Pty) Ltd, has survived structurally in the new South African Rugby Football Union, headed by Van Rooyen. But the powers of the company's decision-makers have been devalued, and those linked to the company are now glorified commercial agents of the game. The downgrading of the company's role forced the resignation of the respected and influential Morné du Plessis as an independent board member. Another independent board member, Alwyn Martin, would quit for the same reason. The biggest disappointment was Du Plessis' departure. He held an unprecedented press conference to express his concerns about the politicking in the corridors of South African rugby.

Du Plessis' resignation was a dagger in the heart of those who still believed in Springbok rugby and the integrity of rugby's new leadership. In quitting South African rugby, Du Plessis delivered the most dramatic blow to the battered image of our game. He detailed the moral corruptness of the new leaders, who purport to be acting in the best interests of South African rugby:

> I cannot stand by idly and witness the deal-making now taking place between provinces that could potentially damage Free State as a rugby power by entrenching the four metropole regions as Super 12 teams. I cannot accept the manner of the decision to revert back to a system of 14 professional teams playing the Currie Cup, which we decided last year would be replaced by strength versus strength.
>
> I also cannot accept the coaching process in appointing the next Bok coach. It is not about individuals on the list. It is the manner in which it was done. I cannot support it. We needed to go looking for the best, regardless of his nationality. I understood my role as an independent director to be that of an independent voice that could contribute positively to South African rugby. My attempts to contribute were met with nothing short of disrespect.

Du Plessis, a global rugby icon and man of integrity, said the South African rugby public were deserving of more than the underhanded politicking he experienced at the new leadership's first think tank. He spoke openly about his disgust at the bartering and trade-offs as provincial representatives pursued individual and provincial agendas at the expense of what was good for the national game. 'I have been in the game so long, so perhaps I should not be so naive,' Du Plessis said. 'But I refuse to be a part of it. Rugby business decisions were taken last year based on research, and each decision was supported by a statistical argument of why it would benefit South African rugby. At the weekend these decisions were changed at a dinner discussion. Minds were not applied and decisions were based on what one province would gain from another province's compromise.'

The Accenture report, which changed the direction of South African professional rugby in 2002, was deleted in a new restructuring. The report of a task team, appointed to improve South African rugby, was dismissed as irrelevant. The opinion of the Sharks' Brian van Zyl, without a doubt South Africa's most efficient provincial managing director, was influential in the report, which took nearly a year to complete.

Among the report's findings was that SA Rugby could not sustain a professional premier competition that had to support more than 600 professional players. The suggested solution was to have a strength-versus-strength first division of six teams and a semi-professional second division of six teams. The game in this country does not have more than 200 professional players, yet more than 600 are trading as professionals when the majority are club players. The new regime ignored the task team report, and Van Zyl, among others, was not even consulted.

According to Du Plessis, there are no independent voices in South African rugby. 'I see no purpose for myself as an independent board member,' he said. 'I have not been able to contribute constructively to any decision and see no way to do so under the current structure. I cannot accept accountability for that which I have no influence over and it is misleading the rugby public to think otherwise.

'It had become clear that I could not work from inside South African rugby to change things. I would have been doing the public a disservice if they thought I could change things from inside. I could not. I have spent two months in an extreme state of confrontation with SARFU president Mr van Rooyen. In the end I have to follow my conscience. This game belongs to the people of South Africa, not to any individual or groups. The rugby people of South Africa are owed some straight talking. I could no longer be Mr Nice Guy.'

Among the many ironies following Du Plessis' dramatic departure was the appointment of Jake White as Springbok coach. Du Plessis had fought for an extended coaching candidate shortlist that included White. He opposed Van Rooyen's original list of four, which consisted of Markgraaff, Chester Williams, Heyneke Meyer and Dumusani Mhani.

The initial thinking had been that Markgraaff would be head coach, Meyer would take the forwards, Williams the backs, and Mhani would be the technical advisor and the black representation in the mix. Only, no one bothered to ask them how they felt about it. Meyer and Williams did not want to work with Markgraaff in a coaching structure, and Markgraaff could certainly not return as national coach. If the world wasn't ready to accept Markgraaff, many in South Africa felt the same way. While the South African government had forgiven him for calling black rugby administrators 'kaffirs', many supporters of the game refused to accept his face as the one to represent a new South African image and Springbok team in 2004.

However, Markgraaff had led the Van Rooyen presidential campaign, and Van Rooyen was therefore indebted to him. When interviewed by Mike Wills on CapeTalk Radio in January 2004, Van Rooyen was asked whether White, then the under-21 coach, was a consideration for the Bok coaching position. Van Rooyen said he wasn't. He was adamant that the list of four was sufficient. Then Markgraaff opted out, Meyer did likewise, and the list was increased to eight, which now included the names Du Plessis had fought for from the beginning.

When Jake White was appointed, Van Rooyen was seated next to him, representing the future of our game. But it should have been Du Plessis next to White. When I spoke to Du Plessis after his resignation, he said he felt that he could do more good from the outside. He insisted that the game belonged to the people and not the individuals with egos and hidden agendas. But the reality is, the public does not own the game. Elected officials who chair portfolio committees control the game. The continuation of the company has simply become a convenient tax benefit.

The game's administration remains in the power of the provincial presidents, which will undoubtedly stifle growth and limit South African rugby's ability to be a competitive player on the global stage. These provincial presidents want to administer the game as in the amateur days, but they also want the financial gains associated with a business. It can never work. In his first few months in office, Van Rooyen made many public statements, slamming the SARFU he inherited as 'rotten', and lashing out at the game's administration for its apathetic approach to transformation. He made bold statements, yet those he criticised are still in power. The 'rotten' people Van Rooyen mentioned still make up the majority of his executive and company board of directors. These faces have not changed. The same blokes who allotted themselves a R1-million-plus package to attend the 2003 World Cup are still in power and controlling the future of South African rugby. And having a new boss hasn't dulled their enthusiasm for rewarding themselves. Van Rooyen and Lategan split the role of SARFU executive chairman and SA Rugby board chairman, and upped their annual retainer.

When Silas Nkanunu was in power, he chaired both the executive and the board, for which he was paid R320 000 a year. Currently, Van Rooyen and Lategan are paid R360 000 each. The executive members have also had their annual retainers increased, while Van Rooyen has made a song and dance about the organisation's need to cut back on staff salaries.

Within the corridors of power, the provincial presidents have looked after themselves and their provinces in a continuation of the kind of provincialism that eventually sapped even Oberholzer's energy – provincialism that was so engrained in the psyche of the rugby administrators that when Oberholzer walked away, it was with the certain knowledge that the provincial strongholds would only grow stronger, and that the national cause would always be threatened because of this mentality.

During my last two years at SA Rugby, I heard it whispered in the corridors that it was time for François Pienaar's reintroduction into South African rugby as managing director or CEO. Unfortunately, it might not be an improvement. In 2002, Pienaar had wanted the Springbok coaching job when Harry Viljoen resigned. Pienaar, who was in South Africa at the time, met with Oberholzer and outlined the way forward for South African rugby. But Pienaar's plan seemed to revolve mostly around him, instead of the interests of South African rugby. Pienaar had initially asked for the meeting to be held at his house in Steenberg. When Oberholzer refused, Pienaar asked if he could see him at the office before the start of the business day. Oberholzer agreed, and when I arrived at work,

Rian called me in to share the details of Pienaar's proposal. The 1995 World Cup-winning captain wanted to be head coach, with Brendan Venter as his assistant. He also wanted to be paid offshore in US dollars, and an incentive of one million pounds to win the World Cup for South Africa.

Oberholzer was not impressed, and he doubted the board would be. He communicated Pienaar's plan and remuneration demands to the board as a matter of course, where it was dismissed very quickly. Provincial presidents and board members were anti-Pienaar. Many still are, even though meetings were arranged between Pienaar and Markgraaff in the run-in to Van Rooyen's election challenge. A truce of sorts was arranged between Pienaar and Markgraaff in the event of the two having to work together. At the time of writing, this scenario had not yet materialised, although Pienaar's name keeps on cropping up as a possible CEO. It also keeps on being dismissed, but for how long is debatable.

Big decisions seldom come down to an in-depth discussion around the boardroom table, as the decisions have usually been made the night before. A study of Oberholzer's and Straeuli's resignations indicates that little has changed in the new dispensation. Correspondence I received from former independent board member Derick Minnie revealed that Van Rooyen had been well aware of Oberholzer's and Straeuli's payouts before his election as president of SARFU. Silas Nkanunu knew that he was not going to win the election, and asked Theunie Lategan to persuade Van Rooyen to agree to the payouts, as he would be the new president.

E-mail correspondence between Lategan and Minnie confirmed this, and Lategan told Minnie that he had informed the board of the situation, in order to clear up any misconceptions that Minnie might have acted unethically in his capacity as chairman of the remuneration committee. Lategan's letter to the board, attached in an e-mail to Minnie and forwarded to me by Minnie, read:

> Upon being approached by Rian and Rudolph (*sic*) last year to negotiate settlement agreements, Derick Minnie and I made it clear to them that we would first have to seek permission from the Board Exco to enter into discussions. I spoke to Silas, Ronnie and Keith who after careful deliberation gave me the go ahead. They, however, made it clear that this matter would have to be cleared by Brian as it appeared as though he was a serious contender for presidency of SARFU. In our negotiations with Rian and Rudolph we made it very clear that only the Board could approve of the exit agreements. The agreements that were drafted made it very clear that this was indeed the case. I circulated the draft agreements to Silas, Ronnie and Keith who commented thereon and cleared same for tabling at the Board meeting. Brian also received copies and phoned me with amendments thereto. I negotiated these amendments with Rian and

Rudolph who reluctantly agreed thereto. The agreements were amended accordingly. At the Board meeting of 4 December 2003 I made it very clear at the outset that I was not seeking a ratification from the board, but an approval of the agreements. After a detailed discussion, such approval was given unanimously. Payment to Rian and Rudolph was made on 2 January 2004 in accordance with the agreements. I spoke to Brian yesterday who confirmed to me that in light of the above the exit payments would not be questioned. I take this as the final chapter on this matter. We cannot operate on the basis of retrospectively questioning matters that were approved by the Board in a transparent and consensual manner.

On 5 December 2004, the day of his appointment as Nkanunu's successor, Van Rooyen expressed surprise at the payouts both men had received. Now it has emerged that he had signed them off. The administrative politics of South African rugby is ugly. Our game needs a truth and reconciliation commission, but this will never happen. At the moment, Van Rooyen and Markgraaff are running the show. In a few years' time, it will be someone else. All that will remain consistent within the administration is the infighting, jockeying for position and political agendas.

The black versus coloured power struggle has almost grown as prominent as provincialism. White South African rugby bosses, in their capacity as a national executive in the unified SARFU, have never addressed the internal politics that existed between black and coloured in the old South African Rugby Union fold – a situation that has never gone away, despite the unification of the game in this country.

This kind of division keeps the white conservatives powerful within the game. They sit back and watch while black and coloured square up to each other, and then align themselves with whoever is the more prominent. For the past five years it was Nkanunu, a black man from the Eastern Cape. When Nkanunu was in control, the conservatives were supporters of everything black. They never challenged Nkanunu for fear of it being 'misinterpreted' as racism, and were also wary of government involvement and disapproval. Publicly, the black leadership was in control, but it did not stop the white conservative element from undermining its influence.

Nkanunu's inability to present a strong public image and his lack of presence in dealing with the players added to the belief that he was only a ceremonial puppet. Nkanunu was well respected within the international rugby community, but was not afforded the same recognition in his own country. His leadership style differed from that of his predecessor, Louis Luyt. As an elected official, he allowed the paid employees of SA Rugby and SARFU to get on with their daily work and make the daily decisions, which was interpreted as him having no say in the decision-making. This was not true, as Nkanunu and Masson would assist Oberholzer in all the major decisions that were presented to the board for discussion and approval.

Gideon Sam, a far stronger personality than Nkanunu, resented the suggestion that blacks could not run rugby. In 2003 he knew that a coalition existed between the conservative coloured and white elements in SA Rugby to derail black empowerment in the game at national level. During the Geo Cronjé–Quinton Davids incident at the Pretoria High Performance Centre, Sam had raged that the coloured element in Cape Town was not anti-Bok but anti-black, and that the blacks would 'show the coloureds', who believed that blacks could not run the game in South Africa, that they were wrong. But instead Sam had it wrong. The coloured leadership has vanquished the black leadership, at least for now.

When I spoke to Van Rooyen in November 2003, he said that he was aware of the complex interracial politics. I asked him how he would deal with it if he were elected SARFU president, and he said, 'It will always be there in our rugby. We have to deal with it and move on.' I asked SARFU CEO Mvuleli Ncula about the hostility between black and coloured, and he took the party line. He said he did not like to differentiate between black and coloured. 'We are all black,' Ncula said. If only it were that simple. Depressingly, the black leadership of SA Rugby has accommodated this attitude since international re-admission in 1992, speaking of the tolerance required to change the inherently racist mindset. Patience, in this case, can be an excuse for weakness in decision-making, and this is one of the reasons why Nkanunu was defeated so easily.

For all his good intentions, Nkanunu never challenged the white presence or mindset. He failed in transformation at the highest level. The dearth of black players in the national team had infuriated the black leadership in the previous regime. In private the talk was more heated than anything said in public. Black administrators don't see coloured players as black. Coloured administrators don't see their players as black either. Blacks don't have an identity in South African rugby because of the complexities of what constitutes black. Black is not coloured and coloured is not black. While this debate continues, the white conservatives sit back and play the role of puppeteer.

The previous black leadership had been silent, and those who remain are equally quiet. These are individuals who in the past had fought hard against white dominance of the sport. Yet once within the system themselves, the rewards have apparently proved too overwhelming.

Nkanunu gave up without a fight, and his conqueror, Van Rooyen, marched in, carried shoulder-high by the white conservatives. It is an open secret within South African rugby that André Markgraaff led Van Rooyen's campaign in the conservative northern provinces. When I recently asked the managing director of SA Rugby, Songezo Nayo, about whether or not Markgraaff had raised R100 000 to assist Van Rooyen's election campaign, he said he couldn't confirm this, but added that everyone in SA Rugby knew that Markgraaff had played a major role in the campaign.

On the provincial pre-election trail, Van Rooyen had made many promises to the provinces. He reintroduced the fourteen-team Currie Cup system, and gave the four main provinces control of the regional Super 12. Commercially, Van Rooyen looked after all fourteen provinces and entrenched the role of the provincial presidents, as well as his position as SARFU president. Many of the changes introduced since Van Rooyen's appointment in December 2003 are political paybacks for getting him elected, rather than decisions taken in the best interests of South African rugby. The company has been turned into a glorified tax front, and elected officials run the professional game by committee. Blacks again represent the minority, and those black officials that there are, are as comfortable in the trappings of the good corporate life as their predecessors were.

Nayo is a very competent person who offered hope for South African rugby. But on 31 May 2004 he resigned, after failing to find common ground with Van Rooyen, who had publicly accused him of incompetence.

A few of the faces in the corridors of power have changed, but the script, alas, remains the same.

Index